**Sampling in Archaeology**

The first overview of sampling for archaeologists for over twenty years, this manual offers a comprehensive account of the applications of statistical sampling theory which are essential to modern archaeological practice at a range of scales, from the regional to the microscopic. Bringing archaeologists up to date with an aspect of their work which is often misunderstood, it includes a discussion of the relevance of sampling theory to archaeological interpretation, and considers its fundamental place in fieldwork and post-excavation study. It demonstrates the vast range of techniques that are available, only some of which are widely used by archaeologists. A section on statistical theory also reviews the latest developments in the field, and the formal mathematics is available in an appendix, cross-referenced with the main text.

CLIVE ORTON is Reader in Quantitative Archaeology at the Institute of Archaeology, University College London. He is the co-author of *Spatial Analysis in Archaeology* (1976) and *Pottery in Archaeology* (1993), and author of *Mathematics in Archaeology* (1982), all published by Cambridge University Press. He has published widely in scholarly journals.

# CAMBRIDGE MANUALS IN ARCHAEOLOGY

*Series editors*

Don Brothwell, *University of York*
Graeme Barker, *University of Leicester*
Dena Dincauze, *University of Massachusetts, Amherst*
Priscilla Renouf, *Memorial University of Newfoundland*

*Cambridge Manuals in Archaeology* is a series of reference handbooks designed for an international audience of upper-level undergraduate and graduate students, and professional archaeologists and archaeological scientists in universities, museums, research laboratories, and field units. Each book includes a survey of current archaeological practice alongside essential reference material on contemporary techniques and methodology.

Already published:

J. D. Richards and N. S. Ryan, DATA PROCESSING IN ARCHAEOLOGY
Simon Hillson, TEETH
Alwyne Wheeler and Andrew K. G. Jones, FISHES
Lesley Adkins and Roy Adkins, ARCHAEOLOGICAL ILLUSTRATION
Marie-Agnes Courty, Paul Goldberg and Richard MacPhail, SOILS AND MICROMORPHOLOGY IN ARCHAEOLOGY
Clive Orton, Paul Tyers, and Alan Vince, POTTERY IN ARCHAEOLOGY
R. Lee Lyman, VERTEBRATE TAPHONOMY
Peter G. Dorrell, PHOTOGRAPHY IN ARCHAEOLOGY AND CONSERVATION (2ND EDN)
A. G. Brown, ALLUVIAL GEOARCHAEOLOGY
Cheryl Claassen, SHELLS
William Andrefsky Jr. LITHICS
Elizabeth J. Reitz and Elizabeth S. Wing ZOOARCHAEOLOGY

# SAMPLING IN ARCHAEOLOGY

Clive Orton
*University College London*

CAMBRIDGE
UNIVERSITY PRESS

CAMBRIDGE UNIVERSITY PRESS
Cambridge, New York, Melbourne, Madrid, Cape Town, Singapore, São Paulo, Delhi

Cambridge University Press
The Edinburgh Building, Cambridge CB2 8RU, UK

Published in the United States of America by Cambridge University Press, New York

www.cambridge.org
Information on this title: www.cambridge.org/9780521566667

First published 2000
Reprinted 2002

*A catalogue record for this publication is available from the British Library*

*Library of Congress Cataloguing in Publication data*

Clive Orton, 1944–
Sampling in archaeology / Clive Orton; illustrations by Gillie Newman
    p.   cm. – (Cambridge manuals in archaeology)
ISBN 0 521 56226 0 (hb) 0 521 56666 5 (pbk)
1. Archaeology – Statistical methods handbooks, manuals, etc.   2. Sampling
(statistics) handbooks, manuals, etc.   I. Title.   II. Series.
CC80.6.078   2000
930 – dc21   99-28846 CIP

ISBN 978-0-521-56226-3 hardback
ISBN 978-0-521-56666-7 paperback

Transferred to digital printing 2009

# CONTENTS

# ILLUSTRATIONS

# TABLES

# ACKNOWLEDGEMENTS

This book is the fulfilment of a long-term ambition to express my views about the current and potential uses of sampling in archaeology. It has been made possible by a generous allowance of time from successive directors of University College London Institute of Archaeology: Professors David Harris and Peter Ucko. A period of part-time study leave, amounting to three days per week for one year (October 1997 to September 1998) has allowed me to finish the book within the scheduled period of two years, something that would otherwise have been quite impossible. Practical help was given by Dylan Edgar and Ian Martin, who contributed the computer simulations in chapter 5, and above all by Gillie Newman, who prepared most of the diagrams, either redrawing them from existing publications or interpreting my rough sketches. The photographs were taken by staff of the Institute's Field Archaeology Unit. My colleagues and students must be thanked for their forbearance during this period, and especially for respecting the arrangement by which I was frequently 'not at home' although clearly visible in office or library. The staff of the Institute library put up with my frequent enquiries with good humour. Several colleagues read a chapter or two, and made valuable comments, especially Kris Lockyear, who has been a constant source of encouragement. Encouragement has also come from my family – Jean, Ruth and David – and my good friend Janet Likeman.

The following are thanked for permission to reproduce copyright illustrations:
Dr Paul Tyers, Figs. 3.2, 3.3; Oxford University Press, Figs. 3.4, 6.8; Hampshire Field Club and Archaeological Society, Fig. 3.5; Professor C. Haselgrove, Fig. 3.7, Dr W. Boismier, Fig. 3.8; Field Archaeology Unit, UCL Institute of Archaeology, Figs. 4.1, 5.1, 5.2, 5.10, 6.2–6.4; Professor S. Shennan, Figs. 4.2, 4.11; Cambridge University Press, Figs. 4.3, 5.14, 5.15, 6.10; Dr A. Voorrips, Fig. 4.4; *Journal of Field Archaeology* and the Trustees of Boston University, Figs. 4.5, 4.8, 5.8, 5.9; Leicester University Press, Fig. 4.6; Professor M. Aston and Dr C. Gerrard, Figs. 4.12, 4.13; Professor T. Darvill, G. Wainwright and Antiquity Publications Ltd, Fig. 4.14; English Heritage and University of Southampton, Figs. 5.3–5.7; UCL Institute of Archaeology, Fig. 5.11; Society for American Archaeology, Figs. 5.12, 5.16–5.18; Professor T. Champion, Fig. 5.13; Research Laboratory for Archaeology and the History of Art, Figs. 6.1, 7.2, 7.4, 7.5; Dr P. Fasham and Dr M. Monk, Fig. 6.5; Rijksdienst voor het

Oudheidkundig Bodemonderzoek, Fig. 6.9; Arnold Publishers, Fig. 6.11; Trustees of the British Museum, Fig. 7.3; Museum of London, Fig. 8.2.

Finally, I would like to thank Jessica Kuper of Cambridge University Press for her trust in and support of this volume.

September 1998

**1**

# ALL THE WORLD'S A SAMPLE

## Introduction

Reading almost any archaeological document, from a research proposal to a fieldwork report, it will not be long before one comes across the word 'sample' in one context or another. A project, whether at regional or site level, will be based on a *sampling strategy*, a research design may specify that features are to be *sampled*, and *samples* of various types will be taken for the delight or otherwise of specialists who wish, or who can be persuaded, to look at them. In fact, almost all archaeology involves sampling; indeed, one could say that there is a sense in which much of archaeology *is* sampling, echoing David Clarke's remark that 'Archaeology . . . is the discipline with the theory and practice for the recovery of unobservable hominid behaviour patterns from indirect traces in bad samples'. (Clarke 1973, 17).

The word sample is all-pervasive, but one soon comes to realise that it does not have the same meaning each time it occurs. This is not surprising, as just one of the six definitions given by the *Oxford English Dictionary* is broad enough to encompass a wide range of meaning: 'a relatively small quantity of material, or an individual object, from which the quality of the mass, group or species, etc. which it represents may be inferred'. At one extreme, one may encounter a 'multi-stage probabilistic sampling strategy', while at the other, one may encounter the casual use of the word sample to refer to collections of muddy objects in plastic bags. Cynically, one might note the existence of piles of 'samples' in dark corners of archaeological stores, whose main role seems to be to get in the way for several years, and then to be thrown away. The word sample has become, through usage, so diffuse that we need to bring it back into focus before we can start to understand what it means, where it comes from, and what implications it carries for the way in which we actually do archaeology.

To try to achieve this focus, we need to split apart the various meanings that have accreted on to the word sample, and look at each separately. As a first step, we can divide samples into:

(a) *Unintentional samples*. Here the sampling has been done, so to speak, before the archaeologist arrives on the scene. We know full well that the material we have painstakingly recovered is not the whole of what was lost or discarded in the course of activities undertaken at its location. Sometimes its condition makes this obvious – for example sherds are clearly only a fraction of the pots that they represent – but at other times its condition may lure us into thinking that we have a 'total sample' (e.g. of coins). But survival does not guarantee recovery; both size and colour, among other factors, may affect the chance of detection, thus imposing a curious form of sampling based on an archaeologist's ability (combined with weather, deadlines, etc.).

(b) *Informal samples.* Next we come to samples whose selection is, to some extent at least, in the deliberate choice of the archaeologist. The choice may be based on archaeological criteria or on those of time, cost and convenience, or on a combination of them. There is a spectrum of intentionality within this group: at one end we might put *purposive samples*, for example carefully targeted excavation units based on topographical features or geophysical survey. At the other end, we might put *haphazard* or *grab samples*, for example the hasty gathering-up of a few objects found on the surface of a potential site. Somewhere between the two might come the idea of a *typical sample*, selected by the archaeologist to represent a collection of objects, though the achievement of typicality is far more difficult than might be expected. What all such samples lack is the potential for generalisation from them: the ability to move from the description of a sample to a reliable statement about some wider entity, usually known as a *population*. Such power is provided by:

(c) *Formal samples.* These are samples selected from well-defined populations according to rigorous statistical procedures. If taken properly, they enable us to make valid statements about the relevant populations, such as estimates of certain parameters (e.g. density of sites in a region, size distribution of inclusions in a ceramic fabric). Equally importantly, they can provide likely margins of error for such estimates, which can not only tell us how 'useful' they are likely to be, but can also help us to determine how large a sample has to be to tell us what we want to know (at least, with a chosen level of confidence). The price of this power is exposure to, or even immersion in, statistical sampling theory, which may seem rather daunting to many archaeologists, but which in many archaeological situations is unavoidable.

It might seem that I am here making the equation: formal = good, informal = bad, but that would be a gross over-simplification. Certainly, there are situations in which this is true: the subjective choice of sampling units, whether at a regional scale or in a museum store, can easily lead to bias (p. 23) and an inability to quote reliable margins of error for one's results. On the other hand, formal methods are to some extent a rational response to a state of ignorance, and the more we know about a situation, the less necessary they may be (Redman *et al.* 1979). For example, to ignore evidence from aerial photographs or geophysical surveys in designing a purely random sample of (for example) test-pits would be wasteful and unproductive, and a more targeted approach would be likely to give more useful results. But there is a contrasting danger, that of the self-fulfilling prophecy – looking only at areas where one expects to

Fig. 1.1 Invasive sampling or the march of the quadrats.

find 'something' may merely confirm what one already knows – and some (lesser) attention should be paid to apparently 'blank' areas. So there needs to be a balance between statistical rigour and the use of what statisticians call *prior information*, in order to make best use of resources and to achieve reliable outcomes. One approach to statistics, known as *Bayesian statistics* (p. 16), seeks to make explicit use of such information, but it requires a higher level of expertise, particularly in modelling, and is only just beginning to make an impact on survey sampling. But even if such advanced theory is not accessible, there is a need to break away from the mental image that equates sampling with an army of small squares marching willy-nilly across the landscape, oblivious of rivers, mountains and any other natural features (Fig. 1.1). This caricature is born of very incomplete understanding of sampling theory, which results in archaeologists using it as a self-imposed straitjacket, against which they rebel. Sampling theory is a good deal more flexible than is sometimes supposed, as we shall see in the following chapters.

First, though, we need to continue to break down the definition of sampling, this time according to the *scale* at which it takes place. In the course of fieldwork, we may be called on to sample from a region, a site, or a feature on a site. In the laboratory, we may need to sample from an assemblage of excavated material, or from within the material of an object itself, such as a pottery sherd or a metal artefact. Even when laid to rest in a store, artefacts may not be free from our attentions, as we may decide to sample them to check that they are not decaying at an unacceptable rate. Activities at these different levels tend to be undertaken by different groups of people, who have built up their own professional expertise and case law. This has tended to obscure the underlying unity, that at whatever the scale it is all *sampling*, and shares common problems and possibly solutions. The unity is provided by statistical sampling theory, which at its core is context free, but which nevertheless seeks to adapt itself to the needs and assumptions of particular situations. A secure grounding in theory can enable one to see where an advance made at one scale can be successfully transferred to another (and, just as importantly, where it cannot). In a discipline which is well known for its penchant for borrowing techniques from other disciplines (p. 171), it is perhaps surprising that there has been so little cross-fertilisation between the sub-disciplines that make up archaeology. Perhaps the reason lies in archaeologists' ambivalent attitudes towards sampling, which could provide the link.

### Attitudes and history

To try to untangle the complex web of feelings and opinions that archaeologists have about sampling, I have created the following series of thumb-nail sketches. Obviously they contain an element of caricature, and archaeologists may well recognise an element of themselves in more than one of them. Nevertheless, they can form a useful basis for exploring the shifts in opinion and practice that have occurred over the years.

> (a)  *Mother's milk.* Sampling is something that all archaeologists do all the time, and as such they instinctively know all they need to know about it. This view is often tacit rather than articulated; when it is expressed, it may be in the form of 'professional judgement'. Found mainly in commercial archaeological units.
>
> (b)  *Black art.* Sampling could be the answer to all our problems, but someone somewhere is withholding a vital piece of information. A magic percentage of our site, region, etc., will tell us all we need to know, if only we knew what that percentage is. Second to (a) amongst field archaeologists.
>
> (c)  *Alien imposition.* Sampling theory is an attempt by statisticians (and like-minded people) to impose their values and methods on an unwilling discipline. Their methodology is inappropriate because archaeology is unique and has nothing to gain from such outsiders. Found amongst those who know enough statistics to recognise the folly of some archaeological sampling schemes, or amongst those who are simply scared of it.
>
> (d)  *Regrettable necessity.* 'Had we but world enough, and time' we would do everything – total survey, total excavation, total record. Unfortunately, we don't, so we have to compromise with the constraints imposed by real life. Sampling is a sell-out, but until we get proper funding, etc., we have to live with it.
>
> (e)  *Passport to respectability.* All respectable scientists sample, so if we are to hold up our heads in the scientific community, then we must do so too. The more explicit the theory the better, and admire my research design. Main habitat is research grant applications.
>
> (f)  *Escape from tedium.* Much archaeological activity consists of the tedious compiling of mountains of low-grade data. Surely we don't

need it *all*? Why not base our analyses and interpretations on just a sample of it, and spare ourselves the effort of measuring another (large number) of (chosen artefact type)? Particularly common amongst finds specialists.

(g) *Framework for research.* We need to ask 'how much work (fieldwork, finds study, etc.) do we have to do to find out what we want to know?' Ask questions, design research to answer them, sample, analyse and interpret, then move on. Target resources carefully.

The history of sampling in archaeology will be examined thematically in chapters 4 to 8, but here we look at it in terms of the attitude behind the practices. Initially, sampling was seen as an intuitive exercise (a) – if, for example, there were more sherds on the surface of a site than you could reasonably collect, then you took what seemed to you to be a 'representative' sample (p. 112). More formal methods started to come in in the 1940s, after the wider dissemination of statistical sampling theory that followed the theoretical advances of the 1930s (p. 15) and their application to quality control in response to the industrial pressures of World War 2. They were used first on dense concentrations of data in small spatial locations (e.g. shell mounds, pp. 145–7), seeming to be motivated by attitude (f).

A turning point in many ways was signalled by Binford (1964), although technically precedence should be given to Vescelius (1960) (p. 68). Binford advocated three changes, one archaeological and two statistical: the promotion of the region to the position of primary unit of archaeological research, the explicit *design* of archaeological research programmes, and the explicit use of sampling theory as the way of linking the two. Although his practical example was rather contrived, this paper had a tremendous impact and did in fact achieve its apparent aims. Certainly, in fewer than ten years, formal sampling had reached such a level that a major symposium could be held on the subject (in San Francisco 1973, see Mueller 1975b), and a series of textbooks and reviews soon followed (see pp. 69–70). It is worth noting that the majority of contributions at San Francisco were on regional sampling, with a minority on site sampling and only one on sampling at a smaller scale. In contrast, at the British counterpart (in Southampton 1977, see Cherry *et al.* 1978), there was a much more balanced representation of the various scales.

Inevitably, there was opposition of one kind or another. At the feature level, the widespread introduction of sieving methods in the 1960s and 1970s led to a growing realisation that sampling was essential to keep the resulting workload down to a manageable volume. At first, this seems to have been done reluctantly, in the spirit of (d) (e.g. Payne 1972a), but later more enthusiastically (e.g. Veen and Fieller 1982; Levitan 1983). At the site level, moves towards more formal sampling were paralleled by realisations that, to answer some questions, larger rather than smaller areas had to be excavated (Biddle and

Kjølbye-Biddle 1969). Although this was initially a reaction against the 'Wheeler system' of excavation, in which a surprisingly high proportion of a site was left unexcavated as baulks, it led to expressions of the view that total excavation was the only 'proper' excavation (e.g. Barker 1977; see Cherry *et al.* 1978, 151). The over-rigid use of sampling designs at regional level was quite rightly criticised (e.g. Hole 1980; Wobst 1983), though at times the concern seems to have been with the idea of sampling rather than with the way in which it was being employed (c).

By the 1980s in the USA and the 1990s in the UK, sampling had become firmly entrenched in the methodology of the 'contract' wing of archaeology (pp. 69, 74), to the extent that one could almost say that the wheel had turned full circle and returned to (a), though at a higher level of self-awareness, and with an element of (b).

### Where this book stands

This book is written from a background of an academic training in mathematics and statistics, favouring attitude (g), and an archaeological career spent mainly in ceramics, a material which leads one towards attitude (f). Attitude (e) is perhaps less important – archaeologists must find a methodology that is appropriate for them, and should not be always looking over their shoulder and worrying about what others might say. From this perspective, sampling is not an option but an imperative that should be embraced willingly, not reluctantly. It is not a 'second-best' strategy forced on us by lack of resources, but a responsible use of whatever resources may be available to us, whether small or large.

The root of the issue is that archaeological fieldwork has the potential to generate enormous, indeed overwhelming, quantities of data. These quantities need to be limited, for both logistical and intellectual reasons. On the logistical front, we run immediately into problems of resources – money, time and scarce specialist expertise. Many fieldwork projects are heavily constrained by the need to obtain the required information (often for external purposes, such as local government planning control) from a very restricted budget in a competitive environment. It would be wrong, from many points of view, to retrieve more material than we can handle, and simply trying to increase our resources does not help, since it will (at least in the short term) only decrease resources elsewhere. The 'free lunch' of volunteer labour is not the answer, since it raises the questions of whether such workers would be better employed in doing something else (either within archaeology or outside it), and of whether we are exploiting them. Finally, all this material must go somewhere; museums in the UK are in a storage crisis brought about in part by the boom in archaeological fieldwork since the 1970s. These arguments involve the whole of archaeology, from 'cradle to grave', one might say; the point is that sampling is unavoidable, and that informed awareness of formal methods gives us the best chance of obtaining the results that we require, from the resources available.

The intellectual arguments are at least as compelling. There is no point in accumulating data, either for their own sake ('stamp collecting') or in the fond hope that they will answer someone else's questions one day. When or if a new 'wonder' technique does arise, the chances are that it will not be our laborious-ly catalogued data or stored material that will answer it. For example, when thermoluminescence was developed as a method of dating pottery sherds, it could not be used retrospectively because information about the nature of their surrounding matrix was rarely if ever available (Aitken 1990, 154). Next, data are subject to a law of diminishing returns. If we double the quantity of data, we do not double the information that (even in principle) we could obtain from them (p. 210). Sooner or later, as the volume of data increases, there comes a point at which further data provide virtually no extra information (e.g. p. 157). Another point is that, within fixed resources, sampling allows us to pay more attention to our material, and so improve the quality of our data. A relatively small quantity of good-quality data is often of more use than large amounts of low-quality data, as many opinion poll specialists would testify. Finally, too many data can actually obscure rather than illuminate any pat-terns that may be present. They can do so either by sheer weight of numbers, so that we 'can't see the wood for the trees', or because the irrelevance of some of the data can obscure patterns in the more relevant data (p. 181).

How, then, can we limit the quantity of data that we retrieve and accumu-late? In a very simple model, we can see data as measurements or other observations made of *variables* on *objects* (using *object* to refer to any archae-ological entity, and *variable* to refer to any characteristic that may vary from one object to another: see below for a more detailed discussion). Under this model, we can reduce the overall quantity of data either by reducing the number of objects (i.e. by sampling) or by reducing the number of variables (which is here called *selection*). Selection is important because it is often the *irrelevant* variables that obscure patterns, while *redundant* ones (i.e. ones that contribute no extra information) just waste resources. But the issue of selection may make archaeologists feel uncomfortable or insecure. Fortunately, it can to some extent be managed by the use of more appropriate data structures or models. For example, in the 1970s British ceramic specialists, under the influence of Peacock (see p. 178) and feeling their way in relatively new territory, recorded many details (e.g. nature, size distribution, frequency and shape of inclusions) about sherds individually, in the belief that it could all be sorted out on the computer (urged on by the siren-like encouragement of data-processing specialists with little connection with archaeology). By and large, it couldn't be, and much effort was wasted. The correct place to sort out ceramic fabrics is at the work-bench: fabrics can be defined (using ranges of values rather than point values of variables) and sherds can be seen and recorded as examples of particular fabrics. This structure of the data mirrors that of the *relational database*, which was coming into general use at about the same time, and which advocated the superiority of several small tables of data over an all-embracing individual one (a lesson that has not been entirely taken on board by all archaeologists). However, improved structuring of the data does not remove the archaeologist's responsibility to select variables sensibly in the first place.

Given that sampling is essential, we need to ensure that it is carried out in a way that enables us to make best use of the data that it provides. The requirement is that a statement that we make, based on data from a sample, should in some measure be true of the corresponding population, and that we should have some idea of how accurate it is likely to be. This is usually expressed by saying that the sample should be *representative* of the population. In terms of strict sampling theory, this is achieved by ensuring that the sample is *random*, i.e. that each element of the population has a certain, known, chance of being chosen to be part of the sample. This requirement, and the variations in sample design that are possible in different circumstances, are described in detail in chapter 2. The problems that arise in reconciling formal statistical requirements with archaeological reality form the 'meat' of this book in chapters 4 to 8. As we have seen in the introduction to this chapter (p. 2), formal sampling does not seem to be the appropriate answer for all archaeological questions. For example, if one wished to date a ditched enclosure, one or more sections cut across the bank and ditch would be a preferably strategy to a random set of trenches across the whole site. If, however, one wished to estimate the density of activity within the site (measured perhaps in terms of the density of features or artefacts), then the latter *would* be appropriate. The difference is that, in the latter case, we wish (in statistical language) to estimate a parameter of the site as a whole, while in the former the estimate we want is based on material that, experience tells us, is more likely to be located in certain parts of the site. The important point is not so much whether a sample is formal or informal, but whether it is *designed* or *undesigned*. Designed samples include formal statistical (random) samples, which are appropriate for many questions but not for all. Obviously, in this book we shall concentrate, but not exclusively, on those situations in which formal sampling methods have the most to offer.

All this discussion of data raises the question of what data actually *are*? The line taken here is that they are characteristics of objects in the real world, which archaeologists can choose either to observe and record or not to observe and record. The role of the archaeologist, and of archaeological theory, is to select relevant variables according to the question in hand, but not actually to create them. Data, of course, are far from perfect. The values that we record depend on a wide range of extraneous factors, over and above the 'true' value of *that* variable on *that* object. Personal and environmental factors can influence the perception of variables such as colour, and even apparently 'objective' variables, such as length or diameter, can be subject to a surprising level of variation, plus the occasional gross recording error, due perhaps to transposed digits or an omitted decimal point. Gross errors can usually be detected relatively easily, because they stand out; more difficult are small systematic errors that may reflect personal biases. For example, I once analysed differences between rim diameters of pots of the same form found on different parts of a production site, only to find that they had been caused by psychological differences between two recorders, one of whom rounded doubtful diameter measurements down to the nearest inch, while the other rounded them up. The allocation of tasks to different workers, to prevent this sort of problem, requires far more attention than it is usually given (but see Daniels 1978).

The use of instrumentation, even expensive instrumentation, does not remove the possibility of error, but brings its own problems. Equipment used in many sorts of elemental analysis may suffer from 'drift', and have to be calibrated from time to time, while rare elements are subject to a 'threshold' effect: values smaller than a certain amount are recorded as zero. If different elements have different thresholds, or (in a comparative study) different instruments have different thresholds, then analysis of the data will at best be very difficult.

In all cases, then, it is important to maintain a critical attitude to one's data, remembering the old adage 'if it looks wrong, it probably is wrong', or even Twyman's Law that 'any figure that looks interesting or different is probably wrong' (Ehrenberg 1975, 10). This is especially true once data have been stored on a computer: the process of data entry itself can create further errors, but data seen on the screen or on a print-out have an annoying way of looking 'right' simply because they are 'in print'.

The quality of data is a general statistical issue, although it also includes aspects that are specific to each discipline. Much work has been done, and continues to be done, on ways to prevent, detect or minimise errors in data, and, although it falls outside the scope of this book, archaeologists are advised to be aware of it.

All that remains in this section is to bring together this view of data with the role of sampling in archaeology, to present a coherent model for the process of archaeological research as a whole. Fig. 1.2 shows just such a model, which is equally applicable to any other data-based discipline. It is quite complex, and needs to be 'unpacked' carefully. The model first makes a distinction between the world of theory (what goes on inside your head) and the real world (what goes on outside your head). Theory is characterised by *hypotheses* (or, more generally, ideas or opinions), and the real world by *data*. It claims that the two interact not directly, but through an intermediary, the *model*. As a simple everyday example, consider the problem of leaving home in time to catch a

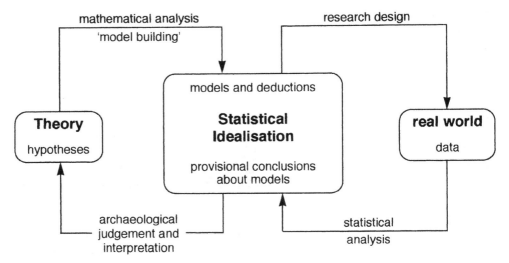

Fig. 1.2 The research cycle.

train. The train (representing the real world), will arrive at the station at a definite but (to me) unknown time. My theoretical task is to judge when I need to leave home. The actual position of the train is of no use to me, because I have no way of knowing it. But what I do have is a model, in the form of the railway timetable plus my experience of how long it takes to walk to the station. Initially, this model provides me with my best guess of when to leave home. Later, it may become modified by experience; if I discover that the train is always at least five minutes late, for example, I may dare to leave home five minutes later. This simple example makes some useful points about models; first, that they are *simplified representations of reality*, and second, that they can be modified in the light of experience.

Having established the main building-blocks of our model, we can now start to see how they relate to each other. The first point to make is that there is no 'correct' starting point: we start from where we are. If we start by thinking about a problem, we are in the world of theory; if we start with a collection of objects, we are in the world of data. For purposes of illustration, we shall start from theory. The first step is to create a model of the situation that we wish to investigate. This may consist of defining the population that we wish to explore, and the variables that we wish to observe. The key questions may well be which population and which variables are relevant to the question that we wish to answer. This step is more difficult than is often acknowledged and may be glossed over. The next step is the well-known one of research design: deciding on the size and design of our sample, and the practical issues of its implementation and analysis. We can then go out to the real world and collect our data. The third step, statistical analysis, should be a formality, since we should have decided how we are going to analyse our data *before* we collect them. Failure to plan for analysis before collecting data is probably the major reason for failure in projects. There is one more step: the statistical results must be interpreted archaeologically and fed back into the theoretical world. Do they support our original ideas? Do they suggest new ones? Or perhaps they were inconclusive and we have to face the whole cycle again.

This is a very short and simplified view of a complicated process; it is expanded in the context of sampling to the twelve stages described in chapter 2 (pp. 27–29).

### Why this book was written, and how to use it

The origins of this book lie in the belief, which gradually grew in me in the early 1990s, that archaeologists were not making the best use of statistical sampling theory in the aspects of their work that involved sampling. There were several strands to this belief:

(a) *Fear.* Many archaeologists are afraid of sampling theory, as indeed they are of statistical theory in general (Nance 1990). It appears to them as a set of arcane and arbitrary rules, which they must obey at the risk of being condemned if they get them wrong. This fear can lead either to a rigid conservatism, only doing what has been done before and has stood the test of time, or to a rebellious kicking over of the traces and rejection of formal constraints on methodology. Neither seems conducive to good practice in archaeological fieldwork.

(b) *Ignorance.* A new generation of field archaeologists has grown up, who have not personally been through the experience of the methodological discoveries of the 1970s. Their appreciation of sampling appears to be based on a perceived need for 'rules of thumb' for the design of fieldwork projects (e.g. site evaluations), combined with a reluctance to get involved with basic principles.

(c) *Time warp.* The sampling techniques used by archaeologists have become locked into the archaeological literature of the 1970s (e.g. Peters 1970; Ragir 1972; Redman 1974; Mueller 1974, 1975b; Jelks 1975; Cherry *et al.* 1978; Plog 1978), which is itself based on statistical work of the 1950s and 1960s. Later archaeological literature has developed the archaeological aspects, but has tended to regard statistics as a fixed and immutable body of theory. But statistical sampling theory is continually advancing and developing, and it seems likely, *a priori*, that some of the advances made since the 1960s would be useful to archaeologists if only they knew about them.

(d) '*You in your small corner*'. Archaeologists use sampling at a range of scales for a wide variety of problems, but it tends to be different archaeologists working at the different scales. There seems to be scope for cross-fertilisation between the different scales of activity, which could benefit all concerned.

It therefore seemed to me that the time was ripe for an attempt to bring the theory of sampling in archaeology up to date, in the hope that if this could be done clearly and enthusiastically, practice would follow. There seemed to be the following needs:

(a)  to present the basic principles of statistical sampling in a simple way, with a minimum of mathematics,

(b)  to explore critically how such principles have been used by archaeologists, at a variety of scales,

(c)  to introduce new developments in statistical theory which archaeologists might be expected to find useful,

(d)  to encourage a more informed and creative approach towards the uses of sampling in archaeology.

A 'manual' seemed a good way to achieve these aims, although this book is not a 'manual' in the traditional sense of series of instructions in the performance of certain tasks. Such a prescriptive approach would simply fossilise practice at a new point in time, and inhibit future developments. Instead, the aim is to provide archaeologists with a soundly based 'jumping-off point', from which they can move in an informed way in various directions: into reading and assessing work done in the past, into establishing criteria and designs for new fieldwork projects, or exploring the potential in their work of new developments in statistical theory.

To use this book, it is probably best to start with the statistical theory of chapter 2. This sets out to provide an introduction to the basic concepts and techniques of statistical sampling theory. In keeping with the rest of the book, this chapter is an 'algebra-free zone': all the necessary algebraic formulae are segregated in a technical Appendix, to which readers can refer as they wish, or which they can ignore as they wish. Chapter 3 is something of a digression, as it looks at the question of whether sampling theory can help archaeologists in their thinking about the processes of site formation, and the interpretational problems that flow from them. Chapters 4 to 7 are very similar to each other in structure, but each deals with a different scale of archaeological research – regional scale, site scale, feature scale and microscopic scale – while chapter 8 deals with sampling in museum stores. The general pattern is to provide a historical introduction, followed by the relevant applied theory, and finally some case studies. The boundaries between the scales are arbitrary, and there are of necessity omissions. In chapters of this size it is not possible to mention, let alone discuss, every project that might be of interest. Case studies have been chosen to illustrate particular points, and their inclusion is neither a seal of approval nor a mark of criticism. Finally, chapter 9 highlights some of the most important points that have been made in earlier chapters.

In using this book, readers will naturally be drawn towards the chapter(s) relating to the scale(s) at which they usually work. But I do encourage you to look at other chapters as well, to broaden your horizons and perhaps to learn from what others are doing.

# 2

# A LITTLE OF WHAT YOU FANCY?

### A brief history of statistical sampling theory

The origins of the fundamental idea of sampling, that a small part can in some way be taken to represent, or stand in for, the whole, are lost in the origins of civilisation itself. There are many everyday, and especially commercial, situations in which the need for sampling, however informal, would have asserted itself. For example, merchants buying grain would wish to test the quality of their purchases, or a community would wish to maintain the standards of the weights and measures of goods (e.g. bread, ale) being sold within it. Such checking is at best time consuming and at worst destructive of the material being checked. For purely practical reasons, a small part had to stand in for the whole. Of course, such a procedure must be seen to be 'fair', to both the producer and the consumer, and this need must have been a frequent cause of disputes. In the absence of any appropriate theory, trust in whoever was doing the checking must have been important, and procedures similar to what we would today call *random selection* (see below) may have grown up.

Later, in the eighteenth and especially the nineteenth century, the need for sampling was felt in other areas, like scientific research and economic and social policy, and more theoretical questions began to be asked. We shall look at the subsequent history of the development of statistical theory and practice mainly through the work of Smith (1976), and will follow this historical account with descriptions of the various ideas and techniques that were introduced (they will be indicated by italics in this section). Early debates focused on the validity of sampling from *finite populations* (the early theory of *inference* was based on the idea of taking large samples from *infinite populations*), and on the methods by which such samples should be taken – *purposive* against *random* sampling. The first was resolved by Kaier (1901) who showed that *stratified* samples could give good estimates of the totals and means from finite populations (Smith 1976, 183). The next step was made by Bowley (1906; 1926), who showed how the accuracy of large samples from large finite populations could be calculated. The second debate was between the concept of random sampling (as then understood, in which every *unit* in the population had to have the same chance of selection), and purposive sampling, in which units were selected according to the values of other, known, *variables* which were thought to be closely related to the variables being studied (this is similar to what is today known as *quota* sampling).

This debate was resolved in a key contribution by Neyman (1934), which also made several other important advances in statistical theory and laid the foundations for modern statistical sampling theory for at least a generation. Indeed, almost all the statistical theory used explicitly by archaeologists can be traced back to this remarkable paper. Neyman's achievements were:

(a) to establish that random sampling yielded *representative samples* from finite populations,

(b) to show that random sampling could give *confidence intervals* for the values of population *parameters* (e.g. means, totals),

(c) to demonstrate the theoretical and practical superiority of random sampling over purposive sampling,

(d) to introduce a criterion, *efficiency*, for the comparison of sample designs, and to show that *stratified* random sampling could potentially be made more efficient than *simple* random sampling by varying the sampling fractions between one stratum and another, and to give a formula for the *optimum allocation* (i.e. the 'best' design of a stratified sample),

(e) to provide a framework for *inference* from *cluster samples* (after Smith 1976, 185).

He later introduced a further key idea, that of *two-stage sampling*. Building directly on his work, *ratio* and *regression estimation* were introduced in the 1930s (Cochran 1942), the efficiency of *multi-stage sampling* was improved by the introduction of sampling with *probability proportional to size* (*pps*) (Hansen and Hurwitz 1943) and the theory of *systematic sampling* was developed (Madow and Madow 1944). The stage was set for the expansion of statistical sampling methods into many walks of life, including archaeology (see chapter 1).

That might appear to be the end of the story, at least from a theoretical point of view. But from the 1950s theoretical statisticians began to realise that, great as Neyman's achievements were, they were not the last word on the subject. The root of the problem was that Neyman's work was, in a sense, *too* general: he made no assumptions about the nature of the population under study, and so developed a theory that can be used in any circumstances. That sounds fine, but it means that if we do have any knowledge about the population, for example a model of the distribution of the variable we wish to study, there is no way we can make use of that knowledge. More recent work has suggested that by incorporating a model of the data into our considerations, we can improve the design of our surveys. This approach has risks – what if the model is wrong? – as well as benefits. The 'Neyman', or *conventional*, approach to sampling (in which almost all archaeological practice is rooted) can thus be seen as both a straitjacket and a safety net: it may prevent gains but it also prevents unquantifiable risks (even confidence intervals have risks – the value may occasionally lie outside them – but such risks are quantifiable and we know where we stand with them).

Despite theoretical work on *model-based sampling* designs from the 1950s through to the 1970s, the actual practice of sample surveys seems to have changed little – much of the real world was still catching up with the theoretical developments of the 1930s and 1940s. The position was summed up thus: 'The impact of newer model-based methods on sample survey practice has been small thus far, partly because I think sample survey theorists are seldom actively engaged in survey practice, and thus tend to write for other theorists' (Cochran 1976).

Some interesting experiments in a radically new, but nevertheless very practical, approach, which became known as *adaptive sampling*, began to appear in the 1980s (Thompson 1988). They were consolidated in a series of papers on *adaptive cluster sampling* (Thompson 1990), adaptive cluster sampling with sub-sampling (Thompson 1991a), *stratified* adaptive cluster sampling (Thompson 1991b) and *multivariate* adaptive cluster sampling (Thompson 1993), culminating in a comprehensive treatment of the whole new approach (Thompson and Seber 1996). The basic idea behind adaptive sampling is that 'the procedure for selecting the sample may depend on values of the variable of interest observed during the survey' (Thompson and Seber 1996, 1). This should appeal to archaeologists (see Shennan 1997, 385–90); it provides a theory for some popular practical techniques (see chapters 4 and 5), and will be discussed further below (p. 34). A related idea is that of *adaptive allocation*, reviewed by Solomon and Zacks (1970), which allows the design of stratified samples (p. 30) to be modified according to the results from an initial part of the survey.

Throughout the history of statistics, there has been an alternative theoretical basis, known as *Bayesian statistics* (after the Rev. Thomas Bayes, who formulated the basic theory (Bayes 1763)). It sees the role of data as modifying our beliefs and opinions about the world, and can be summed up in the deceptively simple equation

prior belief + data = posterior belief,

expressing the view that this should be done in a rational way. Despite its eighteenth-century origins, it made relatively little headway until the 1960s, partly because of the very heavy computation involved in implementing this equation in real situations. This problem is being overcome, partly through theoretical advances, and partly through the ever-increasing power of computers, and the methodology is spreading into various applied fields, including archaeology (Buck *et al.* 1996). The objection is sometimes raised that this approach gives too much weight to the subjective beliefs of the user. The answer is that this is true when there are only few data (in which case we have little to go on except for our beliefs, whatever our theoretical position), but that as more data are acquired, the importance of prior belief diminishes, to a point when it becomes almost irrelevant to our conclusion because it has been overwhelmed by the data. Its possible uses in field survey will be discussed in chapter 5.

### The language of sampling

Like all branches of mathematics, sampling theory has developed a language of its own to express precisely the concepts and techniques that it uses. Such languages are often called 'jargon', and are sometimes seen as a way of excluding outsiders. In reality, they are essential enablers of discussion and explanation between both theoreticians and practitioners. The true criticism of the way in which many specialists express themselves is not in the words that they use, but in the way those words are put together. Specialist terminology requires even greater attention than usual to the syntax in which it is embedded, if it is to be intelligible to the non-specialist.

On the other hand, the non-specialists must attempt to 'get their mind round' the meanings of at least the basic terms that are used, and that may require some effort on their part. 'Nothing is for nothing', as the saying goes. In this section and the next, there are brief non-technical explanations of the terms applied to the basic ideas and the common techniques used in statistical sampling. They are not intended to be rigorous definitions, but to aid the intuitive understanding that will be required in order to follow their use in the rest of this book. More formal and rigorous definitions can be found in many textbooks on sampling and statistics, and there are even dictionaries of statistics (e.g. O'Muircheartaigh and Francis 1981; Marriott 1989) for those who feel the need.

Statistical sampling is part of a bigger field of study known as *inference* (strictly speaking, *inductive inference*). The aim of inference is to draw conclusions about the general from information about the specific; in sampling, the general is the population (p. 18) and the specific is a sample drawn from it. In sampling, as in inductive inference in general, we can never be certain about our conclusions; the best we can do is to express them with a certain level of probability. One of the aims of sampling theory is to control that uncertainty, and achieve a reasonable balance between probability level and cost.

First, the basics: we suppose that we are studying a collection of 'objects', or an aggregation of some material, the chief characteristic of which is that we 'know where its edges are', i.e. given any object or material, we would know whether or not it was inside or outside our field of study. For example, if we are studying voting preferences in a constituency, then people are either on the electoral roll (and thus eligible to be studied) or they are not. If we are studying a region, the boundaries of that region must be clearly and unequivocally drawn. Sometimes it is not so easy to be definite. A study of Roman towns, for example, immediately raises the questions: what is a town? How can we define one? Rules are needed to enable researchers to decide what is 'in' and what is 'out' of the field of study. Once agreed, such a collection or aggregate is known as the *population*. A distinction is often made (e.g. by Cochran 1963, 6; Cherry *et al.* 1978, 5) between the *target population* (the population about which information is wanted) and the *sampled population* (the population from which the sample is actually drawn). Ideally, of course, they should coincide, but in practice there are many reasons why they may not. This is a particularly serious problem in archaeology, where a gap between the two can be opened up by inaccessibility of parts of a region, the pre- or post-excavation destruction of material, and many other factors. The problems are so serious and diverse that a separate chapter (chapter 3) is devoted to them.

What we study is the value(s) of one or more *variables* that could in principle be measured on each member of our population. A variable is just a characteristic that varies from one member to another: for example, the voting preference of an individual, the weight of a bag of crisps, or the number of 'sites' in a geographical area. There are different types of variables; the main ones are:

(a)  *nominal*: simple labels or 'names', with no order implied (e.g. artefact types),

(b)  *ordinal*: variables whose values have a definite order, but do not have equal differences between them (e.g. condition of an object, see p. 194),

(c)  *interval*: variables whose values do have equal intervals between them (e.g. date; the difference between 150 and 100 BC is the same as between 100 and 50 BC),

(d)  *ratio*: interval variables whose values can also be expressed as multiples of each other (e.g. length; 100 mm is twice the length of 50 mm, but 100 BC is not twice the date of 50 BC).

Variables of each type may for convenience or comparison be summarised by *estimates* of their *parameters*, for example estimates of their means, totals and standard deviations. Much of sampling theory is concerned with obtaining the 'best' possible estimates (and of trying to define what we mean by 'best') for a given input (time, money, etc.), or with minimising the costs of obtaining results of a required level.

We may be interested in a single variable or in many: the tendency is to collect many variables at the same time to reduce fieldwork costs (you may have encountered those long lists of apparently unrelated questions with which one is sometimes accosted in the street). The downside of this multivariate approach is that it makes the designing of the sample more difficult; it is straightforward (thanks to Neyman) to optimise the design of a sample survey for any one variable, but to optimise it for several variables at the same time is a complex task, both conceptually and practically.

A further distinction that is sometimes made (e.g. by Cochran 1963, 4) is between *descriptive* and *analytic* surveys. The purpose of the former is simply to obtain information about particular populations; in the latter, comparisons are made between subgroups of the population, or between the different variables observed, to gain greater insights into the factors at work. For example, a descriptive survey of the condition of a museum collection (see chapter 8) would just tell us how many objects were in each condition category, while an analytic survey would seek to relate this information to, for example, location in the store, with a view to assessing problem areas or 'hot spots'.

More recently, Thompson and Seber (1996, 4) divided sample designs into three categories: *conventional* (1 to 4 in the techniques section below, pp. 30–34), *adaptive* (5 in the techniques section, p. 34) and *non-standard*: designs in which the selection of the sample is influenced by values of units outside the sample (this tends to happen by accident rather than on purpose). They also made a distinction (1996, 5) between the *design-based approach* (which makes no assumptions about the nature of the population), and the *model-based approach* (which is based on an assumed model of the population).

Before we can sample, we must divide the population into *sampling units* (called *units* for short). Together they must cover the entire population, but they must not overlap (otherwise parts of the population would have either no chance, or an excessive chance, of being selected for the sample). Sometimes the choice of unit is obvious, e.g. the individual in an opinion poll, but sometimes (and frequently in archaeology) it is far from obvious. If we are surveying land, what are the units? Grid squares on a map? Administrative units (e.g. parishes)? Or something else? Such questions will be discussed in detail in chapters 4 and 5. Two popular units in archaeological fieldwork are the *quadrat* and the *transect*. A quadrat is usually understood to be a grid square (the word itself suggests a unit with four sides), but it *could* be taken to be any regular shape that completely fills a survey area, e.g. rectangles, equilateral triangles or even hexagons. Transects are long thin rectangular strips that stretch across a survey area, for example the area covered by an individual walker in a field. If we are sampling material, the size of the unit is a key question – do we need 100 g or just 1 g, for example? Such questions are looked at in chapters 6 and 7.

Whatever our definitions of units, it must be possible, at least in principle, to create a list of them: such a list is known as a *sampling frame*, and forms the basis of the sample selection. The sampling frame is thus crucial, but it may often be inadequate. Preliminary work may be needed to establish a satisfactory sampling frame before the real business can begin. The next step is the *sample design*, a procedure which says how many units are to be selected, and how this is to be done. Implicitly, it gives the probability of selection of each unit in the population, but it is not usually expressed in this way. The outcome of one selection procedure is a *sample*, which consists of a set of units and the values associated with them. This is contrary to the usual archaeological practice of calling individual units 'samples', which may account for the impression that some archaeologists have, that a 'sample' is a bag of mud lurking in the corner of a store.

The prime requirement of a sample is that it should be *representative*; as we saw above: the part should in some reliable way stand in for, or represent, the whole. Unfortunately, there is no infallible way of ensuring that a sample is truly representative except by comparing it with the population, which removes the need for sampling anyway. The best we can do is to try to minimise and quantify the risk that a sample is not representative, having first defined what representative might mean in any particular situation. It was this need that led to the creation of statistical sampling theory.

Some of the terms associated with the actual choosing of the sample can confuse the non-specialist. First among them is the term *random*, a nettle that must be grasped. It does not mean, as in the everyday sense, haphazard or careless, but quite the opposite. A *random sample* is one that is selected so carefully that we know the probability of any particular unit being selected for it (this is why it is sometimes called *probability sampling*). It is also important, in conventional sampling, that the selections are *independent*, i.e. the selection of a particular unit does not affect the chances of selection of the other units. One radical aspect of adaptive sampling is that it does away with this requirement, under controlled conditions. Originally, it was thought that each unit had to have the *same* probability of selection (see p. 14), but this has long been known not to be necessary, and this special case is known as *simple* random sampling. How can a simple random sample be drawn? The traditional approach is to give each unit a unique identifying number, and to draw the required number of numbers from a book or table of random numbers. Such books, which do not make the most exciting reading, have been available since at least the 1920s (e.g. Tippett 1927). Today, the numbers are often drawn by computer programs called *random number generators*, which, strictly speaking, generate *pseudo-random numbers* not genuinely random numbers. Usually, the difference is of no practical importance unless very large samples are drawn, or unless sampling is repeated on separate occasions, in which case the user must make sure that a different starting point, or *seed*, is given to the program (Freeman 1988, 142).

One ramification of random sampling is the distinction between *sampling with replacement* and *sampling without replacement*. In the former, units once selected are returned to the 'pool', and so become available for selection again, while in the latter they are not. Sampling with replacement has the advantage of making the statistical theory rather simpler, but the disadvantage that in practice it seems a very strange thing to do, and is difficult to defend. It is probably best to assume that archaeologists will want to sample without replacement, and accept the slight inaccuracies that may result in some of the formulae.

It is worth noting that the Bayesian approach (p. 16) does not have the requirement of random sampling. Instead, it has the concept of *exchangeability*: 'units are said to be exchangeable if our beliefs about the value of a characteristic of one unit are the same as our beliefs about the same characteristics of another' (Buck *et al.* 1996, 72). This means that a representative sample can consist of any units drawn from a collection of exchangeable ones (1996, 74).

All other ways of sampling are sometimes lumped together as *non-random* (or *non-probability*) sampling, although a variety of other terms are used: *judgement* or *purposive* sampling suggests care in the selection, while *grab* sampling suggests just the opposite. Often it depends on who is describing whose methods. One variant that has been particularly well developed is *quota* sampling, much used in opinion surveys. The idea is to match the characteristics of the sample to those of the population by ensuring that they (the sample and the population) have the same proportions of men and women, different age groups, etc., so the surveyor is given quotas of so many middle-aged men, etc., to interview. If you feel rejected when you are studiously ignored by a pollster in the street, it's nothing personal: they have just already filled their quota of whatever category you belong to. The value of quota sampling is hotly debated, even today: it can give good results, but is can produce disasters, perhaps linked to the under-representation of categories which are not mentioned explicitly in the definitions of the quotas, e.g. possibly the disabled.

Judgement samples are sometimes justified on the grounds that experienced practitioners can use their experience to select samples of 'typical' units, and so avoid the problem that a random sample might by chance include some very atypical units. One danger is that this approach is likely to under-estimate the variability of a population: this may be an important parameter in its own right, or it may just lead to over-confidence in the results. Another is that it is extremely difficult to achieve. As a simple experiment, lay out a population of twenty to thirty similar items on a table (e.g. pencils of different lengths, pebbles of different sizes), and ask people to select a sample of, say, five typical ones. Then compare the sample means of, for example, lengths or weights with the overall mean. This should destroy any faith you may have in judgement sampling.

Somewhere between random and judgement sampling comes *systematic* sampling. The idea is to simplify or speed up the process of selection by choosing units at equal intervals throughout the sampling frame, with only the first being selected at random. For example, if the *sampling fraction* is 1 in 10 (see below), a random number between 1 and 10 is drawn (say 6), and then the 6th, 16th, 26th, . . . units are selected. As only one random number is needed, instead of one for each member of the sample, the process is much quicker. It

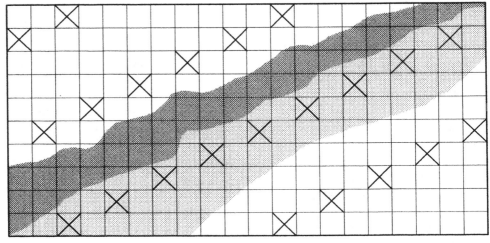

Fig. 2.1 A problem of using systematic sampling in areal surveys. A systematic sample of 1 in 9 squares is taken, indicated by crosses. The topographical zone indicated by light tone is heavily sampled, while the adjacent zone indicated by heavy tone is not sampled at all.

has the apparent advantage of distributing the sample more evenly across the population than a simple random sample would. Some practitioners worry that a truly random sample has the appearance of clustering (this is especially true of spatial sampling), and seek to avoid it; systematic sampling is one way of doing so. The big disadvantage is that the sampling interval may by misfortune (or Murphy's Law) relate to some regularity in the frame or in the data. For example, when sampling grid squares on a map, systematic sampling may generate diagonal lines of sampled squares, which in turn may relate to natural topographical or geological features (Fig. 2.1). On the other hand, there are situations in which systematic sampling can perform much better than simple random sampling. As Cochran (1963, 214) said: 'A knowledge of the structure of the population is necessary for its effective use.'

This discussion leads naturally to considerations of *sample size* or *sampling fraction*. The latter is just the fraction of the population that is to be sampled, e.g. '5%' or '1 in 20'. So we have the simple equation

$$\text{sampling fraction} = \text{sample size/population size.}$$

The inverse of the sampling fraction is sometimes known as the *raising factor*, because it is the number by which we must multiply (or *raise*) the sample values to get the population values. We will see later how to calculate the sample size that we need for a particular purpose. Here you should note the more general point that the important factor is sample size, *not* sampling fraction. The *precision* (see below) of our results depends on the size (and of course the design) of the sample, not on the fraction. There seems to be a myth, not only that the sampling fraction is what really matters, but that there is a 'minimum viable percentage' (e.g. 2%) that will, as if by magic, make a sample respectable. It cannot be stressed too strongly that none of this myth is true. What can be said is that the sampling fraction does have a slight effect on precision, in that sampling errors are reduced by what is known as the *finite population correction* (or *fpc*), which is given by the equation

$$\text{fpc} = \text{square root of } (1 - \text{sampling fraction}).$$

This obviously only matters if the sampling fraction is not small, i.e. bigger than say 10%.

Another term that causes endless confusion is *bias*. This usually crops up in questions like 'Is my sample biased?', which betrays the confusion because bias is not, strictly speaking, a property of an individual sample. Mathematically speaking, bias is the difference between the true value of a parameter (e.g. the mean of a population) and the *expectation* of the mean for a particular sampling procedure, i.e. the mean of the means of a very large number of samples, all taken according to that procedure. It can arise from one or more of:

(a) *Faults in the sampling procedure.* The classic case, often quoted, is of the voting intentions survey that used phone directories as a sampling frame, and predicted victory for the wrong candidate in a USA presidential election.

(b) *The nature of the estimation procedure.* For example, if the sampling units vary in size, taking a simple average of the figures from each will give a biased mean (but note that a *small* bias can be tolerated for the sake of computational simplicity or better precision).

(c) *Errors in the observing or measuring process.* An instrument may consistently read high or low, or an observer may consistently round up or round down. Such errors are known as *systematic errors*, to distinguish them from the more tractable random errors.

(d) *Differential response rates from within the sample.* For example, the visibility of archaeological sites may vary on different geological strata (see *detectability*, below).

The important point to note is that bias cannot be eliminated by increasing the sample size or by taking more samples; in fact, large samples may make matters worse. It is often a procedural problem, introduced by (for example) allowing too much discretion to the surveyors, rather than a purely statistical problem. There are techniques for detecting and/or reducing some sources of bias (e.g. frequent calibration of instruments, checking for inter-observer bias in the field), but the most common sources of undetected bias are probably errors in sample design and inappropriate calculations.

Yet more confusion arises from the term *significance*, an over-worked word that can carry at least three distinct meanings: *statistical significance, practical significance* and *archaeological significance*. Here I shall try to disentangle the first two; the third will be tackled in chapter 4. It is important to understand that the term statistical significance can only be applied to *differences*, not to individual statistics; we can say 'is the difference (e.g. in site density) between these regions statistically significant?' but we cannot say 'are the results from this region statistically significant?' (i.e. by themselves). What it means is 'can these samples *reasonably* be regarded as having been selected from the same population?' If they can, then we say that the difference between them is *not statistically significant*, and, by inference, we regard the populations as in some sense 'the same'. The word *reasonably* here reflects that fact that we can never be certain, but can only express our conclusion to a certain level of probability. For example, if we say that the difference between the samples is 'significant at the 5% level', what we are saying is that, *if* they had been selected from the same population, there would only be a 5% (or 1 in 20) chance that the difference between them would be as great as (or greater than) the difference we have actually observed. This is a back-handed way of saying that it is unlikely that they *did* come from the same population, i.e. that the two populations are likely to be different. We are *not* saying 'there is only a 5% chance that they come from the same population'; either they do or they don't.

The major problem with the idea of statistical significance is that it depends heavily on the sample size (see, for example, Cowgill 1977). If we increase the size of the samples, and the difference between them happens to stay the same, its statistical significance would *increase*, i.e. the probability of obtaining a difference that large from two samples from the same population would *decrease*. A point will come when any difference, however small, can be deemed to be statistically significant because the samples are so large. We keep our feet on the ground by introducing the idea of *practical significance*, and say that differences of less than 'so much' will be regarded as *practically insignificant*, even though they may be statistically significant. What this strange situation is trying to tell us is that the samples are too large (something that archaeologists find very hard to believe). Conversely, if the samples are very small, a difference may appear large, but fail to achieve statistical significance; in this case, the samples are too small (or the sample design is inefficient).

Closely related to the idea of significance is the technique of *hypothesis testing*, also called *selection* (Cowgill 1975), although this term has other meanings (p. 7). The idea is that we have a hypothesis about the parameter(s) of one or more populations, which we wish to test by means of observations made on samples taken from those populations. For example, the populations might be geographical zones, and the parameters the densities of sites in them, or they might be stores, and the parameters might be the proportions of objects in them requiring urgent treatment. We form a simple (or *null*) hypothesis, which usually represents 'no difference' (between populations) or 'no change' (between the same population on different occasions). We then either *accept* or *reject* the hypothesis by applying an acceptance rule to data from the sample(s) (e.g. 'accept the hypothesis if the difference between the sample means is less than a certain value, known as the *critical value*'). This raises the possibility that we may be wrong; we may reject the hypothesis when it is true (called a *type I error*) or we may accept it when it is false (called a *type II error*) – or, of course, we may be right in our acceptance or rejection. We need a strategy for handling these potential errors; the problem is that the smaller we make one, the larger we make the other. The classical hypothesis approach (and there are others, see for example Lindley 1985) is to choose an acceptable chance of making a type I error, which is called the *size* or more commonly the *significance level* of the test. From this, the sample size(s) and the variability of the data, the appropriate critical value can be calculated. The chance of not making a type II error (i.e. the chance of correctly rejecting a false hypothesis) is known as the *power* of the test. It depends on *how* false the hypothesis is – the bigger the discrepancy, the more likely we are to be able to detect it. So it makes sense to talk about a *power function* – the relationship between the size of the discrepancy and the power of the test, and for statisticians to seek to provide us with powerful tests. Since archaeologists find such ideas very difficult, a useful related concept may be that of an *indifference zone*, i.e. a range of values for which we do not mind whether the hypothesis is true or false. For example, we might say that we are not concerned with identifying changes in site density of less than (say) 10%, but we want to be 95% certain of detecting a change of 10% or more, as well as 95% certain of not saying it has changed if there was no change. This approach was used successfully by Bayliss and Orton (1994) in analysing scientific dating determinations.

As might be expected, this whole approach suffers from the same problem (crucial dependence on sample size) as discussed above in the context of statistical significance: if a sample is large enough, a hypothesis may be rejected on the basis of a very small discrepancy which may not be archaeologically significant (p. 24). Two other serious objections are as follows.

(a)   It is essentially a conservative procedure, in that it favours the *status quo*. Usually, a hypothesis is rejected only if the evidence against it is overwhelming. A null hypothesis may be preferred to a more plausible alternative simply because it is the null hypothesis.

(b)   It forces a rigid yes/no, accept/reject decision in circumstances when this may not be appropriate. The outcome may in fact be ambivalent, suggesting the need for further work, but this can easily be overlooked.

An important criterion that has already been mentioned is *precision*. It represents the average size of the difference between the true value of the parameter, and estimates obtained from a series of samples. It is thus a property of a particular sample design, and can be used to indicate the effectiveness of that design. A small value indicates a 'good' design, that is likely to produce a sample with a 'good' estimate, though even good designs can occasionally produce rogue samples. The design of a sample is often based on the need to achieve a specified level of precision for a minimum cost.

The precision of an estimate can be shown by expressing it as a range of possible values (a *confidence interval*) rather than as a single value (a *point estimate*). Together with the range of values, one must quote the probability that the true value lies in that range (this is known as the *confidence level*), because there is no range which one can be *certain* will include the true value. The greater the confidence we wish to place in it, the wider the interval will have to be. Much of sampling theory is involved with achieving useful confidence intervals with an adequate confidence level at an acceptable cost.

Precision is closely related to, but should not be confused with, *accuracy*. The accuracy of a sample is the difference between that sample's estimate and the true value of the parameter. As such, it is usually unknown (we can only know it if we know the true value, in which case why take a sample?), but we hope it will be small. What we can say is that precise procedures are likely to give accurate samples.

Another related concept is that of *relative efficiency*. If one sample design has a lower value of precision than another of the same sample size, it is said to be more efficient. If the designs are both unbiased, the relative efficiency is just the ratio of their variances (p. 29); if one or both is biased, the formula is more complicated but the general idea is similar.

The idea that objects may not be observed, even when they are present in a sampling unit, is well known in archaeology, but has only relatively recently received serious statistical attention, under the name of *detectability* (Shennan 1997, 390–3). Ways of dealing with it in conventional sampling are given by Steinhorst and Samuel (1989) and Thompson and Ramsey (1987), and in adaptive sampling by Thompson and Seber (1994; 1996, 211–33). Statistically, it is one among many sources of *non-sampling errors*, alongside *non-response* and *measurement errors*. Archaeologically, it is probably the most important of them.

Each object in a survey (e.g. site in a region, feature in a site) has a detection probability; it should be 100%, but may frequently be less, a situation known as *imperfect detectability*. The probability may depend on the sample design as well as on the object itself; for example, features may be less visible in small test-pits than in larger trenches, or in machine-dug trenches than in hand-dug ones, and so have a lower detection probability under those circumstances. The theory divides initially into two parts: when all objects have the same detection probability, and when the detection probability varies from object to object. Both parts can be divided into situations when the detection probability is known and when it must be estimated. The situation is more complicated for adaptive samples than for conventional ones, because in an adaptive design the presence of imperfect detectability will change, not just the estimates of

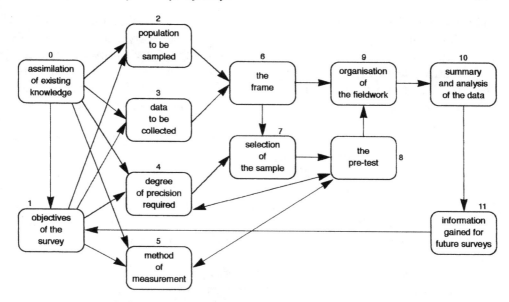

Fig. 2.2 Steps in the undertaking of a sample survey.

totals, etc., but also the design itself. In all cases, the basic idea is simple enough: we must adjust our estimates (and their standard errors) upwards to allow for imperfect detectability. How this is done is covered below (p. 39).

### The techniques of sampling

Before looking at the details of different sampling schemes (or strategies) that might be adopted, it is worth setting the question of choice of scheme in its wider context, by looking at the overall process of sample surveying. Cochran (1963, 5–8) gave a list of eleven steps in the overall process, to which I have added a twelfth (Fig. 2.2). They are:

0   assimilation of existing knowledge
1   objectives of the survey
2   population to be sampled
3   data to be collected
4   degree of precision required
5   method of measurement
6   the frame
7   selection of the sample
8   the pre-test
9   organisation of the fieldwork
10  summary and analysis of the data
11  information gained for future surveys.

This list may seem to play down the importance of the design and selection of samples, which only appears as no. 7 on it. That is probably a good impression to create – obviously design is important, but there are many other issues which may make or mar a sample survey, and to which careful attention must be paid. No amount of expertise in design can compensate for failings in other areas. It is therefore worth looking briefly at them before looking at the options available for design.

0 *Existing knowledge.* Archaeological sampling, in particular, is rarely carried out *in vacuo*, except for peculiarly innovative research, which is perhaps not as common as archaeologists would like to think. Almost always, we are adding to existing knowledge; this should be reflected in our aims, needs and design. Formally, it may be possible to incorporate existing knowledge through the use of Bayesian methods (p. 16); in general, any project should start with a clear summary of existing knowledge and its implications for the work to be done.

1 *Objectives.* Without clear objectives, a sample survey lacks focus and is not likely to succeed (indeed, it is difficult to tell what would constitute 'success'). In a multi-disciplinary project, the competing claims of different disciplines must be carefully weighed.

2 *Population.* The target population must be clearly defined, and the question of which parts of it are actually available for survey (the sampled population, see p. 18) must be considered. It is better, if possible, to discover which areas of a field survey (for example) are 'out of bounds' *before* the sample is designed, than to discover them in the course of fieldwork and have to redesign the survey 'on the fly'. Problems likely to arise from transformation processes (see chapter 3) should also be considered at this stage.

3 *Data to be collected.* A sample survey is selective in two ways – in the choice of units to be surveyed, and in the choice of data to be collected (variables to be measured). The temptation to collect as many data as possible 'in case it comes in useful' must be resisted: the chosen variables must be strictly related to the objectives of the survey.

4 *Degree of precision required.* How precise should our results be? For example, do we want to know the number of objects in a museum store that require immediate attention with an error margin of 100? or 1000? or 10% of the estimated number? And why? Such specifications are vital to the design of the sample. They may even challenge the viability of our survey – if we cannot achieve the required precision with the resources available, why are we doing the survey?

5 *Method of measurement.* In archaeology, this is often a matter of setting academically viable and practically usable definitions, e.g. how do we define 'condition' of an object? Or, in the field, what is a 'significant archaeological remain'?

6 *The frame.* What will our units be? There may be more flexibility than we think. For example, field surveys do not have to be based on grid squares or

transects; other shapes (even ones without straight edges) are statistically permitted (see chapter 4).

8 *The pre-test, or pilot survey.* One of the problems of survey design is that it is best done when the survey is over (because then we have all the information we need), but by then it is too late. This problem can be overcome to some extent by carrying out a small *pilot* survey, to get some idea of the variability in our population, and hence the size and design we shall need for our main survey. Pilot surveys also have the valuable role of discovering the 'bugs' in our system: difficulties of definition, ambiguous questions on a form, unrealistic time schedules, etc. It is always worth carrying out a pilot survey, if it is at all possible.

9 *Organisation.* The pilot survey can help here, by answering questions like 'how long will it take a team of *n* to fieldwalk *x* hectares under certain conditions?' or 'how long will it take a surveyor to assess the condition of *m* objects in a store?' (probably not as long as it takes to find them). As always, it is a question of matching resources with needs.

10 *Summary and analysis.* At this level of an overview, a few general points can be made. First, sufficient time must be allowed for this stage, and over-runs on fieldwork should not be allowed to erode it. It always takes longer than you think. Above all, think about this stage when planning the survey: don't call up your tame statistician with a pile of forms or computer print-out and ask him what to do with them. He will probably tell you.

11 *Information gained for future surveys.* As John Donne might have said, 'no survey is an island' (even if it is of an island). Your experiences, if properly digested and reflected on, will help you to improve your next survey, or help someone else to avoid the mistakes you made. So take time to reflect, be self-critical, and honest enough to make available a critique of your work.

Having set the question of sample design in context, we can now look at some of the options that are available, in terms of sample design (options 1 to 5) and methods of estimation (options 6 to 7). We start from the baseline of simple random sampling (p. 14), and look at some techniques that have been introduced to improve efficiency, to control error, or to make surveying more practicable. The statistical formulae that are needed to implement the various techniques are given in the Appendix; they are referred to here by formula numbers which are given in **bold type**. We start with formulae for estimates and standard deviations under simple random sampling, noting that there are different formulae according to whether we wish to estimate the mean or total of a value that is measured on each object (e.g. length) (**2.1, 2.2**), or whether we wish to estimate the proportion of objects of a particular type in an assemblage (**2.4, 2.5**). All these formulae can be 'reversed' to give the sample size needed to achieve a required level of precision (expressed in terms of the standard deviation or its square, the variance) (**2.3, 2.6**).

*1 Stratification*

This is an unfortunate parallel use of a 'jargon' word. It has nothing to do with archaeological or geological stratification (except as an analogy), but is the process of dividing the units of our population into subgroups, called *strata*. It was originally seen as a way of ensuring a balanced representation of different subgroups in a sample, since the same sampling fraction could be applied to each stratum in turn (this is known as *proportional allocation*). With simple random sampling, there is always a risk of an imbalance between subgroups (e.g. men and women in an opinion poll; different topographical zones in a field survey). It was developed by Neyman (p. 15), who

(a)   showed that, if the strata were appropriately defined, the use of different sampling fractions in different strata could reduce the sampling errors for a given overall sample size, and

(b)   gave a formula for the *optimum allocation* of units from different strata to the sample, i.e. an optimum set of sampling fractions (**2.9**).

This raises the question of how to define the strata or subgroups. The guiding principle is to minimise the variability within the strata, and to maximise it between the strata. For example, if we believe that the condition of objects in a store may vary from one end of the store to the other (perhaps because of environmental conditions), it would make sense to divide the store into 'vertical strata' along its length (Fig. 2.3). It might not make sense to use shelves (running from end to end of the store) as strata, because each might be just as variable as the whole store.

Stratification increases the complexity of the calculations that follow the survey, because the results for each stratum must be calculated separately, and then they must be aggregated to give overall results (**2.7, 2.8**). The only exception occurs when stratification is undertaken for purposes of control, and all strata have the same sampling fraction (*proportional allocation*), in which case the sample is known as *self-weighting* (Cochran 1963, 89) and the formulae for simple random sampling can be used.

Once again, the formulae can be 'reversed' to give the sample size needed to achieve a required level of precision; formulae for proportional and optimum allocation are given (**2.10, 2.11**).

*2 Cluster sampling*

This refers to a method of sampling in which each sampling unit consists of a group or *cluster* of smaller units, which Cochran (1963, 234) called *elements*. He put forward two reasons why one might wish to use cluster sampling.

(a)   The list of elements in the population is either unreliable, not available or too expensive to create. He gave the example of samp-

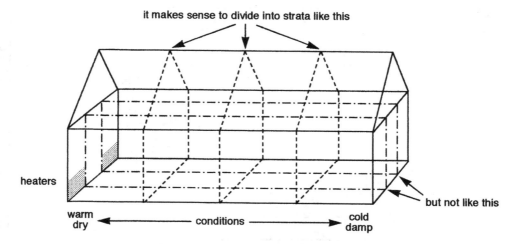

Fig. 2.3 An example of choosing a criterion for dividing a population into strata. The store is divided into strata each of which is as homogeneous as possible.

ling households or farms, where the cluster is a geographical block of land. In archaeology, one might encounter a similar problem in a regional survey, and decide to use quadrats or transects of land as clusters of archaeological 'sites' or other forms of evidence (Mueller 1975a); while at the other end of the scale, the collection of inclusions visible in a ceramic thin-section through a graticule might be taken as a cluster sample of inclusions.

(b)    Even when a reliable sampling frame is available, it may be more economic to sample blocks of (for example) addresses, rather than ones selected individually. The reduction in cost and time in travelling from one element to the next makes it possible to sample more elements in the same time or for the same cost (e.g. see Brand 1992).

This approach immediately raises the question – what is the 'best' size of unit? We shall see in detail how archaeologists have tried to answer this in chapters 4 to 7, but some preliminary general ideas may be useful. From a purely statistical point of view, smaller units are usually more efficient than larger ones (i.e. they have lower standard errors for the same total area surveyed), because the values at adjacent small units are often positively correlated, and thus going from (for example) a 1 km square to a 2 km square (4 sq km) does not give us four times as much information (Fig. 2.4). However, in a field survey, the nature of the fieldwork cost plays a large part in determining the optimum unit (Cochran 1963, 245). The cost of locating and travelling to a unit will be approximately the same, whatever its size; only the cost of actually surveying it will vary. So, for example, it might cost the same to sample only three separate 1 km squares as one 2 km square. Which is the more efficient will

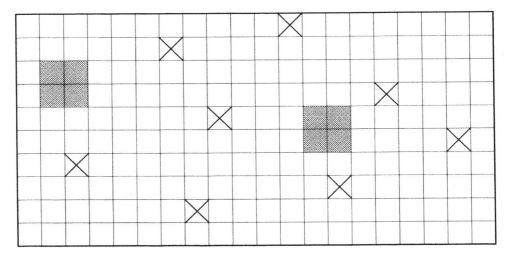

Fig. 2.4 Contrast between the efficiency of four 1 km squares and one 2 km square. Each group of four isolated quadrats, indicated by crosses, is likely to be more informative that the corresponding block of four adjacent ones, indicated by toning, because the data in adjacent quadrats are likely to be correlated.

depend on the correlation between the smaller elements in the larger unit, as well as the details of the cost function: both can only be assessed by a pilot survey, or perhaps by experience of a previous survey in similar terrain.

In archaeology, we often have to deal with cluster units of unequal sizes. For example, the number of sites discovered in each unit (e.g. quadrat) may vary greatly, as may the number of ceramic inclusions per unit area. This is permissible within the theory of cluster sampling, but raises the possibility of a choice of estimates of (for example) the population mean. The best is often found to be the *sample mean per element* (**2.12, 2.13**); it has a slight bias but this is often offset by a better precision than the unbiased estimate, especially if the number of elements varies greatly from one unit to another.

Another common situation is that of sampling cluster units of unequal sizes for proportions of different types of objects in the samples; this often arises in soil sampling (chapter 6). The usual approach is just to treat the whole sample, however it is taken, as a single unit, and use the standard formulae (**2.4, 2.5**) for estimating proportions and their standard deviations. However, this is incorrect as we are dealing with cluster samples, not simple random samples, and the formula will tend to under-estimate the variability, sometimes seriously. If several samples are taken (and not aggregated), the appropriate formulae are **2.14, 2.16**, and the change (usually an increase) in the variance is given by **2.17**. If only one sample is taken, or if multiple samples are aggregated, there is no way of estimating the variance (since the sample size is 1; for example, the statistical size of a soil sample is one unit, even though it may contain hundreds of bone fragments or seeds, see chapter 7), and hence no way of attaching error margins to the estimated proportions. Examples of improper use were given by Kish (1957).

### 3 Multi-stage cluster sampling

Here 'multi' is used to mean 'more than one'; the cluster sampling procedure discussed above should properly be called 'single-stage cluster sampling'. It is often desirable, or even necessary, to take sub-samples from a sample of primary units. For example, we may want to survey a sub-sample of fields from a primary sample of parishes, or a sub-sample of thin-sections or chemical analyses from a sample of sherds. The theory varies according to whether the primary units are of equal or unequal size; the latter is more likely to be encountered in practice, and is also the more flexible statistically, giving us ranges of options on

(a)   the selection of primary sampling units,
(b)   sub-sampling fractions, and
(c)   methods of estimation.

The approach can also be combined with stratified sampling (p. 30), by treating each stratum separately and aggregating the results.

(a)   Primary units can be chosen with (i) equal probabilities, (ii) *probability proportional to size* (*pps*), or (iii) *probability proportional to estimated size* (*ppes*) (see below, p. 34), if the exact sizes are not known. The 'size' of a unit is the number of elements in it.
(b)   Sub-sampling fractions can be chosen to be equal across all primary units (this is often associated with choosing primary units with equal probabilities), or can be chosen to make the probability of selection of an element the same regardless of the unit to which it belongs (this is often associated with pps sampling of the primary units).
(c)   In either case of (b), the resulting sample is *self-weighting*, i.e. the mean per element can reasonably be used as an estimate of the population mean (**2.18**). This is an important consideration, since it greatly reduces the complexity of the post-survey calculations.

More complicated schemes can be devised, and may result in some improvement in precision, but this is rarely worth the extra effort, risk of calculation errors, and the hassle of trying to explain it to colleagues. Overall, it can be seen that 'the efficient design of a multi-stage sample with primary units of unequal size requires a good deal of preliminary work' (Cochran 1963, 322).

There is no reason why we cannot have more than two stages, i.e. why we cannot sub-sample from our sub-samples (e.g. transects within field within parishes), but the added level of complexity makes it even more important to keep the basic principles simple.

### 4 Sampling with probability proportional to size (pps) or estimated size (ppes)

If the numbers of elements in each primary unit are known, pps sampling can be a very attractive option. It is easy to achieve; for example, if we list the primary units in random order, cumulate their sizes, and draw a systematic sample (p. 21) from the cumulated sizes, we have a pps sample of the units (Hartley and Rao 1962) (Fig. 2.5). A possible problem is that large units may be selected more than once. This is only a problem if the sampling fraction is large and some primary units are much larger than others; special techniques have been devised to deal with such situations (Cochran 1963, 260–2).

If the number of elements in each primary unit is not known, an estimate of it can be used as a proxy and we have ppes sampling. How 'good' a sampling method it is depends fairly obviously on how good an estimate we have; ideally, a measure of size that is likely to be proportional to the item totals of the primary units is best.

### 5 Adaptive sampling

As we have seen above, adaptive procedures allow for the possibility of sample designs being modified by values obtained in the sample (p. 16). It is probably best to try to understand this through a simple example of adaptive cluster sampling. Suppose we are surveying a region for 'sites', using quadrats as our sampling units. Conventionally, we just sample so many units, count the sites, perform some calculations, and that's that.

In adaptive cluster sampling (see Thompson and Seber 1996, 94–5), we first define a *neighbourhood* of units belonging to each unit: it might consist of every adjacent unit, every unit with a common edge, or some more complicated pattern (Fig. 2.6). We then survey a sample of units and, for every unit that meets a certain pre-assigned condition (e.g. that it contains more than a certain number of sites), we additionally sample all the units in its neighbourhood. If any of these units meet the condition, we sample all the units in their neighbourhood, and so on until the process stops. If a unit does not meet the condition, we do not sample any additional units. The final sample consists of one or more *clusters* of units, each of which is bounded by a series of *edge units* that do not meet the condition (Fig. 2.7). Because edge units can belong to more than one cluster at a time, Thompson and Seber (1996, 94) define the *network* of a unit as all those units in the same cluster as it, excluding the edge units; any unit that does not meet the condition is defined as a network of size 1. Thus every unit belongs to just one network, and the selection of any unit in

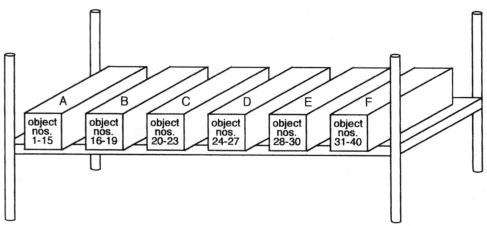

Fig. 2.5 Example of the selection of a pps sample of primary units, in this example boxes on a shelf. A systematic sample of every 12th object, starting with no. 7, would select boxes A, B and F, but not C, D or E. If all of each selected box is then examined, their selection was with pps. The 'larger' boxes have a greater chance of selection, but any box could be selected.

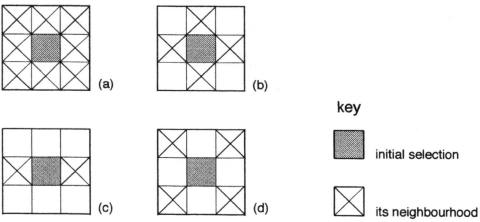

Fig. 2.6 Examples of neighbourhoods in adaptive cluster sampling: (a) all adjacent squares, (b) all squares sharing a common edge, (c) all squares 'east' and 'west' of the initial selection, (d) all squares touching the initial selection diagonally. In each case, the initial selection is indicated by a heavy tone and the squares in its neighbourhood by crosses.

a network leads to the selection of all the units in that network. Having selected the sample, how do we estimate (for example) the number of sites in the region? And what is the precision of this estimate? Formulae for an unbiased estimator and its variance are given in equations (**2.19, 2.20**). The approach can be quite flexible; for example, one could combine initial transects with additional quadrats added at points where the condition is met (Thompson and Seber 1996, 121–3) (Fig. 2.8).

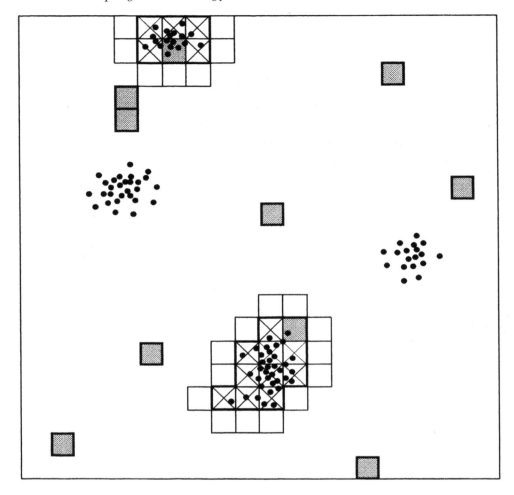

Fig. 2.7 Example of an adaptive sample, showing initial selection (indicated by heavy tone), networks (additional squares indicated by crosses) and edge units (outlined only).

At this point, the archaeologist might well ask:

(a)  How does this precision compare with that of a conventional cluster of the same size?

(b)  And how can I cost a survey when I don't know in advance how many units will be sampled?

(a) *Precision*. The efficiency of adaptive cluster sampling in comparison with a simple random sample of primary units depends on the characteristics of the population – sometimes one scheme will be more efficient and sometimes the other. It is therefore important to know the circumstances in which adaptive

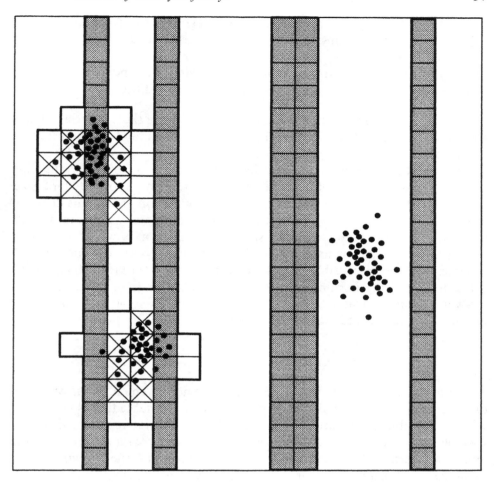

Fig. 2.8 Example of adaptive sampling, using transects as initial units (indicated by heavy tone) and additional quadrats (crosses for those in the networks; edge units outlined only).

cluster sampling is likely to be the more efficient. Thompson and Seber (1996, 159) listed several criteria which indicate when this is likely to be the case.

(i)   The population is clustered or tends to aggregate.
(ii)  The number of units in the population is large compared to the number that satisfy the condition, i.e. the study area is big relative to the area in which sites (or other archaeological objects) are likely to be encountered.
(iii) The expected final sample size is not much larger than the initial sample size.

(iv)   The costs of observing units in clusters or networks is less than the cost of observing the same number selected at random throughout the region.

(v)    The cost of observing units not satisfying the condition is less than the cost of observing units satisfying the condition.

It seems likely that a field survey might satisfy enough of these criteria to make a *prima facie* case for adaptive sampling, while an examination of inclusions in a thin-section (for example) might not.

(b) *Cost*. The first point to make is that the cost of adaptive cluster sampling is usually less than that of a conventional cluster sample of the same size, because less travelling time will be involved (see criterion 4). But this does not overcome the point that we do not know, before we start, how many units there will be in an adaptive cluster sample. By criterion 3, we would not be using adaptive cluster sampling if the difference were great, so it should, with some experience, be possible to make a notional allowance (e.g. 50%) for the extra units, bearing in mind that they will be cheaper than the initial units anyway. Thompson and Seber (1996, 159–61) made some suggestions for limiting sample size and dealing with the unexpected.

### 6 Ratio and regression estimation

Sometimes it is possible to make a considerable improvement in the precision of a survey's results by making use of an *auxiliary* variable that is correlated with the variable that we are studying. If we know the total (or the mean) of this variable in the whole population, we can estimate the total (or mean) of the 'unknown' variable by multiplying the total (or mean) for the known variable by the *ratio* of the unknown variable to the known variable in the sample. Such estimates are known, not surprisingly, as *ratio estimates* (**2.21**). They are biased, but the effect is negligible if the sample size is large, and often more than compensated for by the lower standard error (**2.22**).

They appear to be rarely used in archaeology, but would seem to have uses in situations where the auxiliary variable can be measured 'in bulk'. For example, if we want to estimate the average capacity of a collection of whole pots of similar form, we could weigh them all together, then select a small sample, weigh them individually and measure their capacities, and use the ratio of capacity to weight in the sample to convert the total population weight to an estimate of total capacity, and hence to average capacity. This is likely to be more precise than just taking the average capacity of the pots in our sample.

Regression estimates are similar to ratio estimates, but are appropriate to use when the relationship between the unknown and the auxiliary variable, although still linear, does not pass through the origin, i.e. both variables are not zero at the same time. This approach can be useful in estimating the time needed to carry out a survey; a pilot sample could give us the time taken to survey a few units of varying sizes, and the results could be scaled up to predict the time needed for the whole survey. Regression estimates are more satisfactory than ratio estimates here because survey overheads mean that a simple ratio is not appropriate (it does not usually, for example, take twice as long to survey ten objects in a store as it does to survey five).

### 7 Adjusting for imperfect detectability

If the detectability is constant, and the design is conventional, adjustment is simple: estimates of totals are just scaled up by dividing by the detection probability, and there is a simple formula for the increase in sampling error (**2.23**, **2.24**). If the detectability has to be estimated (but is still assumed to be the same for all objects) then estimation remains the same, but the sampling error is increased and its formula becomes more complicated. Increasing levels of complexity (variable detectability, estimates of variable detectability, and finally applications to adaptive designs) were covered by Thompson and Seber (1996, 211–33).

A particular problem for archaeologists is that their detection probabilities may be neither known nor estimated, but, to put it crudely, *guessed*. It could be argued that a guess is just a type of estimate, but a crucial difference is that while estimates come with standard errors attached to them, guesses do not, and the formulae require standard deviations. Archaeologists will have to assess what confidence they can put on their guesses (e.g. does 50% mean 'between 40% and 60%', or 'between 25% and 75%', or what?), and work from such margins to notional standard deviations (in these examples, perhaps 5% and 12.5% respectively, if the ranges are taken as notional 95% confidence intervals). In the longer term, as experience accumulates, it may be possible to derive such figures from previous work, and the problem will be overcome.

### Conclusion

This chapter has set out the bare bones of sampling theory and practice in a very general way. Chapters 4 to 8 will show how the flesh can be put on these bones in some of the wide range of circumstances in which archaeologists may find themselves, from the regional to the microscopic level.

**3**

# IF THIS IS THE SAMPLE, WHAT WAS THE POPULATION?

### Introduction

Before moving on to look at the applications of statistical sampling theory and practice at a range of archaeological scales (chapters 4–8), we first make a diversion into archaeological theory. In this chapter we shall consider what insights the statistical theory of chapter 2 might be able to give us into the broader question of archaeological *inference*, that is, of inferring past activities from present-day archaeological remains. Archaeological inference is of course an enormous topic (see Sullivan 1978 for an overview; for a more recent view see Adams 1991), deserving of a book in itself, and it is not my intention to cover its full breadth here. But an approach grounded in statistical theory may at least help to clarify some issues, and to suggest appropriate methods of recording and analysis in certain situations.

It is a truism that archaeological remains, whether in the form of features or of artefacts, are rarely the totality originally created by, or used in, the activities that they now represent. In a sense, they are a 'sample' from some original but unknown 'population'. For example, coins found on the site of a Roman town may be regarded as a sort of sample of those in circulation at that location at a certain period, or the sherds from a waster dump at a pottery production site may be regarded as another sort of sample of the pottery produced there. The big question is: *what sort* of a sample? Are the processes that intervened between production and retrieval regular or predictable enough for the characteristics of the modern retrieved assemblage (such as its *composition*, see p. 157) to be a reliable guide to the characteristics of the archaeological population from which they have been derived? This question goes to the heart of archaeological inference; if the processes are so variable, irregular or unpredictable that we cannot make a link, then for what are we excavating or undertaking an archaeological survey? Certainly, quantified data would, under such circumstances, be of little use, and even qualitative data (e.g. presence/absence) would not be reliable, subject as they are to problems such as those that arise from variations in sample size (see pp. 171–6). It is always possible to compare present-day archaeological assemblages, using a growing range of statistical techniques; the problem lies in deciding whether any patterns that we may observe are due to patterns in the original populations, or to patterns within the processes that led from one to the other (or, quite possibly, to both).

A common approach to this problem is to make a firm distinction between the *target population* and the *sampled population* (e.g. Chenhall 1975; Cherry *et al.* 1978, 5). The former is defined (e.g. by Mood and Graybill 1963, 141) as the totality of elements which are under discussion and about which information is desired. It must be capable of being precisely defined, although it may be real or hypothetical. It is often impossible to select a random sample from the whole of such a population, in which case it must be selected from a related smaller population, the sampled population, which can be defined as the population from which our sample can reasonably be though to be a random sample (Mood and Graybill 1963, 142). The relationship between the sample and the sampled population can then, it is argued, be treated as a statistical problem, whatever the discipline, while the relationship between sampled population and target population is for the theory of the discipline concerned. The latter relationship may be seen as a 'black box' with inputs and outputs that we seek to model, or it may be broken down into a series of step or discontinuities, each of which must be taken into account. Collins (1975, 29) listed them as follows:

(a) Not all behaviour patterns result in patterned material culture.
(b) Of those which do, not all will occur where there is an opportunity for inclusion in archaeological context.
(c) Of those so occurring, not all will be included in such context.
(d) Of those which are included, not all will be preserved.
(e) Of those which are preserved initially, not all will survive.
(f) Of those surviving, not all will be exposed to, or by, the archaeologist.
(g) Among patterns exposed to the archaeologist, not all will be perceived or properly identified.

The difference between these approaches can be seen graphically in Fig. 3.1.

In this chapter we shall look first at the history of this approach, trying to avoid entanglement in the wider issues of archaeological inference and interpretation as far as is possible. Then we shall look at two areas in which statistical sampling theory may have a useful contribution to make:

(a) the comparison of artefact and ecofact assemblages, which will be useful background to chapter 6,
(b) the use of surface remains, both in their own right and as a predictor of sub-surface remains, in archaeological survey, which will be useful background to chapters 4 and 5.

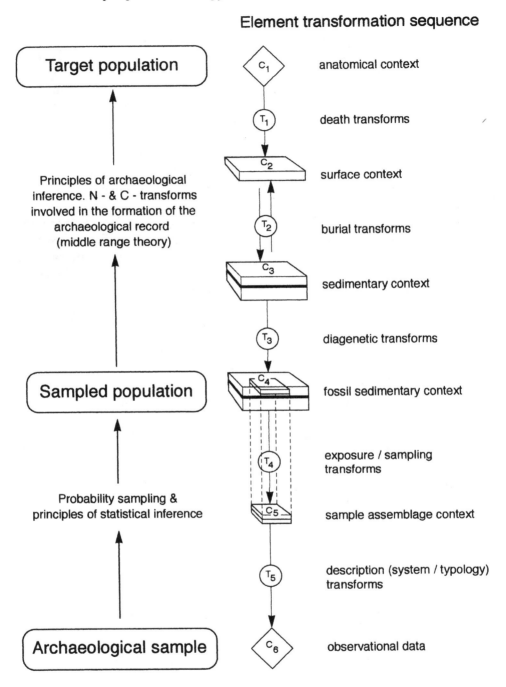

Fig. 3.1 The relationship between target population, sampled population and sample, expressed as 'black boxes' (*left*) or as a series of steps (*right*) (redrawn from Cherry *et al.* 1978, 5 and Gifford 1981, 387).

### History

Researching the history of this approach has reminded me of the saying that 'the surprise is that the dog did nothing in the night' (*The Memoirs of Sherlock Holmes*). Once archaeologists started to use quantified data to compare assemblages, as they were doing from early this century for purposes of seriation (Orton *et al.* 1993, 11) their analyses were vulnerable to the sorts of problems mentioned above. And yet, so to speak, the dog did nothing: discussion of the biases in the archaeological record due to post-depositional factors does not seem to start until the late 1960s. An early mention of the contrast between the *target* and *sampled populations* (p. 41) was made by Ragir (1967; 1972, 184), based apparently on the analogous problem in palaeontology (Krumbein 1965); the general problem was well stated by Cowgill (1970). A study of modern artefacts in a state of decay (Ascher 1968) has been seen as an early general approach (Schiffer 1987, 9).

The general statement of the problem in terms of stages of decay and/or transformation between the living assemblage and the excavated assemblage rapidly became part of the conventional wisdom (e.g. Daniels 1972; Clarke 1973) and was well established by the time of the San Francisco Symposium, where it was stated in detail by Collins (1975). Explicit use of sampling theory, in contrast to the voicing of general concern, was left to specialists in particular topics (e.g. animal bone, Krantz 1968, Fieller and Turner 1982; pottery, Orton 1975), perhaps because the wide differences in behaviour between different classes of material makes a general theory extremely difficult to achieve. The most determined attempts to establish a general theory have been those of Schiffer (e.g. 1976; 1987).

The question remains – why did the dog do nothing for at least fifty years? A possible explanation is that the older 'inductive' or culture history school, which predominated until the 1950s/early 1960s, was simply not interested in such questions, or did not have the mathematical expertise needed to pursue them, for 'archaeologists have tended not to use mathematical models to define either the archaeological record or past phenomena or the relationship between the two' (Fritz 1972, 142). The 'new' archaeologists of the 1960s and 1970s, with their emphasis on deductive reasoning, tended to bypass the problem by choosing the variables least likely to be affected by it. It was left to archaeologists in neither school (e.g. Cowgill) to voice the question.

Since the 1970s, debate has continued at the level of the specific topic (see case studies below), rather than at a more general theoretical level, with some notable exceptions (e.g. Cowgill 1994). This may be because, once again, such questions were not of concern to the current generation of those who saw themselves at the forefront of archaeological theory. That does not mean, however, that the topic has gone away, or that it can be ignored. The following studies show that it can be of great concern to practising archaeologists.

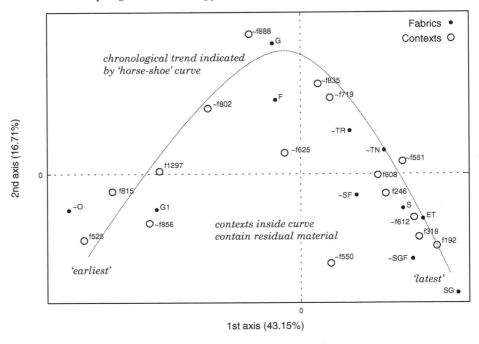

Fig. 3.2 Seriation of first-century AD pottery from Silchester, using correspondence analysis (Tyers 1996, Fig. 22).

### Assemblages of artefacts and/or ecofacts

The characterisation of a single assemblage, for example in terms of its *composition* – the proportions of different types of objects (artefacts and/or ecofacts) in it – is of relatively little use in itself. Such data gain value by being compared to data from other related assemblages (Orton 1993). A chronological study may concentrate on the comparison of assemblages from the same location over a period, perhaps by the use of *seriation* (Marquardt 1978) (Fig. 3.2), while a distributional study may compare more-or-less contemporaneous assemblages from across a region (Fig. 3.3), perhaps to shed light on methods of distribution from production centres (e.g. Fulford and Hodder 1974). Within a site, spatial differences between assemblages may perhaps be ascribed to functional or social differences (e.g. Barclay *et al.* 1990; see Fig. 3.4). The nature of the explanation depends on the archaeologist's research intentions and the potential of the data to answer them, and need not directly concern us here; the point is that it is based on the comparison of two or more assemblages.

Typically, archaeologists use statistical techniques such as the *chi-squared test* (accounts can be found in almost any textbook on statistics) to compare the counts of objects of each type in each assemblage (it is to be hoped that they use the counts, not percentages, see Cowgill 1975). This technique itself carries

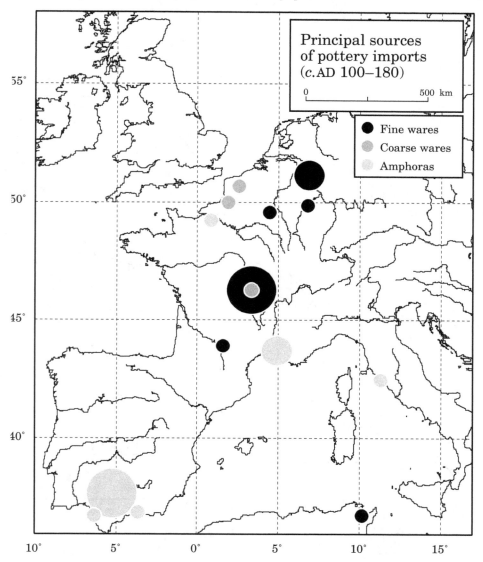

Fig. 3.3 Quantified sources of pottery imported into Roman Britain in the second century AD (Tyers 1996, Fig. 39).

an implicit assumption that the assemblages are random samples from populations, and that we are interested in seeing whether patterns in the assemblages reflect real variations in the populations, and are not just sampling variation (Cowgill 1970; Juhl and Marksted 1991). This is a good start, but only a start, because it begs the question of whether they are random samples, and if so, of what population? Looked at another way, is it possible to define populations from which they *could* be considered to be random samples (Orton 1978)?

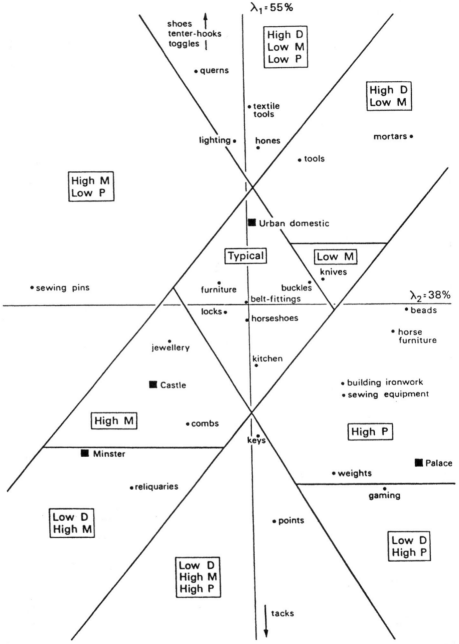

Fig. 3.4 Correspondence analysis plot showing the associations of different types of artefact with different types of site in medieval Winchester. The plot has been divided into zones according to whether each type of find is more common than expected ('High') on a particular type of site, or less common than expected ('Low'). 'Typical' finds occur in roughly the expected proportions on all types of site. (Barclay *et al.* 1990, Fig. 6, by permission of Oxford University Press.)

We shall approach this question gradually, through a series of case studies of increasing complexity. The 'choice' of the relevant populations is crucial for interpretation, since they must be populations about which we wish to say something.

There seems to be a sort of 'trade-off' here: the more 'useful' (from an archaeological point of view) a population is, the less likely it is that an assemblage can reasonably be seen as a random sample from it . For example, suppose we are studying the distribution of a particular type of pottery within a region. Looking at any one settlement site in the region, the target population might be the totality of pottery discarded at that site in a certain period (or there might be several target populations, each relating to a different period). What sort of assemblage might relate to such a target population? The assemblage from a single feature (e.g. a pit) of the appropriate date would be easy to define, but its target population might well be too narrow, relating to only a part (and not necessarily a representative one) of the site. At the other extreme, the totality of pottery from the site would be equally easy to define, but its target population might well be too broad, comprising pottery from several periods. The 'happy medium' would be a target population of all the pottery discarded at the site in a certain period; this might be much more difficult to define, especially if residuality is a serious problem. Thus the easily defined assemblage may be of relatively small interpretative value, while the assemblage needed for interpretation may be very difficult to define.

Simple random sampling is a very strict assumption to have to make, and we might reasonably try to find weaker assumptions that still meet our needs. *Stratified sampling* (p. 30) is a possible candidate, with the different types forming the different strata, and having potentially different *sampling fractions* (p. 22). This would introduce a *bias* (p. 23) into each assemblage, in that it would not accurately reflect the composition of its parent population, but nevertheless *differences* between populations could be reflected by differences between assemblages, and *vice versa*.

To make progress at this point, we need to think through the stages that might intervene between the target population and the sampled population. We are here in the realms of *site formation processes* (Schiffer 1976), or, looking particularly at the effects on objects (artefacts and/or ecofacts), in the sub-discipline of *taphonomy*. This is a term coined by Efremov (1940) for a sub-discipline of palaeontology, from the roots *taphos* (tomb or burial) and *nomos* (law or system of laws) (Gifford 1981, 366), which has since become a thriving branch of archaeological research (e.g. Noe-Nygaard 1987; Lyman 1994), as well as a major contributor to palaeontology.

A primary distinction that must be made is between a *life assemblage* and a *death assemblage*, for example between the assemblage of pots in use at a certain location at a certain time, and the assemblage of pots discarded at that location over a certain period. The distinction is, so to speak, demographic, and the differences between the two depend on the different use-lives of the types of pots in the assemblage (see Orton *et al.* 1993, 207–9, for a fuller discussion). The distinction can also be seen as that between the *stock* of objects within a system at a point in time, and the *flow* of objects through that system over time. There is as yet no convincing way of estimating relative use-lives of archaeological objects (and there may never be one), so recourse is made to ethnographic parallels (e.g. DeBoer 1974), which show that wide variations can exist.

From this point on, another distinction must be made – that between at least four classes of archaeological objects:

(a)  those that are usually found in a complete, or near-complete, state (e.g. coins),
(b)  those that are usually found in a broken state, but different parts of which are usually likely to have the same post-depositional history (e.g. pottery),
(c)  those that are commonly recycled (e.g. glass),
(d)  those that are usually found broken, but for which different parts may have different histories (e.g. animal bones).

Objects of each class have different probabilities of being included in the archaeological record, of being preserved to the present day, of being retrieved in the course of fieldwork (excavation or surface survey), and of being recognised and identified. Much can be, and has been, written about each of these stages, but as we are here looking specifically at the contribution statistical sampling theory might make, I shall treat the whole process as a series of 'sampling events', interspersed if appropriate with 'breakage events'. Further complications can be caused by differences between archaeological workers, both at the retrieval stage (Haselgrove 1985, 23) and at the stage of identification or classification (Beck and Jones 1989). The use of statistical sampling as a metaphor for all these processes suggests that we should concentrate on the relationship between the sample and the target population, rather than on the two separate relationships between sample and sampled population, and between sampled population and target population, because any deliberate sampling that we may employ is just one amongst several stages of sampling.

A good example of the first class of object is that of coins. They have been extensively studied, and, for at least some periods and some parts of the world, can be classified with considerable confidence. Databases are beginning to be made available, including discoveries from many sites in a region, so that data can be analysed and re-analysed (e.g. Reece 1995). What can they tell us? What can our samples tell us about our target populations, for example about the discard patterns on sites in Roman Britain? Using the sampling metaphor, we cannot say anything from the overall size of a sample assemblage, since we do not know the *sampling fraction* (which stands for the overall level of survival

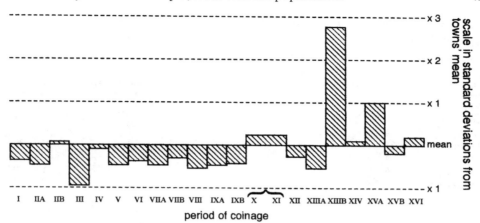

Fig. 3.5 Example of a comparison of the chronological profile of the Roman coin assemblage from a site (Neatham, Hampshire) with a hypothetical 'norm' (the average assemblage for Romano-British towns). This was used as the basis of an argument for above-average activity at Neatham from period XIIIB (AD 330) onwards. (Millett and Graham 1986, Fig. 4, by permission of the Hampshire Field Club and Archaeological Society.)

combined with the intensity of fieldwork). We *could* compare the totals from two sites, but only if we are prepared to assume an equal sampling fraction at each (i.e. equal rates of survival and intensity of fieldwork). However, one of the main uses of coin data is to provide a chronological *profile* of a site, i.e. the proportions of the total assemblage that can be assigned to different periods within a site's life. The term *profile* is thus similar to *composition*, except that it carries an ordering of the categories as well as a breakdown into the proportions in each category. For a single site, such a use raises archaeological problems, since coins of a certain period may be less valuable than coins of another, so that a larger sample may not necessarily reflect increased economic activity. But suppose we compare two sites? Surely then these factors 'cancel out', and we can safely say (for example) that site A was more 'active' at one period and site B at another (Fig. 3.5)? This argument carries an implicit assumption that the sampling fractions of different types of coins at site A are proportional to the corresponding sampling fractions at site B, which is not necessarily the case. If, for example, the methods of retrieval were different (e.g. chance collection, systematic fieldwalking, sieved or unsieved excavation, metal-detecting), then the relative sampling fractions of different types of coin may vary from site to site, and we may find that we are studying, not so much differences between sites as differences between methods. For example, in Roman Britain the bronze coinage of the first to second centuries AD tends to be large, while that of the third to fourth centuries tends to be small, some very small. The different modes of retrieval listed above are likely to have different relative probabilities of retrieving large, small and very small coins, and so have different relative sampling fractions. Comparison of the profiles in ignor-

Table 3.1 *Numbers of finds from excavations in medieval Winchester, by find type and context date (from Barclay et al. 1990, 54, Table 9; my bolds).*

| Find type | context date by latest century to eleventh | eleventh | twelfth | thirteenth | fourteenth | fifteenth | sixteenth | later | total |
|---|---|---|---|---|---|---|---|---|---|
| beads | 1 | 2 | 1 | – | 4 | 2 | 8 | 19 | 37 |
| belt-fittings | 5 | 8 | 5 | 12 | 17 | 27 | 4 | 13 | 91 |
| buckles | 4 | 14 | 17 | 57 | 55 | 44 | 34 | 33 | 258 |
| building ironwork | 25 | 20 | 24 | 58 | 39 | 21 | 19 | 24 | 230 |
| combs | 9 | 12 | 6 | 2 | 2 | – | 4 | 10 | 45 |
| furniture | 16 | 10 | 6 | 20 | 8 | 4 | 8 | 8 | 80 |
| gaming equipment | 8 | 6 | 9 | 10 | 7 | 5 | 4 | 8 | 57 |
| hones | 17 | 28 | 17 | 42 | 29 | 23 | 5 | 9 | 170 |
| horse furniture | 5 | 8 | 6 | 26 | 12 | 5 | 4 | 11 | 77 |
| horseshoes | 23 | 36 | 52 | 104 | 63 | 17 | 19 | 33 | 347 |
| jewellery | 24 | 17 | 13 | 25 | 21 | 10 | 8 | 22 | 140 |
| keys | 12 | 32 | 23 | 38 | 21 | 15 | 10 | 19 | 170 |
| kitchen equipment | 11 | 6 | 13 | 13 | 9 | 6 | 12 | 10 | 80 |
| knives | 38 | 56 | 42 | 66 | 48 | 22 | 34 | 44 | 350 |
| lighting equipment | 5 | 20 | 35 | 50 | 19 | 7 | 2 | 6 | 144 |
| locks | 7 | 9 | 6 | 12 | 10 | 5 | 5 | 3 | 57 |
| mortars | – | – | – | 7 | 14 | 14 | 4 | 8 | 47 |
| points | – | – | 6 | 3 | 3 | 13 | 43 | 77 | 145 |
| querns | 7 | 18 | 7 | 10 | 6 | – | 1 | 1 | 50 |
| reliquary fittings | 8 | 21 | 25 | 24 | 15 | 17 | 6 | 6 | 122 |
| sewing equipment | 2 | – | 4 | 2 | 8 | 1 | 3 | 21 | 41 |
| sewing pins | 1 | 1 | 1 | 16 | 15 | 39 | 64 | 242 | 379 |
| **shoes** | **60** | **27** | **6** | **13** | **–** | **–** | **1** | **–** | **107** |
| tacks | 19 | 16 | 20 | 21 | 7 | 13 | 5 | 13 | 114 |
| tenter-hooks | 2 | 3 | 9 | 43 | 18 | 5 | – | 2 | 82 |
| textile tools | 16 | 34 | 30 | 36 | 19 | 5 | 1 | 9 | 150 |
| toggles | 2 | 2 | 2 | 5 | – | 1 | – | 1 | 13 |
| tools | 26 | 52 | 11 | 20 | 16 | 10 | 7 | 12 | 154 |
| weapons | 5 | 2 | 5 | 25 | 6 | 5 | 5 | 11 | 64 |
| weights | 1 | 5 | 4 | 3 | 5 | 3 | 6 | 6 | 33 |
| Total | 359 | 465 | 405 | 763 | 496 | 339 | 326 | 681 | 3834 |

ance of the methods of retrieval would be dangerous because the relative sampling fractions would be unknown. Even with knowledge of the methods, some empirical evidence on relative retrieval rates would be needed to enable a fair comparison between the sites to be made.

Sometimes, the problem may lie more in differential survival than in differential retrieval, thus widening the gap between the sampled population and the target population. For example, we consider the counts of artefacts of different functional types from the excavations in medieval Winchester (Barclay *et al.* 1990). They are of sufficient quantity to, on the whole, provide a reliable pattern of varying usage, both through the centuries and across different parts of the city. But they cannot be used uncritically; for example, the distribution of types by date (Table 3.1) appears to show a rapid decline in the number of shoes recovered from deposits dating to the twelfth century, and almost none from fourteenth-century or later deposits. What does this mean? Did people stop wearing shoes in the twelfth century in Winchester? Obviously not. What happened was that many of the excavated earlier deposits were waterlogged and so preserved organic remains (including leather shoes) while corresponding later deposits did not. So the difference was one of survival, not one of use or even of retrieval. In sampling terms, there was a catastrophic decline in the sampling fraction for one type of find against the others, leading to biased chronological comparisons.

To sum up the 'whole objects' situation, we can say that the comparisons of totals, or the interpretation of a single profile or composition, depends on assumptions of equal sampling fractions, either between sites or between types of finds, which may not be easy to justify. We may be on safer ground in the comparison of profiles, but even this carries the built-in assumption that the relative sampling fractions between types do not vary from one site to another (or one period to another, etc.) – technically known as the assumption of *no interaction*. Sometimes this is justified and sometimes it is not (e.g. for organic vs. inorganic finds), but we need to be always aware that we are making it.

Dealing with broken material, such as pottery, is made more complicated by the fact that, although the target population consists of whole objects (e.g. pots), the sample (and probably the sampled population) consists of fragments (e.g. sherds). Archaeologists initially avoided this issue by behaving as if sherds had never been anything else, until the *quantification* of pottery (i.e. saying how much pottery there is in an assemblage, and what the composition of an assemblage is) became a theoretical issue from the 1960s onwards (see Orton 1993 for a detailed historical account). The next source of confusion was the wish of archaeologists to characterise assemblages by attempting to say how many vessels are represented by their collections of sherds. This is essentially a futile exercise, because

(a)   it is of no use, and can be actually misleading, in the estimation of the characteristics of populations, such as their compositions (Orton 1993, 180);

(b)   it can be very difficult, if not impossible, to calculate, because of the problem of identifying non-joining sherds to vessels with certainty.

But it does seem to make archaeologists feel comfortable. However, the root of the problem is that, for purposes of interpretation, we need to estimate past populations, not characterise present samples.

Site formation processes can be modelled most simply as a breakage event and a sampling event, although each may have taken place over several stages. The breakage rate depends on both the context and the type of pottery, while the sampling fraction should depend only on the context. As an example, we shall use this point of view to evaluate two ways of quantifying pottery: sherd

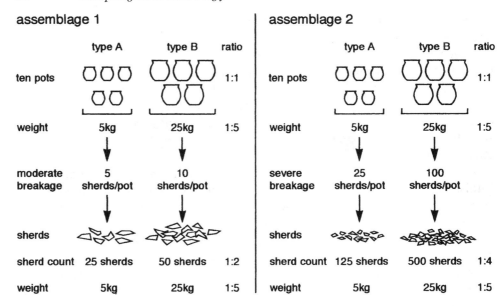

Fig. 3.6 Illustration of the effects of using sherd count and weight in the comparison of ceramic assemblages. Two hypothetical assemblages have equal proportions of type A and type B pots. Because the weights of the types differ, weighing them gives a biased ratio (1:5 instead of 1:1), but as this ratio is the same in both assemblages, weighing correctly indicates that the proportions are the same in both assemblages. In contrast, sherd count incorrectly suggests a higher proportion of type A in assemblage 1 than in assemblage 2 (1:2 compared to 1:4), because the pottery in the latter is more broken.

counts and weights. Fuller discussions, about a wider range of measures, can be found in Orton (1993) and Orton *et al.* (1993, 166–81). Since breakage rates vary between types, sherd counts cannot be used to estimate the compositions of population assemblages. Nor can they be used to compare assemblages, because the relative breakage rates are likely to vary according to the intensity of the breakage (for example, a type that is twice as 'breakable' as another will break into twice as many sherds after one breakage event, four times as many after two events, and so on). The sampling fraction is irrelevant to this argument. In contrast, breakage does not affect the composition of assemblages measured in terms of weight, since overall weight is not itself affected by breakage (Fig. 3.6). Weight is changed by sampling, but since all types should have the same sampling fraction, the relative proportions should remain unchanged. Weight should therefore give unbiased estimates of the compositions of target populations, and also of comparisons between them. There are problems that come from extreme conditions; for example, if a particularly fragile type breaks into fragments so small that some are not detected, that type will clearly be under-estimated. But weight minimises this effect, since the 'missing' sherds are also the lightest. So sampling theory suggests very strongly that weight is superior to sherd count as a measure of quantity.

The statistics of animal bones are more complicated than those of ceramics, for at least two major reasons:

(a)   there are two distinct scales of breakage – the 'breakage' of animals into individual bones, and the breakage of those bones into fragments;

(b)   there is the likelihood of selection of different bone elements for different purposes (e.g. food consumption, or industrial purposes), and the possibility of deliberate fragmentation of some elements, e.g. for the extraction of marrow.

An interesting account of the sorts of problems that can arise even when these two factors are not major sources of difficulty was given by Robertson (1989). Small wonder that animal bone assemblages have been described as 'one of the most awkward of all types of data used in archaeology' (Ringrose 1993a, 122).

In this discussion I shall used the terminology established by Ringrose (1933a, 122–5). The term *element* is used to mean an anatomical part of an animal, *bone* to mean an element of a particular animal, and *specimen* to mean a piece of recovered faunal material (whether complete or fragmentary). He distinguished between two broad approaches to the data: the *palaeozoological* (where the interest is mainly in living communities) and the *zooarchaeological* approaches (where the interest is mainly in the *deposited assemblage*). His model of the taphonomic processes encompassed five stages: the *living community* (also known as the *life assemblage*), the *death assemblage*, the *deposited assemblage*, the *fossil assemblage* and the *sample assemblage*, with a potential loss of material and data incurred in passing from each stage to the next (Fig. 3.1). Finally, he listed various measures that had been used to quantify faunal material:

NISP    number of identified specimens
MNI     minimum number of individuals
LI      Lincoln Index (alias Petersen Index)
MNE     minimum number of elements
MAU     minimum animal units
TMAU    total minimum animal units

noting that some have more than one definition.

The aim of quantification is commonly said to be the assessment of the relative frequencies of different species. This rather bland statement hides several disagreements, for example:

(a)   Frequencies in what? In the sample assemblage, the deposited assemblage, the life assemblage, or in something else?

(b)  Are absolute numbers required, or just relative proportions?

(c)  Should those proportions be expressed as percentages, or just as a ranking of relative frequencies?

(d)  Should the proportions be in terms of numbers of animals, or of some derived statistic, such as meat weight?

The debate was opened in the USA by White (1953), although his methods had been anticipated in the late nineteenth century (in Belgium by Dupont (Charles 1998), and in Russia by Inostrantsev (1882), see Casteel 1977, 125). White proposed the use of the MNI statistic as a way of deriving meat weights and hence the relative importance of different species in the diet. His method of calculating MNI for a species was to determine the most abundant element of that species, and to take the greater of the number of 'left' and 'right' examples of that element. MNIs could then be totalled across species, and relative proportions could be calculated. These are clearly descriptive statistics of the sample assemblage; any interpretation must rely on a whole series of unspoken assumptions about both taphonomic processes and methods of retrieval. Although the use of meat weights was later discredited (e.g. see Grayson 1979, 224), the use of the MNI statistic survived and underwent several refinements (e.g. Chaplin 1971, 74; Casteel 1977; Grayson 1979; Watson 1979; Nichol and Wild 1984). All, however, were concerned with obtaining as accurate a count as possible of 'the number of animals whose bones lie on the table' (Fieller and Turner 1982, 50). MNI was generally seen as an improvement on NISP for calculating relative proportions, mainly because it was thought to be less affected by problems of fragmentation (Ringrose 1993a, 125). The point was also made (Watson 1979, 127) that until the introduction of sieving (p. 149), any differences in statistical method were likely to be outweighed by inadequacies in excavation techniques.

Sampling as an explicit consideration seems first to enter the discussion in the work of Krantz (1968), who saw the aim of quantification as one of estimation rather than description, and devised a formula for the estimation of 'the actual number of animals represented by the excavated bones' (1968, 288) (**3.1**). The formula was based on the idea of matching pairs of bone elements; in a population, there are equal numbers of left and right elements. As the population is reduced by sampling effects, some left and some right elements are removed, leaving unmatched left elements, unmatched right elements, and matching pairs. The smaller the sampling fraction, the smaller the proportion of matching pairs is likely to be. The numbers of unmatched left and right elements, and of matching pairs, can thus be used to estimate the original size of the population, given assumptions about the nature of the taphonomic processes (p. 215).

A more definitive statement of this approach was made by Fieller and Turner (1982), although they were apparently anticipated by Poplin (1976) (see

Ringrose 1993a, 128). They showed that Krantz's formula and a similar approach due to Lie (1980) were both wrong. They made an analogy between the survival of left elements, right elements and matching pairs and the capture-recapture methods used by ecologists to estimate the size of living populations, thus opening up a wide range of existing statistical techniques to archaeological use (p. 215). They showed how ecology's Petersen Index could be used to create a *Petersen estimate* (**3.2**) of the number of animals in the original population (i.e. in the death assemblage, not the life assemblage). On the positive side, this was the first such estimate to which confidence intervals (p. 26) could be attached (Fieller and Turner 1982, 55). The main weaknesses were:

(a)   the estimate would be inflated if matching pairs were missed, thus putting a premium on reliable matching techniques;

(b)   two assumptions were built in,

   (i)   that left and right bones have equal probabilities of survival (which seems reasonable and could be tested statistically), and

   (ii)   that the loss of an individual's left and right bones from an assemblage are independent of each other (which is more problematic and difficult to assess) (Fieller and Turner 1982, 58).

This approach led to some initial controversy (Horton 1984; Turner and Fieller 1985), and exposed some confusion between the processes of description and estimation.

In a similar vein, Gilbert and Singer (1982) considered the representativeness of bone samples, that they called the problem of 'faunal bias'. They saw two ways forward:

(a)   the study of such biases as a way of reconstructing past behaviour,

(b)   the correction of presumed biases as a way of working backwards from recovery frequencies of skeletal remains to species ratios of carcasses originally exploited,

with (a) seen as the more promising. It is worth noting in the context of (a) that bias is not always something to be eliminated, but can on occasions be in itself a useful source of information. To explore (b), they devised both deterministic and stochastic formulae (Gilbert and Singer 1982, 32–7) for the decay at various stages of the taphonomic process (Fig. 3.1), and suggested that these equations could be reversed to enable frequencies to be estimated. Unfortunately, they did not follow up this suggestion, which would have involved some very difficult problems of estimation.

Yet another approach involving the explicit use of sampling or probabilistic considerations was put forward by Chase and Hagaman (1987), who looked at the problem of estimating proportions in the deposited assemblage. They examined MNI and several rival measures in terms of their vulnerability to various biasing factors, primarily the recovery rate $r$, but also the fragmentation rate $f$ and the number of skeletal parts $s$, using sampling theory to estimate the expected value of MNI for chosen values of $r$, $s$ and $n$ (the original number in the population). They concluded that MNI is inferior to other measures such as TMAU.

To sum up the debate so far, we turn to Ringrose (1993a). He clarified the definition of MNE as a sort of NISP for each skeletal part (possibly correcting for fragmentation), and the MAU as the MNE divided by the number of examples of that part in a living animal. He saw Chase and Hagaman's (1987, 81) TMAU as a sort of MAU, averaged across the skeletal elements. He then asked what each measure was actually measuring or estimating (something that had not always been clear in the earlier literature) (Ringrose 1993a, 132–6). In this light:

NISP   was best seen as an estimate of the number of specimens in the fossil assemblage, but suffered problems from fragmentation.

MNI   was usually a conservative estimate of the number of animals in the fossil assemblage, but (like NISP) could not be used to say anything directly about the living community, the death assemblage or the deposited assemblage.

LI   could in principle be used as an estimate of the death assemblage, but was not generally applicable, and was vulnerable to errors in the identification of matching pairs, as well as to fragmentation.

He saw it as sensible to use all measures except LI to estimate aspects of the fossil assemblage, and then to try to get back to earlier assemblages by any means available.

In this case study, the use of probabilistic/sampling thinking has provided a much-needed framework within which the claims of competing measures can be assessed, as well as providing an ingenious device (the LI) for potentially estimating further up the sequence of assemblages than more conventional measures.

In this section we have seen how arguments based on probability or sampling theory can allow us to climb painfully back up a sort of taphonomic 'ladder' of successive assemblages (Fig. 3.1), provided we are prepared to make certain assumptions, e.g. about the independence of observations (p. 20), or the absence of interaction between two or more factors (p. 51). Clearly, the further we go, either the less we can say and/or the stronger are the assumptions that we must make – a complicated three-way trade-off. A fruitful area of study is to consider which measures are most likely to survive post-depositional processes without the need for 'heroic' (i.e. unjustifiable) assumptions. By their very nature, totals will not survive however they are measured, so they should not be a research aim. Estimation *via* the LI may be possible in certain restricted circumstances, but its assumptions need careful testing. Compositions of individual assemblages have greater possibility of survival, but only if the combined breakage/survival rate is the same for each 'type'. Some measures may be able to achieve this (e.g. weight of pottery), provided that the material does not become so broken that it is not discovered. But such statistics may not be particularly useful for interpretation. Comparative data may be the most useful; their use depends on the discovery of measures that are likely to preserve statistical patterns (which we might call *invariants*, see p. 66) through the post-depositional processes. Such considerations have led to the recommendation of the *eve* statistic (the *estimated vessel-equivalent*) for pottery (Orton 1993) and a related statistic for animal bone (Moreno-García *et al.* 1996). These are not likely to be the 'last word' on the subject, and further studies are needed, particularly on the rates at which materials can be removed from the archaeological record altogether. The long-term aim should be to integrate assemblages of different classes of material, so that patterns between classes (e.g. the relationship between coins and pottery, or between pottery and animal bones), as well as within classes, can be studied.

### The relationship between surface and sub-surface archaeology

The question of whether surface remains give a reliable indication of subsurface remains is a key issue for the practice of archaeological survey, at both the regional and the site level (chapters 4 and 5 respectively). Opinions, both as expressed and as implicit as fieldwork practices, seem to vary widely. In a sense, to carry out any sort of surface fieldwork is to put one's faith in the relationship between surface and sub-surface remains (or, more precisely, between surface remains and the totality of the archaeological record, both surface and sub-surface), although the value of the surface remains in their own right has been stressed (e.g. Dunnell 1990). On the other hand, there is evidence (much of it anecdotal) for the unreliability of surface evidence, and the practice of machining off 'unstratified' surface deposits in site evaluations indicates what some archaeologists think of them. The issue focuses in particular on the status of artefact distributions both within and on the surface of the *plough-zone* – that depth of soil on arable (or once arable) land that is (or has been) subjected to regular ploughing (or *tillage*, which includes other agricultural activities, such as harrowing and sub-soiling) – which can be regarded to some extent as 'homogenised'. There are other issues, such as *trampling* (Villa and Courtin 1983), which will not be considered here.

The problem can be divided into two:

(a) the relationship between surface finds and the entire contents of the plough-zone;
(b) the relationship between the plough-zone and the deposits beneath it.

Both can be expressed in terms of the 'sampled population' of which the collected or excavated finds are a sample, and any related 'target population'. In case (a), the question is whether the entire plough-zone, which is the target population, can reasonably be also considered to be the sampled population (Ammerman 1985, 34). In case (b), the question is less simple: regarding the sub-plough-zone remains as a target population is not adequate, because

- (a) they may no longer exist, and
- (b) if they do exist, they may themselves not be representative of the original archaeological distribution before ploughing took place. For example, ploughing may have destroyed shallow features such as post-holes, and left only deep features such as wells and storage pits, in which case the sub-plough-zone remains are at least as biased as anything in the plough-zone may be, and possibly more so (Fig. 3.7).

The plough-zone may thus contain the only surviving evidence for important activities. The target population is probably best thought of as the deposited archaeological assemblage before ploughing, which itself raises interesting questions about the representivity of plough-zone finds.

As often happens in archaeology (p. 43), such questions had a long period of latency before being brought out into the open, in this case in the explicitly problem-stating period of the 1960s (Binford *et al.* 1970; Redman and Watson 1970). There was a series of observations and experiments from the 1970s onwards (see below), and as the issue grew in importance in the CRM era (p. 69) a series of conferences and syntheses aimed at clarifying the issues and bringing them to a wider audience (e.g. Hinchliffe and Schadla-Hall 1980; Lewarch and O'Brien 1981; O'Brien and Lewarch 1981; Haselgrove *et al.* 1985; Wandsnider and Ebert 1988; Schofield 1991b). The period of experimentation continues to this day (Boismier 1997), and we clearly do not yet know all the answers.

The 'observational' phase consisted mainly of the verification of several factors that, *a priori*, might be expected to make a surface collection less representative of its target population than it otherwise might have been. They included the following.

- (a) The surface density of finds can be affected by the depth of overburden between cultural deposits and the surface (*attenuation*) (Tolstoy and Fish 1975).
- (b) Local movement of finds can cause those derived from separate clusters to appear to coalesce (*merge*) (Tolstoy and Fish 1975).
- (c) Surface finds are likely to move down a slope over time, the rate of movement depending (*inter alia*) on the type of object (Rick 1976).

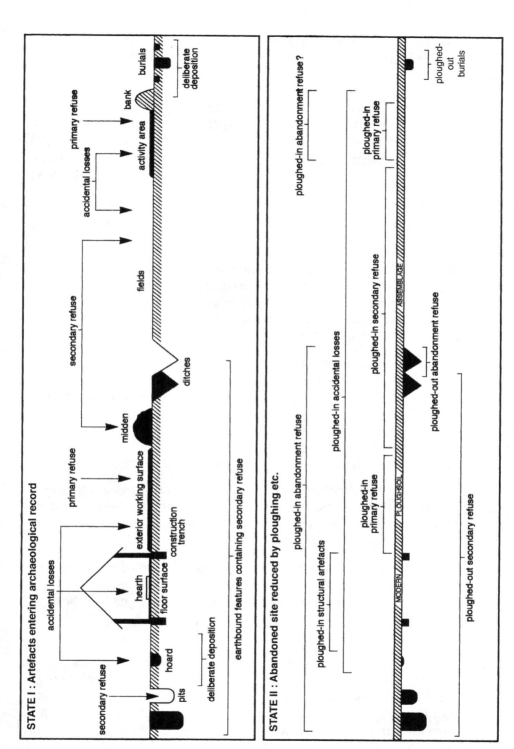

Fig. 3.7 Comparison of assemblages surviving in the plough-zone and below the plough-zone (redrawn from Haselgrove 1985, Fig. 1.3).

(d)   The distances between joining fragments of the same artefacts might give an estimate of the horizontal displacement (Roper 1976).

(e)   Collection rates can be affected by short-term factors, such as recent rainfall or agricultural disturbance (Hirth 1978).

(f)   Collection rates depend on the efficiency of individual workers (Woodman 1981–2; Haselgrove 1985; see also p. 105, Fig. 4.11).

(g)   Spatial patterns can be confused by the effects of manuring fields from middens (Wilkinson 1982; Gaffney *et al.* 1985; see also p. 105).

(h)   Tillage can cause damage to artefacts that could be confused with use-wear (Mallouf 1982).

(i)    The density of finds can vary greatly from one period to another, making direct comparisons between periods unreliable (Millett 1985).

Taken together, these factors suggest that surface collections cannot be taken at face value, and they demonstrate the need to assess the scale of such effects, and the circumstances under which they are likely to be serious.

Experiments were aimed at resolving questions in one or more of five areas (Frink 1984; Ammerman 1985):

1   the proportion of material in the plough-zone that is visible on the surface at a given time,

2   the nature of the 'sampling' process that produced a surface assemblage,

3   the vertical displacement of artefacts,

4   the horizontal displacement of artefacts,

5   the degree of breakage caused to artefacts by tillage.

They were divided by Ammerman (1985, 34–5) into two generations: the first examined the congruence between surface and sub-surface, while the second concentrated on the behaviour of the processes within the plough-zone itself. Methodologically, they can be divided into three groups:

1   those based in an initial survey, followed by (a) excavation, or (b) further survey,

2   those based on the survey of objects 'planted' as part of the experiment,

3   computer simulations.

1a The early experiment of Redman and Watson (1970) was of this type, but it is difficult to assess because very few of the areas from which collections were made were later excavated. A more extensive experiment was carried out by Howell (1993), who examined the accuracy of auger tests for identifying the density of sub-surface cultural deposits and the location of sub-surface cultural features at the site of Mixtequilla in the Veracruz region of Mexico. His samples consisted of twenty 1 m square excavation pits and a corresponding auger hole, 0.1 m in diameter, at the south-west corner of each; both were recorded in levels of 0.1 m depth. The sherd counts for each auger level were plotted against the corresponding counts for the excavated pit (the first two levels were amalgamated in each case). The statistical correlation ($r^2$) between these counts was very low (only 0.13); even aggregating all the levels in an auger hole and its pit only increased the figure to 0.39. He ascribed these low values to the presence in some areas of small local concentrations of sherds; when sampling units with such deposits were removed from the analysis, the correlation increased to $r^2 = 0.73$. The auger tests were thus quite good at detecting the presence of extensive deposits, but much less good at detecting the presence of small localised deposits, as indeed one might expect.

1b An alternative approach to excavation is to return to the area in successive years, and to compare the collections made in each year. Frink (1984) described the collection of lithics on two sites after ploughing for three consecutive years, showing that the average weight of artefacts varied considerably from year to year, the average length varied less and the average width even less. More controversially, he suggested, on the basis of the observed decline in the number of finds collected each year, that about 15% of the plough-zone assemblage was being collected each year – a rather higher figure than that suggested by most other work.

Verhoeven (1991) analysed the effect of revisiting a field on the recorded presence or absence of finds, within the Agro Pontino Survey (p. 78). He discovered statistically significant differences between successive visits. The most important cause appeared to be differences in 'dust conditions' (i.e. whether or not it had rained recently). He also observed that the effect on flint and obsidian appeared to be greater than that on ceramics.

2 Two experiments in tracking buried objects will be mentioned here: one using ceramic 'tiles' (Ammerman 1985) and one using chipped stone (Odell and Cowan 1987). Ammerman buried 1000 small (25 by 25 by 5 mm) tiles 20 mm below the surface in a ploughed field near Acconia (Italy) in 1977. The locations of tiles visible on the surface were recorded on six occasions (two in 1979, two in 1980, one each in 1981 and 1983). He reported that the proportion visible on the surface varied around 5 to 6%, and that after four visits displacements of up to 2 m had occurred. Large down-slope displacements between the fourth and fifth visits appeared to have been caused by an unusual down-slope ploughing. Little breakage was observed. Ammerman (1985, 40) concluded that, although the results were interesting, longer-term experiments were needed.

Odell and Cowan (1987) buried 1000 pieces of chipped stone of various sizes, painted blue to aid visibility, 0.1 to 0.15 m below the surface of an area of about 15 m square in a flat field. The procedure was for the field to be ploughed and disked; surface material was then recorded (but not removed) after the next rainfall, in terms of its location and any damage. The whole cycle was repeated twelve times in two years. The main conclusions were:

(a)  the recovery rate varied around a mean of 5.6% (about the same as other experiments);

(b)  recovery was highest in the spring and autumn;

(c)  large pieces were discovered more frequently than small ones (the *size effect*);

(d)  the mean displacement was about 1 m after one cycle, increasing to around 2 m after all twelve cycles;

(e)  the dominant displacement was in the direction of ploughing;

(f)  contrary to the conventional wisdom, no correlation between object size and displacement was observed.

3 A common feature of such experiments is the inability to observe more than a few ploughing cycles, in contrast to the dozens or even hundreds to which some archaeological sites must have been subjected. Since it is not possible to undertake such long-term experiments, some form of extrapolation or 'accelerated aging' is needed, and can in principle be supplied by computer simulation.

Van der Velde (1987) simulated the joint effect of two processes – natural decay (including bioturbation) and 'mechanical interference' (i.e. effects of human activity) – on the patterning of archaeological distributions. He assumed that decay would progress with an exponential distribution (analogous to radiocarbon decay, see **3.3**), but that the 'half-life' would depend on the material and size of the object as well as the nature of its burial context. On one particular site he estimated the half-life of small animal bones to be about 700 years, and that of pottery sherds to be about 1500 years (1987, 170). He modelled the effects of ploughing as the smearing out of horizontal distributions and the shattering of larger objects, and concluded that 'small scale patterning is rapidly lost with time. On the other hand, general patterns remain visible even after considerable loss of content, and the better structured an initial distribution of artefacts has been, the clearer the original general pattern can still be recognized even after so many rounds of natural and mechanical decay' (1987, 173). This may not appear to be a startling conclusion from an archaeological point of view, but it does demonstrate the ability of computer simulation to produce realistic outcomes under these circumstances.

Perhaps the most comprehensive computer simulation study of the effects of tillage is that of Boismier (1997), who aimed to 'develop a more comprehensive understanding of the movement of portable artefacts in the ploughzone, how they make their appearance on the surface, and how tillage-induced changes in pattern characteristics may affect interpretation' (1997, 7). He asked three fundamental questions which sum up the problems discussed in this section.

1 To what extent do the patterns characteristic of the surface artefacts approximate to those of the parent populations?
2 Is the assumption of distributional stability or equilibrium in pattern characteristics on the surface through time valid?
3 Do pattern characteristics on the surface reflect not only large-scale occupational patterning but also small-scale intrasite patterning? To what extent do quantitative differences in these characteristics reflect not only tillage-induced patterning but also their original patterning, and can these two classes of patterning be analytically distinguished in artefact distributions? (Abbreviated from 1997, 7.)

He used a model, with assemblage composition and spatial configuration, slope gradient and direction, and number of tillage events as controlled variables, to 'disturb' two artificial artefact distributions in a series of six experiments. Unlike van der Velde, he specifically excluded the effect of decay from the model. Since many tillage cycles were simulated, he selected only six of them (numbers 3, 6, 12, 24, 48 and 96) for detailed analysis (1997, 9) (Fig. 3.8).

The conclusions drawn from the experiments were tentative in nature, but seem to indicate the following answers to the above questions (1997, 234–7).

1 Proportions of relatively abundant categories of objects in the population were generally well represented in the surface samples, but those of less abundant categories were less so, tending to be either absent or over-represented because of sampling effects (this is similar to the well-known problem of estimating the proportion of a rare category from a sample). Also, larger examples of a particular category tended to be better represented than smaller examples.
2 Dispersion is a cumulative process, with no evidence that stability is reached as the number of tillage events increases. If a slope is present, the distribution will tend to be biased down the slope, as might be expected. There is no evidence that the distance of dispersion depends on the size of the object.
3 Small-scale patterning is lost very quickly, and clusters increase in size and decrease in density as the number of tillage events increases. The shape of clusters tends to become more circular and less distinct, and adjacent clusters tend to merge into one another. Tillage may under some circumstances induce spurious patterns.

This work has shown just how complicated the interpretation of surface artefact patterns can be. Some aspects of patterning may be preserved, but many are lost. A key factor is the extent to which tillage has taken place: has it been a regular event over a long period, or a rare and spasmodic event? This is important because the comforting belief in an eventual state of equilibrium has been shown not to be well founded.

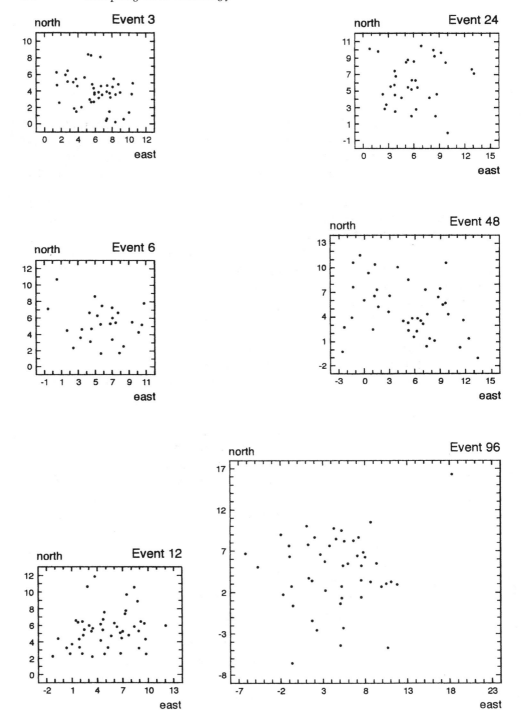

Fig. 3.8 Effect of series of ploughing events on spatial distribution of surface artefacts (redrawn to common scale from Boismier 1997, Fig. 10.4).

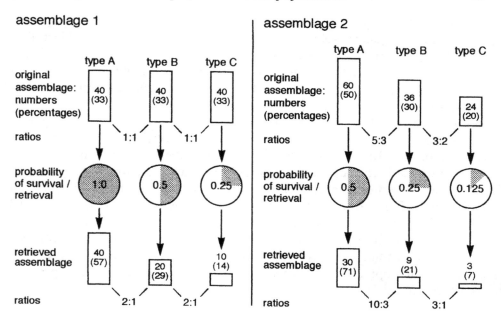

Fig. 3.9 Effects of differential survival/retrieval rates on comparisons between proportion of different types in different assemblages. In the original assemblages, the ratios of type A to type B are 1:1 (assemblage 1) and 5:3 (assemblage 2). In the retrieved assemblages, the corresponding ratios are 2:1 and 10:3, apparently quite different. But the ratios of the ratios are the same for each assemblage, being 1:2 in each case. So although the compositions of the retrieved assemblages do not reflect the compositions of the original assemblages, the comparison between the two retrieved assemblages does reflect the comparison between the two original assemblages.

## Conclusions

Statistical sampling theory does not in itself provide answers to the sorts of archaeological questions we have looked at in this chapter. It does, however, provide a language in which such questions can be articulated and discussed, and finding an appropriate language is an important first step in discussing a problem. The concepts of target and sampled population, a proper understanding of the over-worked and misunderstood concept of bias, and the idea that we are in the business of making inferences, or perhaps verifying hypotheses, about populations on the basis of data from some sort (perhaps a very strange sort) of sample, all help us to get to grips with these real and fundamental problems of archaeology.

The picture at this stage may look bleak – we cannot say anything about the sizes of populations, because we have no way of knowing about effective sampling (or survival) rates (with the possible exception of the LI, p. 53). Even estimating the composition of an assemblage requires the possibly unpalatable assumption of equal sampling fractions for different categories of object. But, as we have seen (p. 44), the value of compositions lies not in them individually but in comparisons between them. Although the sampling rates for different assemblages may differ, and the rates for different categories within them may differ, we might be prepared to assume that the relative rates between categories within assemblages remain more-or-less the same (we would have to check that there were no gross differences in circumstances, as happened at Winchester (p. 50)). In statistical jargon, we could then say that there was no interaction between the assemblages and the categories, and we could safely compare the compositions, even though we would not trust any of them individually (Fig. 3.9). We could say that (to borrow some more mathematical jargon) the comparisons remain *invariant* under the transformations brought about by site formation processes. The hunt for the invariants then becomes a foundation for reliable interpretation, since through them interpretation can be based on population patterns (comparisons), and not on any possible transformations.

# 4

## COVERING THE GROUND

### Introduction

The regional archaeological survey is an instrument whose nature and status have changed throughout this century, and particularly since about 1970. Four main reasons have been put forward for undertaking such surveys:

(a) *discovery* of sites, or *prospection*,
(b) *estimation* (e.g. of site densities or numbers),
(c) *characterisation* or *specification* (Wobst 1983, 37) (of the archaeological distribution within a region), and
(d) *hypothesis testing* (Wobst 1983, 40).

The emphases both between and within these aims have shifted over the years, following changes in academic and legal climates.

As a preliminary, we need to establish what is meant by both a region and a site. Although the term region may have a definite administrative meaning in some countries (or even several conflicting ones, as in the UK), it is used very broadly in archaeology to denote a spatially defined unit of territory, ranging from a few sq km in the British 'Parish Survey' (e.g. Aston and Gerrard 1995, 5) to 10,000 sq km or more (Read 1986, 479). The smaller examples can be thought of as 'samples of size 1' within larger regions, while the regions *per se* should exhibit some sort of topographical or cultural coherence (for example, an island (e.g. Cherry 1982, 13), a drainage basin (e.g. Read 1986, 477; Barker 1995), or a distinct topographical zone such as the English Fens (Hall 1987) or the Agro Pontino in Italy (Voorrips *et al.* 1991)). The extent to which the very small examples (e.g. Parish Surveys) can individually represent anything except themselves is debatable (Cherry and Shennan 1978, 25), but at the very least they perform a valuable local role, and can form the building blocks of a wider comparative study.

If we find it hard to define a region, then the definition of a 'site' is even worse. Ask archaeologists what it means, and they will probably say something like 'I can't define it precisely, but I know one when I see one.' Some authors (e.g. Binford 1964) used the term as if it were 'given' and there was no need to discuss its meaning, while others have struggled to produce definitions. Examples range from the deliberately vague 'a target or place with definable physical properties' (Krakker *et al.* 1983, 470), or 'the smallest unit of space dealt with by archaeologists' (Willey and Phillips 1958, 18), through 'a high density area of artefacts' (Schiffer *et al.* 1978, 2, and 14 for a more detailed discussion), to the more precise 'a discrete and potentially interpretable locus of material. By discrete we mean spatially bounded with those boundaries marked by at least relative changes in artifact densities' (Plog *et al.* 1978, 389) to the very precise 'one with a minimum of fifteen pieces of artefactual material recorded from an area of 10 m by 10 m in 10 minutes' (Hall, quoted by Sylvester 1991, 9). In contrast, Shott (1985, Table 1) implicitly suggested that the presence of a single artefact in a shovel-test (see this volume, p. 71) is enough to indicate the presence of a site. A good discussion of various attitudes and definitions was given by Gallant (1986, 408). The need for consistency on the small scale (e.g. workers in the same team at the same location) is clear, but it is also clear that no single definition is likely to be appropriate for all conditions of terrain and land use. Some workers (starting with Thomas 1975, see below) did not see the site as a useful concept in this context, and prefered to see the archaeological record as a continuously varying set of variables across a region (see below).

### Historical overview

Archaeological survey can be said to have its roots in the tradition of travelling antiquarians such as Leland and Camden in the sixteenth and seventeenth centuries (Daniel 1981, 25–6), and in the tradition of scientific expeditions that started in the nineteenth century (see, for example, Wauchope 1965; Von Hagen 1973). Initially, the aims were simply discovery – and there was much to discover – and survey was seen as a necessary but rather mundane prelude to the real business of excavation, or of recording standing monuments. More systematic work followed through the 1920s to 1940s (e.g. Braidwood *et al.* 1937; Lloyd 1954). Growing interest in settlement patterns (Fox 1923) led to a broadening of the aims of surveys in this direction, i.e. towards characterisation, as in the Virú Valley survey in Peru (Willey 1953), and a corresponding improvement in the intellectual standing of surveys. Sampling was not practised explicitly – hardly surprising as the statistical theory was still under development (see pp. 14–17) – and such surveys have reasonably been criticised for having a 'large-site bias' (Wobst 1983, 43).

The idea of using probabilistic sampling methods explicitly in archaeological survey is usually attributed to Binford (1964); similar ideas had been put forward by Vescelius (1960), but were apparently not acted upon. Probabilistic sampling was employed at the site level slightly earlier (p. 113). Binford stressed the idea of the region as a natural unit of archaeological study, and, admitting the impossibility of total coverage at this scale (1964, 427), advocated probabilistic sampling techniques as the way of achieving representative and reliable data with less than total coverage. Perhaps fortunately, he was less explicit about the methodological details, discussing simple random sampling (see p. 20) and stratified sampling (p. 30) in the context of a hypothetical 20% coverage of 'squares equaling one-half square mile' (1964, 434), using systematic sampling (p. 21) as suggested by Vescelius (1960). One outcome was to move the 'discovery' aim of survey towards the discovery of representative samples of sites, rather than of sites in general; a second was to establish the multi-stage nature of archaeological survey (see also Redman 1973). It is unfortunate that both archaeologists and statisticians have adopted the term *multi-stage*, with rather different meanings: to the archaeologist, it means a survey which is not all carried out in one stage (e.g. one season of fieldwork), and in which the earlier stages inform the aims and design of the later; to the statistician, it means a survey design in which the sampling is carried out in stages – first-stage units are selected, then second-stage units are sub-sampled from them, and so on (p. 33). Confusion can result if this distinction is not kept in mind.

There followed a burgeoning of large-scale surveys using probabilistic sampling. Whether this was due to Binford's influence, or to the passage of laws in the USA requiring environmental impact assessments or similar studies to be made (e.g. the National Historical Preservation Act of 1966 and the National Environmental Policy Act (NEPA) of 1969), is difficult to tell from this side of the Atlantic. This legal change, and the injection of funds that followed, led to the creation of almost a sub-discipline within American archaeology, that of cultural resource management (CRM – McGimsey and Davis 1977), also known as contract archaeology (Schiffer and House 1975), public archaeology (McGimsey 1972) and conservation archaeology (Lipe 1974; Schiffer and Gumerman 1977); an early review was by Goodyear *et al.* (1978). Four main problem areas can be observed:

(a) the design of large-scale ('regional') projects (the main subject of this chapter),
(b) the design of small-scale projects (see chapter 5),
(c) the integration of small-scale projects into regional research designs (outside the scope of this book, but see Goodyear *et al.* 1978, 163; Powell and Rice 1981),
(d) the assignment of relative importance, or significance, to sites once discovered (see below).

By the early 1970s the subject had apparently developed enough to justify the publication of textbooks on the subject (Mueller 1974; Redman 1974; Jelks 1975), and computer programs to aid archaeologists (e.g. Burton 1977). Such books have in some quarters been dismissed as 'cookbooks' (e.g. by Wobst 1983, 48); certainly they tended to neglect the full range of statistical theory available even then (see pp. 30–34) and had difficulty in getting to grips with the interface between archaeological and statistical theory. One problem that was raised by those uneasy about random sampling methods was the so-called 'Teotihuacan effect' (Flannery 1976b, 134), which in the UK should probably be called the 'Alton effect' (Shennan 1985, 15); Alton was the only town in Shennan's study area. The problem as expressed was that a statistically valid random sample (e.g. of quadrats) could easily miss the largest site in the study area, thus giving a completely false impression of the pattern of sites (particularly if there was one dominant site in the region). The answer is that surveys do not usually take place in a state of total ignorance, and the existence of any dominant site would probably already be known (see stage 1 below), and if not, it would probably be revealed by the preliminary work needed to set up a viable sampling frame or to test survey procedures (stages 6 and 8 below). The 'problem' is best seen as an attempt to find a stick with which to beat statistical sampling methods.

Regional sampling featured strongly in the San Francisco symposium of 1973 (Mueller 1975b), alongside within-site sampling (chapter 5 here) and artefact sampling (chapter 7). There was a strong emphasis on the comparison of different sample designs (in practice, between transects and quadrats, different sizes of each, systematic and simple sampling, stratified and not), by the criterion of relative efficiency (see p. 26), or, where population data were available, by accuracy (p. 26) (Judge *et al.* 1975, 94–121). It is clear from the high level of experimental resampling (often done by computer simulation), combined with the occasional 'howler' (see Chenhall 1975 for a self-confessed one), that the subject was still in a 'growth' or 'experimental' phase. Increased stress was laid on aim (b) – estimation – because the formal criteria associated with statistical sampling all point in that direction. It is very easy for the statistics to develop a life of their own, especially if computer simulations are used, and for more practical archaeological considerations to be overlooked.

After growth and experimentation comes consolidation and even opposition. The consolidation can be seen in a series of thoughtful reviews of the late 1970s and early 1980s (Plog 1978; Plog *et al.* 1978; Schiffer *et al.* 1978; Ammerman 1981; Nance 1983), whose valuable bibliographies show the extent of the work carried out in the previous decade or so. A language for the problems encountered by archaeologists, such as *obtrusiveness* and *visibility* (Schiffer *et al.* 1978, 6; see below) had begun to develop, as had an appreciation of the sorts of questions that probability sampling appeared to be good, or not so good, at tackling. Opposition came from two directions: from the belief that interesting questions could only be answered by total coverage (Fish and Kowalewski 1990) and from the belief that sampling, and indeed statistics as a whole, was dehumanising and best avoided (Hole 1980). Certainly, plenty of mistakes were made during the 1970s (see Chenhall 1975; Thomas 1978), and techniques were often applied too rigidly, but the overwhelming argument of the cost of the alternative to sampling could not seriously be gainsaid. Perhaps the most cogent criticism came from Wobst (1983), who contrasted the level of technical discussion over the details of sample design with the lack of a coherent theory, based on the modelling of archaeological distributions, to form a bridge between archaeological needs and statistical techniques. Many of the points he made will recur in the discussion below.

So far, regional sampling had been concentrated in arid and semi-arid areas, mainly but not exclusively in the south-west USA, where the visibility of archaeological remains on the surface was good. *Fieldwalking*, or *pedestrian survey*, was thus an appropriate technique, and large areas could be covered at a reasonable cost in terms of time and labour. Sampling fractions could be relatively high, and in some cases (e.g. Sanders *et al.* 1979, 14; see also Fish and Kowalewski 1990) 'total coverage' was claimed, although the *intensity* of some surveys (i.e. the spacing between workers) must cast some doubt on such claims (see Cowgill 1990). However, valuable spin-offs of such surveys were models of archaeological distributions, which could inform the design of work in other similar regions where sampling was deemed necessary (Wobst 1983, 67). In other parts of the world (or of the USA), conditions are completely different. The land surface may be covered in grassland, arable crops or forest, so that even the ground itself, let alone any archaeological remains, may not be visible. The question of the relationship between what is visible on the surface and what is beneath the surface (e.g. as in walking ploughed fields) is an important theoretical issue that has been discussed in chapter 3.

The question of what to do when nothing is visible was broached by Lovis (1976). There followed much exploitation, and a considerable literature (e.g. Nance 1979; Lynch 1980; 1981; Stone 1981; Krakker *et al.* 1983; McManamon 1984; Shott 1985; 1989a; Lightfoot 1986; 1989; Nance and Ball 1986; 1989) on what became known as *shovel test-pit*, or *STP*, sampling. Compared to earlier work, such sampling was characterised by very small sampling units, ranging from 0.25 m square to over 1 m square, but typically 0.5 m square, and consequently to very small sampling fractions in areal terms (typically between 0.1% and 0.001%) (these figures are based on Wobst 1983, 61). Foci of concern were problems of definition and detectability – what was a 'site' and how did you know if your sample had 'hit' one? Perhaps not surprisingly, many writers expressed scepticism about the approach, but were unable to offer a constructive alternative. Wobst (1983, 66–7) put the criticism into a broader context by linking the approach to an administrative need to define 'sites' as islands of archaeology in a sea of nothingness, so that they could be 'managed' at the expense of any information that might be contained in their surrounds – a problem that is very much with us today. McManamon (1984) compared shovel-testing with three other methods of sub-surface probing – *coring* (Stein 1986; 1991; Schuldenrein 1991), *augering*, and *divoting* (Lovis 1976) – in the light of their ability to detect five types of evidence for sites: artifacts, features, anthropic soil horizons (middens), and chemical and instrument anomalies. He concluded that, although it was not possible to establish a rule that would be

Fig. 4.1 Fieldwalking at Bullock Down, Sussex (photo: Field Archaeology Unit).

appropriate in all circumstances, in general shovel-testing was the most effective of the probing techniques, especially if the excavated soil was screened ('sieved' in the UK) (McManamon 1984, 261). Even allowing for the labour costs, shovel-testing appeared to be the most effective technique in terms of time taken per unit volume of soil examined. The efficiency and effectiveness of various designs of shovel-test surveys was further discussed by Kintigh (1988).

McManamon also examined techniques that would now come under the heading of geophysical prospection, in particular resistivity, magnetometry and ground-penetrating radar, concluding that they were better suited to examination of known sites than to the discovery of new ones (see chapter 5). Techniques have advanced rapidly in the past decade, especially in terms of their speed of operation (David 1995; Clark 1996), and now seem able to take their part in regional survey (Gaffney and Gaffney 1986; Bintliff 1992; Gaffney and Leusen 1996). At the other end of the spatial scale there are the large-scale remote-sensing techniques, such as vertical and oblique aerial photography (Palmer 1978; Ebert 1984) and the many forms of imaging possible from satellites (Adams 1981, 33; Ebert 1984; Gaffney *et al.* 1996). Satellite images in particular can form a very useful basis for planning surveys (McManamon 1984, 250). Since sampling is rarely an issue at this scale, they will not be discussed in this chapter, except to note that aerial photography suffers from problems of visibility related to those encountered in fieldwalking (chapter 3), and that similar considerations of detection probabilities come into play (Gould 1987). The challenge today is to integrate the growing number of different ways in which the same area can be surveyed (Limp 1987; Gaffney and Leusen 1996).

Since the early 1980s there seems to have been a shift away from aim (b), estimation, towards aim (d), hypothesis testing, and a related shift within aim (a), discovery, as exemplified by Read (1986) and Sundstrom (1993). These changes seem to be related to the sorts of statistical problems posed by the *STP* approach, and in particular to the statistical meaning of negative evidence. Does it really mean there is nothing present, or have we just been unlucky? and how do we cope with large parts of our region where we expect the site density to be very low? Statistically, there was a move away from precision (see p. 25) as a criterion, to the use of explicit probability statements, e.g. of not detecting a site of a certain size and/or rarity in a sample of a given size. This is a sort of 'quality assurance' approach, in effect specifying in advance the probability of making various errors, and making use of the power (p. 25) of statistical tests.

It would be wrong to give the impression that the use of probability sampling in regional survey is a peculiarly American preoccupation. Only four years after the San Francisco Symposium (p. 70), a conference was held in Southampton to discuss the implications for British archaeology (Cherry *et al.* 1978). Part of the reason was to expose British archaeologists to developments in the USA in this area since Binford (1964) had put the topic firmly on the map, but which were not readily accessible in the literature. The value of probability sampling as a methodological tool was discussed at a variety of levels, reflected in this and subsequent chapters of this book.

There has long been a tradition of archaeological survey carried out by British archaeologists, usually in more hospitable climes than the British Isles, such as the Mediterranean lands (see for example Renfrew and Wagstaff 1982; Keller and Rupp 1983; Macready and Thompson 1985; Barker and Lloyd 1991). What was relatively new at the time of the 1977 conference was an emphasis on survey in Britain (for an early expression see Fowler 1972), together with a feeling that all this work was generating undigested data rather than useful knowledge (Cleere 1978). Cherry and Shennan (1978) saw the intensive survey of probabilistic samples as bridging the gap between the two forms of survey common at the time: the extensive regional survey and the intensive local survey, both of which were proving unsatisfactory, for different reasons. The need for more standardised methods was also highlighted at this time (Shennan 1980), leading to the production of fieldwalking manuals (e.g. Fasham *et al.* 1980; Hayfield 1980). One of the early implementations of this approach was the East Hampshire Survey (Shennan 1985), seen initially as a pilot first-stage sample area for a wider Wessex Survey (Schadla-Hall and Shennan 1978), in which the first-stage units would be selected purposively to cover the major geological and physical divisions of the region; they would in turn be sub-sampled by systematic transects (see case studies below).

The way that CRM developed in Britain did not lead to a large number of regional-scale surveys, as had been seen in the USA. Instead, emphasis was placed on

(a)    enhancing the coverage of information at relatively local level through the county Sites and Monuments Records (SMRs) (Lang 1992; Fraser 1993),

(b)    thematic surveys, dealing with particular risks, such as gravel extraction (Benson and Miles 1974) or the potential drying-out of wetlands (e.g. in the Fens (Crowther *et al.* 1985; Hall 1985; 1987; Sylvester 1991) or in the North-West (Middleton and Winstanley 1993)), or with national problems, as in the Buildings at Risk Survey (Brand 1992) and the Monuments at Risk Survey (MARS, see below: Darvill and Wainwright 1994; Bell and King 1996),

(c)    surveys based on particular research problems, such as the apparently anomalous Roman town at Wroxeter (Gaffney and Leusen 1996).

Particularly following the issuing of the Guidance Note PPG 16 in 1990 (Department of the Environment 1990) the bulk of CRM work has been carried out at 'site' level within a framework of local SMRs and Development Plans, and so comes under chapter 5.

The continental European picture tends to divide into two, with work in northern Europe facing broadly similar problems to those in Britain (and the north-eastern USA), for example in Denmark (Thorpe 1997) and northern France (Astill and Davies 1985; Haselgrove 1989; Haselgrove, Lowther and Scull 1990; Haselgrove, Lowther, Scull and Howard 1990). The southern, 'Mediterranean', parts, by contrast, have larger and more visible remains, and problems more akin to those encountered in the south-western USA (Barker 1991). But less visible sites can easily be overlooked, and intensive survey and attention to problems such as visibility is still needed (e.g. Verhoeven 1991, and see chapter 3).

### Theory and practice

In this section we shall examine how the general principles of sampling (see pp. 27–9 and Fig. 2.2) can be implemented in practice in the specific situation of regional survey. In later chapters the same principles will be applied to different scales of survey and sampling. To do this we need to use an appropriate terminology, referred to above as the 'language of sampling' (pp. 17–27), augmented by some terms which are more restricted in their scope.

*discovery probability*: the likelihood that, given certain archaeological materials and environmental characteristics of the study area, archaeological materials (sites and artefacts) relevant for estimating target parameters will be encountered (Schiffer *et al.* 1978, 3);

*extensive survey* (or *non-systematic survey*): a survey in which priority is given to the broad, comprehensive coverage of a region, and no systematic attempt is made to obtain information on site function (Ammerman 1981, 73);

*intensive survey* (or *systematic survey*): a survey which sets out to achieve 100% coverage of all, or a defined part (e.g. a sample), of a study region;

*recovery theory*: specifies how discovery probabilities vary with the archaeological and environmental characteristics of the study area, and particular techniques (Schiffer *et al.* 1978, 3);

*abundance*: the frequency or prevalence of a site or artefact type in the study area (Schiffer *et al.* 1978, 4);

*accessibility*: the variability in the effort required to reach any particular place, i.e. constraints on observer mobility (Schiffer *et al.* 1978, 8–9); can have a serious effect on discovery probabilities;

*clustering*: the degree to which archaeological materials are spatially aggregated (Schiffer *et al.* 1978, 4);

*effectiveness*: measured by the number of sites that can be recovered for a given expenditure of resources (Read 1986, 483);

*intensity*: the amount of effort devoted to inspecting surveyed areas. It can be measured directly by the spacing interval between crew members using the pedestrian tactic, and indirectly by the number of person-days per unit area inspected. It has a profound effect on discovery probabilities and parameter estimation (Schiffer *et al.* 1978, 13);

*microstratification*: a kind of purposive sampling where the study area is divided up, on the basis of various criteria, into small units of space (*microstrata*) which have a high probability of containing certain site and artefact types (Schiffer *et al.* 1978, 5–6);

*obtrusiveness*: the probability that particular archaeological materials can be discovered by a specific technique (Schiffer *et al.* 1978, 6);

*reliability*: the proportion of the variation in the observed values of a variable that is due to variation in the underlying true values, in contrast to that due to random errors (Nance 1987, 249);

*sensitivity*: the expected prevalence of archaeological remains (Wobst 1983, 59);

*visibility*: the variability, dependent on the environment, in the extent to which an observer can detect the presence of archaeological materials at or below a given place (Schiffer *et al.* 1978, 6–7); obtrusiveness and visibility together seem to equate to the statistical idea of *detectability* (p. 26).

We can now turn to the twelve stages (p. 27).

### Assimilation of existing knowledge

It is virtually impossible today to undertake a survey in a region about which nothing is known archaeologically. There is bound to be something known about the area, and from the point of view both of the formulation of hypotheses or objectives, and of the efficient use of resources, it would be foolish to ignore it. Unfortunately, this is easier said than done. The information is likely to vary greatly in its nature, scope, extent and quality. There may well be records of chance finds made at any time in the last few centuries, with often only a vague find-spot indicated, and probably only related to highly notable categories of finds (e.g. coins). There may be antiquarian records of more substantial sites, such as earthworks or burials, for which perhaps a plan but no precise location was given. If they have since been levelled by intensive agriculture, or buried under urban sprawl, we may be left with a quite detailed account of a large monument whose location is imprecisely known. For example, the Iron Age hillfort of Uphall Camp, Ilford (east London) was recorded by John Noble *c.* 1735, covered by factories and housing in the early twentieth century, and rediscovered by the Passmore Edwards Museum in the 1980s (Greenwood 1989).

When we come to systematic archaeological fieldwork, the situation is better, but not to the extent that one might expect. Different parts of our region may have been surveyed by different workers, at different times, and for different purposes; the extent to which archaeological distributions reflect simply the distribution of archaeological fieldwork is well known (Hodder and Orton 1976, 19–24; Fitzpatrick 1987). Massagrande (1995a) gave an example from Spain where an apparently bimodal distribution was caused by the activities of two local teams, each wary of trespassing on the territory of the other, leaving a relatively unsurveyed area between them.

The data are not only archaeological. Human activity in the area will have been influenced by many environmental and topographical factors, which must be recorded and taken into account. Many of them may be available before the survey starts, e.g. from topographical, geological, soil and land-use maps; sometimes such data will need to be checked and refined in the field, and other types of data (e.g. palaeoecological data) may have to be collected as part of the survey (Schofield 1987; Stafford 1995).

One modern response to such problems has been to use Geographical Information Systems (GIS) to bring together the many different sources of evidence that may be available (e.g. Dobbs 1993; Massagrande 1995b). This certainly helps, especially in terms of presentation, but still leaves problems of interpretation (e.g. see Boaz and Uleberg 1993). If some parts of a region have been intensively surveyed, then findings from intensive survey and previous (extensive) fieldwork in those areas can be compared, possibly with a view to calibrating the results of extensive fieldwork in other areas, so as to predict what more intensive survey might reveal. This can be carried a step further by bringing in environmental and topographical variables (e.g. soil, hydrology, elevation, slope, aspect) to predict likely site densities in different areas, a process known as *predictive modeling* (Hamond 1978; Warren 1990; Brandt *et al.* 1992; Leusen 1993; Wheatley 1996); it can be applied generally or to specific periods (Hoffecker 1988). Although it can be criticised as a resurgence of environmental determinism (Wheatley 1993), it can be useful in creating a framework for regional survey. Another important use of GIS may be to highlight problem areas (both geographical and chronological), and thus provide valuable input into the next stage.

### Objectives of the survey

It should go without saying that any survey, especially ones on this scale, should have well-defined objectives, which may of course vary depending on the underlying reasons for the survey, the state of knowledge about the region concerned, and the particular interests or theoretical orientation of the person or organisation responsible. Two main reasons can be discerned: management of the archaeological resource of the region, and research into its past. In practice one hopes for a symbiotic relationship between the two, but this cannot be taken for granted. Other reasons may sometimes be inferred: for example, use as a training exercise, or even the wish to spend part of the year in a congenial climate (which may help to explain the preponderance of Mediterranean surveys). A more important secondary reason is the methodological one: to experiment with and improve the methods of field survey (Shennan 1985; Gerrard 1990). The management reason is generally to provide an inventory of resources ('sites') of an area, perhaps for long-term purposes such as a Sites and Monuments Record, or perhaps for a short-term purpose such as specific 'threat' (flooding by a reservoir, motorway building, etc.). As this usually requires a 'census' (100% coverage), it will not be examined closely here, except to note that there may be a conflict between management and research aims at this scale, just as at the site scale (see chapter 5), and to note that archaeologists have shown remarkable ingenuity in interpreting the former in terms of the latter (see Schiffer and House 1977, and compare the requirements of the Army Corps of Engineers (p. 44) with the final aims and design of the project (p. 47)).

Generally, the objectives are stated as either questions to answer or hypotheses to test, with questions possibly including the estimation of parameters of interest (e.g. densities of sites of different types), or relating to the archaeological characterisation of the region (see p. 67 above). It is interesting to look at the stated objectives of some surveys.

> *Discovery*: Chevelon Archaeological Research Project: 'to obtain a substantial, representative sample of sites from the Chevelon drainage to be used for a variety of research purposes' (Read 1986, 479).
>
> *Hypothesis testing*: Reese River Ecological Project: 'to test Steward's theory of Shoshonean settlement patterns' (Thomas 1975, 63).
>
> *Question*: Southwestern Anthropological Research Group: 'Why did prehistoric population locate sites where they did?' (Plog and Hill, quoted in Goodyear *et al.* 1978, 167).
>
> *Characterisation*: Basin of Mexico Survey: '(1) to describe the socioeconomic institutions of cultural systems at different times . . .; (2) to explain . . . the ecological processes of evolutionary change by which these cultural systems evolved . . .' (Sanders *et al.* 1979, 12).
>
> Melos Survey : 'the diachronic investigation of human settlement on, and adaption to, the Melian island environment, with particular reference to those intra- and inter-systemic factors which served to control major episodes of change and stability' (Cherry 1982, 13).
>
> East Hampshire Survey: 'an understanding of . . . (i) variation in the density and distribution of human activity loci through time, (ii) the relationship between human exploitation and ecological variables, (iii) the degree of variation between human activity loci and the relations between those which were contemporary with one another' (Shennan 1985, 2).
>
> Shapwick Project: '(a) the systematic field survey of the area and the study of the finds recovered, (b) the assessment of the nature, extent and importance of the archaeological resource represented within the study area, (c) to generate a corpus of base-line archaeological field data with a view to constructing a pottery type series and recorded finds series for use in future studies, (d) to enable any modifications to the design of future fieldwalking programmes to be made at the earliest opportunity and help develop a sound methodological foundation on which further research could be built' (Gerrard 1990, 21).
>
> Agro Pontino Survey Project: '(1) to describe the distribution of archaeological surface materials in the Agro Pontino as accurately as possible, (2) to place these materials in a rough chronological

framework, and (3) to determine for each prehistoric period the factors ... contributing to the distribution observed' (Loving *et al.* 1991).

Biferno Valley Survey: 'to document the long-term settlement history of a typical Mediterranean landscape, to try to understand how and why it developed in the way it did' (Barker 1995, xvi).

Thy Archaeological Project: 'As objects and processes for investigation, we have recognised three major complexes: the variable and changing availability of resources, the economic relationships of production and exchange, and the sociopolitical and ritual actions that constitute social groups' (Thorpe 1997, 72).

In this far from random sample of projects, it seems that the predominant objective is some form of characterisation of the archaeological distribution of the region, although this is seen differently in different places and at different times.

The more general objectives are sometimes recast as a series of 'estimation' type questions, for example (Cherry 1982, 14):

'1  How many sites of all types and sizes are there in the area?
2  how are these sites distributed by period and function?
3  how does this distribution relate to various environmental variables?
4  how do the sites relate to one another?'

If formal statistical methods are to be used to determine sample size, then reformulation of the objectives, either on such lines or as hypothesis tests, are an essential prerequisite. If this cannot be done (and it is in no way a criticism of the objectives if they cannot), then one is forced back on less formal criteria.

### Population to be sampled

This concerns the definition of the study area. A region must be defined spatially, but on what criteria? Four sorts of boundaries can be suggested: archaeological, topographical, administrative and arbitrary. Ideally, the boundary should correspond to the confines of the objectives of the survey, but in practice this is not likely to be possible (or the objectives are drawn up in the light of the choice of region), not least because archaeological boundaries are likely to change between one period and another. Topographical boundaries are probably the best practical alternative; many surveys cover 'natural' areas such as islands or river catchments, and this seems a very sensible approach. Administrative boundaries (e.g. parishes, counties, countries) are likely to be arbitrary in relation to archaeological problems, but may be forced on us by the policy of the funding body (no one wants to pay for work on someone else's 'patch'). Completely arbitrary boundaries (e.g. cartographic grid units) are rarely used; they have the apparent benefit of simplicity, and may work well when situated entirely within a single administrative unit (e.g. the East Hampshire Survey, see pp. 101–3), when they can be thought of as a single large first-stage sampling unit, but they may cause difficulties if they cross administrative boundaries. Theoretical issues about regional boundaries were discussed by Kowalewski *et al.* (1983).

Having decided on spatial extent, we need to consider the third dimension. In other words, will the survey be a surface survey or a sub-surface one (or a combination of the two)? This brings us up against the problem of target vs. sampled population (see pp. 41–2). Presumably our target population comprises *all* archaeological evidence in the region, not just that on the surface. Whether it is reasonable to adopt the surface as a sampled population for the entire archaeological record depends on a series of factors such as obtrusiveness and visibility (p. 75), as well as the major theoretical question of the extent to which surface remains represent the corresponding sub-surface remains. This issue is considered in chapter 3. But surface sampling (e.g. fieldwalking) is much cheaper than sub-surface sampling, and enables spatially much larger samples to be taken (recent costs of sub-surface sampling have been given by Champion *et al.* 1995, 59; they are compared with figures for fieldwalking in Table 4.1). Intermediate levels of survey may be possible in special circumstances, such as the examination of the sides of drainage ditches in the Fens that led to the discovery of the important Flag Fen site (Prior 1991, 39). The balance between cost and sample size on the one hand and the representativeness of visible surface remains on the other, which itself depends on ground cover, geomorphology, etc., is a very difficult one to achieve. It may be that different strategies will be needed in different parts of a region, and that multi-stage sampling (in the archaeological sense, p. 69) will be needed, with sub-surface testing following up an initial surface survey.

Yet another problem, accessibility (p. 75), stands between the target and sampled populations. We are bound to encounter in our fieldwork areas that are inaccessible for practical or legal reasons (e.g. urban or forested areas for a surface survey, or 'difficult' landowners). If encountered after the sample has been designed, they will have the effect of either reducing the sample size, or causing much extra work in redesigning the sample to restore its designed size. For example, in the East Hampshire Survey large parts of the sample transects were not actually surveyed, for just such reasons (Shennan 1985, 17–20) (see Fig. 4.2). If possible, it would be preferable to define such areas at an earlier stage, and exclude them from the sampled population. This could lead to a very oddly shaped sampled population, which in turn might have implications for the sampling frame (see below). Either way, the exclusion of such areas immediately raises the possibility of bias (p. 23); statisticians have for long recognised this problem, which they call *non-response*, and have developed

Table 4.1 *Relative costs of fieldwalking and various forms of sub-surface survey (from Fasham et al. 1980, 9; and Champion et al. 1995, 59).*

| *Amount per person-day*: | | |
|---|---|---|
| Line walking: | | |
|    Lines 3 m apart | | 1000–2500 m² |
|    15 m apart | | 3300–6600 m² |
|    30 m apart | | 6600–10000 m² |
| Excavate, monitor and backfill 2 m-wide machine-dug trench | 70 m | 140 m² |
| Dig, sieve and record 1 m by 1 m test-pits | 4 pits | 4 m² |
| Hand-excavation of site trenching once overburden has been removed | | 9 m² |
| Machine operator can trench (at an equivalent cost of 2.5 person-days) | 140 m | 280 m² |

various strategies for dealing with it (Cochran 1963, 355–74; Thompson and Seber 1996, 90–1).

## Data to be collected

A primary decision here is the choice of the *unit of analysis* (Foley 1978, 51). Is it to be, for example, the artefact, the assemblage, or the site? This depends on our mental model of the archaeological record: is it (to use mathematical terms) a continuous or discontinuous distribution? The traditional view, with its emphasis on distinct sites, sees the record as basically discontinuous. A more recent view, that seems to have started with Thomas (1975) and to have been developed by Foley (1978; 1981a and b), Dunnell and Dancey (1983), Bintliff and Snodgrass (1988), Dunnell (1988), Schofield (1989; 1991a) and Rhoads (1992), emphasises the distribution of activity and artefacts between the so-called 'sites', and is thus sometimes called *non-site* or *off-site* survey. There are practical and theoretical grounds for this approach. The practical ones are the difficulty and arbitrariness of defining a site on the ground during a survey. For example, the Cambridge/Bradford Boeotia Expedition (Bintliff and Snodgrass 1985) started with the idea of using pottery distributions to separate habitation sites from 'off-site activity areas', but was forced off this approach by the sheer density and ubiquity of pottery scatters (Bintliff and Snodgrass 1988, 506). Dunnell and Dancey (1983, 271) made the crucial point that 'distinguishing a site and settling its boundaries is an archaeological decision, not an observation'. The theoretical grounds are that to ignore what goes on between the 'sites' is to miss out much information about the use of the landscape. For these reasons, much survey work has, either explicitly or implicitly, been going over to this approach (see the objectives listed above).

It is likely, then, that a modern survey will concentrate on the spatial recording of artefactual material. This raises three questions: whether to collect the material physically or to record it *in situ*; whether to record all categories of

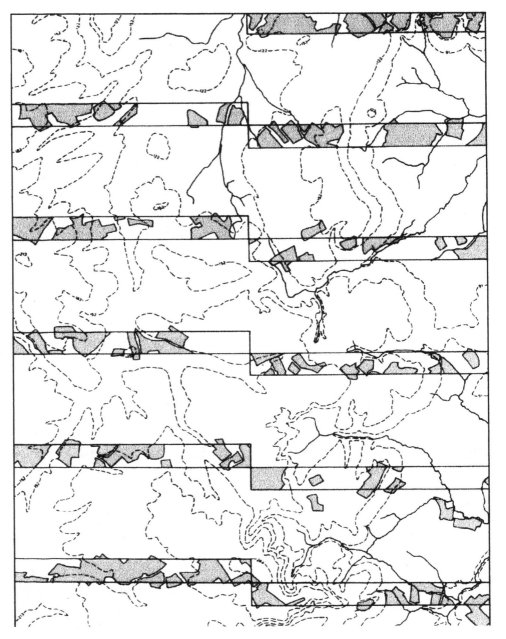

Fig. 4.2 Comparison of sample transects and fields actually walked in the East
Hampshire Survey (Shennan 1985, Fig. 2.7).

material or to be selective; and what level of aggregation and of spatial accuracy is required in the recording.

The arguments against collecting material are that it damages the archaeological record (Cherry 1982, 19), slows down the survey (Cherry *et al.* 1992), and increases transport and processing costs (see discussion by Schiffer *et al.* 1978, 15). Against these, the 'total collection strategy' is favoured because it prevents rare categories from being missed altogether (Sylvester 1991, 8), and because it does not rely on the ability of workers to recognise categories in detail (Shennan 1985, 8). Gerrard (1995, 13) argued that it does not slow down data collection. Many survey reports make the point that, when a concentration of material is found, a 'representative sample' is taken (whether or not material is collected elsewhere) (for example Sylvester 1991, 9; Barker 1995, 46), but it is not clear how this is to be achieved. Many surveys attempt to filter out modern and undiagnostic material; Shapwick is unusual in that natural material 'alien to the area' was collected (Gerrard 1990, 25).

It is more difficult to ascertain the level of spatial aggregation employed in the recording and presentation of finds, although some theoretical criteria have been suggested by Rogers (1982). The collective bagging of finds from 10 m or 20 m squares seems commonplace in the more intensive surveys, with plotting perhaps by 100 m squares (e.g. Gerrard 1990, 25). The question of accuracy with which the location of a sampling unit, let alone a find, can be recorded, needs to be addressed. Global Positioning Systems (GPS) have been suggested as a possible solution (Belli 1997), and with the imminent possibility of linking 'palm-top' computers to GPS (Pascoe *et al.* 1997; for current possibilities see Carver *et al.* 1995) great improvements in both speed and accuracy may soon be possible.

### Degree of precision required

This stage is likely to present archaeologists with a dilemma. On the one hand, it provides essential input into the calculation of sample size (see p. 22), but on the other hand, archaeologists find it very difficult, if not impossible, to be precise about the degree of precision they require. Indeed, the whole idea may be alien to their way of thought.

In the 'estimation' approach (p. 70), they would have to specify a particular variable (e.g. total number of sites in a region), and to specify both a required margin of error (in either absolute or percentage terms) and an acceptable probability of achieving a result within this margin. For example, 'I want to be 90% certain that my estimate of site density is within 10% of the true value.' The problems for the archaeologist are:

(a)   there may not be a single variable whose estimation is of prime importance to the survey – there may be several, or none – and

(b)     there may be no obvious archaeological criteria for choosing a margin of error and the associated probability.

Criteria based on several variables can, in principle, be combined (but the mathematics is very heavy, see Cochran 1963, 120, and the number of arbitrary decisions to be made is multiplied).

The situation may be easier if the objectives are couched in 'hypothesis testing' terms (p. 78). As a bare minimum, the archaeologist has to specify the *size* of the test (p. 24), i.e. the acceptable probability of rejecting a true hypothesis, for example that site density does not change between period A and period B. But this says nothing about the *power* of the test (p. 25), and leaves wide open the chance of accepting a false hypothesis, e.g. of saying the density has not changed when in fact it has. This risk does not seem to bother most archaeologists, but those who want to consider this issue more deeply may find the 'indifference zone' approach (p. 25) useful.

In the 'discovery' mode (p. 68), the steps are:

(a)     to specify a minimum size of site that 'ought' to be discovered,
(b)     to specify the acceptable probability of *not* finding such a site, given that it would be detected if 'hit' by a sampling unit, and
(c)     to follow the sorts of procedures suggested by Read (1986) or Sundstrom (1993).

But even this apparently straightforward situation can be complicated by the question of imperfect detectability (p. 39): what corrections must be made to allow for the possibility of 'missing' a site that is included in a sampling unit?

The 'characterisation' situation is perhaps the most difficult of all. Estimating a distribution from samples taken across it requires a degree of interpolation that must be based on either (a) some statistical model of the distribution itself, or (b) an assumption that the distribution is at least 'smooth', i.e. that it suffers no sudden 'jumps' or discontinuities. The former seems to beg the question: if we know so much, why are we doing the survey? The latter seems to deny the existence of sites, which could be defined as discontinuities in artefact distributions. One possible approach might be *kriging* (Zubrow and Harbaugh 1978). Other suggestions were made by Wheatley (1996).

Overall, then, this is a difficult issue for the archaeologist. The hypothesis testing approach seems the most promising; if a relatively simple null hypothesis could be distilled from the survey's objectives, then it could at least provide a 'baseline' figure of precision with which to proceed to the calculation of sample size (see below). Since we are usually interested in comparisons rather than absolute values, the hypothesis should be couched in terms of 'no difference' (e.g. between values in two periods, or two areas), rather than in terms of a hypothetical single value. The temptation to bypass this stage without serious thought, and to rush for a sample design (and especially a sampling fraction) on the grounds that so-and-so recommended it, or that it worked well on such-and-such a survey, must be resisted at all costs. Every survey is different, and such rules of thumb are rarely useful.

### Method of measurement

In archaeology, this is so closely related to *data to be collected* (see above) that the two cannot really be disentangled. This is in contrast to social surveys, in which the same question may be asked in different ways (e.g. by mail, telephone, or face-to-face interview). One point which archaeologists do have to consider here is the design of the recording form. Obviously, standardised recording is needed to ensure consistency, as far as possible, between workers and between seasons within a project. Two points must be kept in mind:

(a) workers must understand the form and be comfortable with it, to the extent of having been involved in discussions on its content (possibly) and design (certainly), and

(b) it must be suitable as an entry document for a database of some sort.

The database design, and indeed the structure of the output tables envisaged, should logically come *before* the design of the form. It is too late to collect all the data and then worry about how to analyse them. These points apply equally to paper records and to direct input into data-logging devices. As mentioned above, the imminent possibility of direct input of spatial data from GPS is likely to make a considerable impact.

### The frame

Here we come to issues which have caused much debate over the past thirty years or so – the shape and size of the sampling units (p. 19). Formally, the only requirement is that the units cover all the study region and do not overlap one another. In practice, two issues tend to dominate the discussion: the argument between quadrats and transects (p. 19) for pedestrian survey, and the layout of the units for sub-surface sampling. We shall look at each in turn.

### Pedestrian survey

Both quadrats and transects have been widely used in practice: examples of the use of transects are Melos (Cherry 1982) and Agro Pontino (Loving *et al.* 1991) (Figs. 4.3 and 4.4), as well as East Hampshire (Fig. 4.2); examples of the use of quadrats are the Chevelon Archaeological Research Project (Read 1986) and the Biferno valley (Barker 1995) (Figs. 4.5 and 4.6). Theoretical discussions and experiments on their relative merits (Plog 1976; Plog *et al.* 1978; Schiffer *et al.* 1978, 11) have tended to favour transects, although the conclusions are not clear-cut. Since a transect could be thought of as a series of quadrats placed

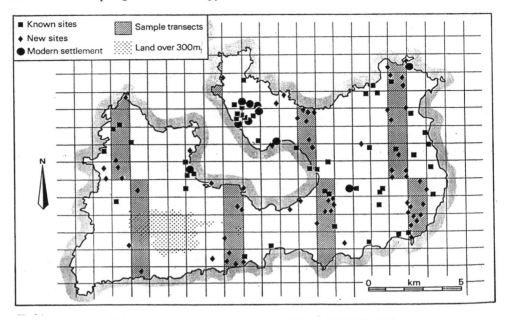

| Known sites | Sample transects |
| New sites | Land over 300m, |
| Modern settlement | |

Fig. 4.3 Sample design for Melos Survey (Cherry 1982, Fig. 2.1).

end-to-end, there is an *a priori* case for suggesting that quadrats might be more efficient, especially if spatial autocorrelation (p. 31) at the scale of the quadrats is a potential problem. But such arguments have tended to show relatively small differences in efficiency, and are usually based on comparisons in which the same total area is surveyed by each method. This is probably not a fair comparison, favouring quadrats because it ignores the costs of locating the sample units before they can be surveyed. Quadrats are likely to be more expensive than transects in this respect, so that, in a given time, they are likely to result in the surveying of a smaller total area. A fair comparison would thus be even more likely to favour transects.

However, the statistical position is more flexible than archaeologists seem to realise. There is no reason why a sampling unit has to be square, or even has to have straight edges. It is perfectly possible to construct a sampling frame from 'natural' units (e.g. fields or other units of land use; units bounded by coastlines, watercourses, geological boundaries, watersheds, contours, etc.), provided only that they follow the statistical rule given at the start of this section. Such a scheme was used by Rogge and Fuller (1977), but this approach seems to have been little used since, whether through ignorance or deliberate avoidance is not clear. The ensuing variation in unit size is not a problem, since selection can be made with probability proportional to size (pps) (p. 34), and methods of estimation are only a little more complicated. More preparatory work may be needed to define the frame, since nothing is easier than slapping a grid across a map, but the payoff comes in the practical ease of locating and

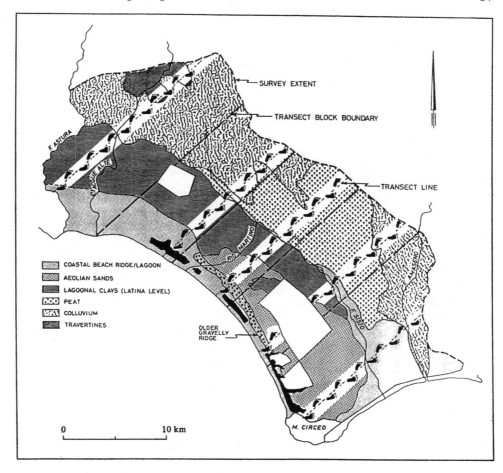

Fig. 4.4 Sample design for Agro Pontino Survey (Loving *et al.* 1991, Fig. 3).

defining units on the ground. The approach also avoids the problem of those awkward quadrats that consist mostly of water, bare rock or other sterile areas. It might run into difficulties if a survey were to be repeated on successive occasions (e.g. in monitoring the condition of monuments in a region), since apparently well-defined topographical boundaries can vanish (e.g. by removal of hedgerows to form larger fields), and its benefits may be diminished by increasing use of GPS to locate quadrats or transects (p. 83).

In the choice of size of unit, there is a tension between theory, which favours small units, especially for purposes of estimation and hypothesis testing, and practical considerations, which favour larger units, on the grounds of the overhead costs of travelling to and locating a multitude of small units. The theoretical position has been caricatured by Hole's remark that 'by planning infinitely small sample units, one could know everything about an area by

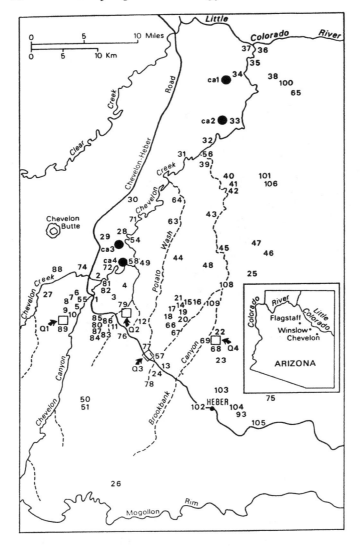

Fig. 4.5 Sample design for the Chevelon Archaeological Research Project (Read 1986, reprinted with the permission of the *Journal of Field Archaeology* and the Trustees of Boston University).

looking at nothing' (1980, 226). The objective of characterisation would also favour larger units, since the scale and nature of inter-site patterns are not apparent unless the units are larger than that scale. Again, comparisons of efficiency must be based on equal resources (time and/or money), not equal areas surveyed and certainly not on equal numbers of units. In practice, 'large' quadrats seem to mean 1 km (Plog 1976) or 1.5 km (Schiffer *et al.* 1978) squares, and 'small' quadrats range from 0.1 km (Schiffer *et al.* 1978) to 0.5 km (Plog

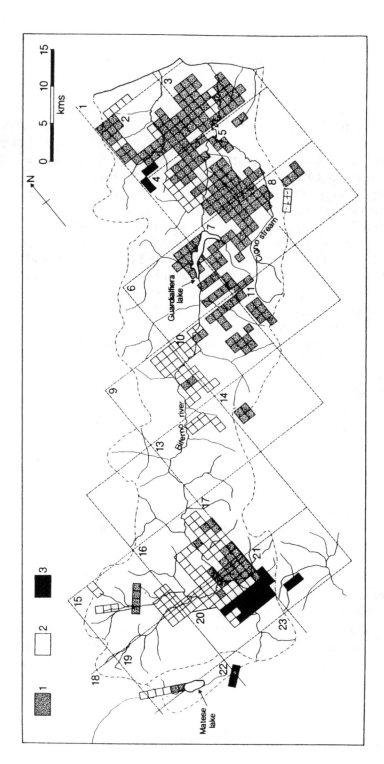

Fig. 4.6 Sample design for the Biferno Valley Survey (redrawn from Barker 1995, Fig. 21, by permission of Leicester University Press an imprint of Cassell, Wellington House, 125 Strand, London WC2R 0BB, England).

1976) squares. The width of transects may vary from 75–150 m (Plog 1976) to 0.5 km (Shennan 1985) to 1 km (Cherry 1982). In this context, fieldwalking should usually be seen as systematic sub-sampling (p. 21) by transects. If the spacing between walkers is more than about 5 m (depending on the terrain), then total coverage is not achieved and there is *de facto* systematic sampling, although it is often disguised by the term *intensity* (p. 75).

*Sub-surface sampling*: A good starting point is to consider the probability of intersecting a circular site of a certain size with a grid of shovel-test-pits (*STP*) of a certain spacing. This probability depends partly on the ratio of site diameter to grid interval, and partly on the shape of the grid itself. Krakker *et al.* (1983) showed that for a rectangular area, a staggered grid is considerably more efficient than a square grid, and that a hexagonal grid is slightly more efficient still (Fig. 4.7 and (**4.1**)). Kintigh (1988, 688) showed that this also holds for transects, which are just long thin rectangles. The increase in probability is shown in Fig. 4.8. However, detection is not the same as intersection. Two further probabilities must be taken into account: the probability that a unit contains any artefacts (which depends on the density of the artefact distribution and the size of the units), and the probability that an artefact contained in the unit would be detected by the archaeologist (which depends, *inter alia*, on the nature of artefacts likely to be found, and whether the contents of the unit are screened) (1988, 689). Kintigh carried out computer simulation tests on the effects of combining these three probabilities, across different values of the underlying factors, for a hypothetical but 'typical' situation. He concluded that, although much can be done to improve efficiency by tailoring a design to the circumstances of a particular survey, any survey of an affordable intensity is likely to miss a considerable proportion of sites, especially the smaller ones (1988, 706). Krakker *et al.* (1983, 479) also pointed out that the high cost of implementing such criteria would prohibit the use of *STP* across areas of regional scale. It is therefore best seen as a technique to be used at 'site' level (chapter 5), or as a sub-sampling technique in regional survey (see below).

*Common issues*: The possibility of stratification (p. 30) of the survey region should always be considered. The definition of strata could be based on any factor, or combination of factors, such as geology, elevation or aspect, that is thought likely to affect the parameters under study (e.g. site density), provided that the strata do not overlap and together comprise the whole region. Archaeologists are sometimes reluctant to vary the sampling fraction between strata, on the mistaken grounds of 'bias', but this is not a problem provided that the results from each stratum are properly weighted.

The multi-stage (in the statistical sense, p. 33) nature of most sample surveys needs to be acknowledged. For example, test-pits within transects, and field-walked transects within quadrats or 'natural' units such as fields, constitute

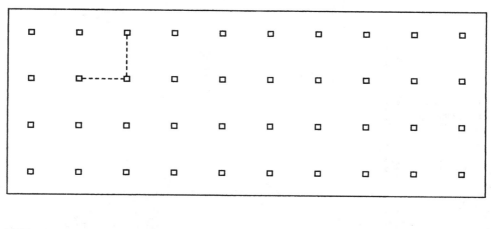

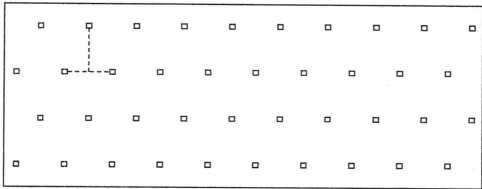

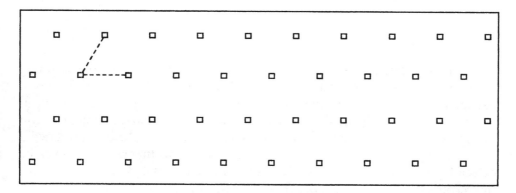

Fig. 4.7 Three possible grids for locating test-pits: (top) square grid; (middle) staggered square grid; (bottom) hexagonal grid (based on Kintigh 1988, Fig. 1).

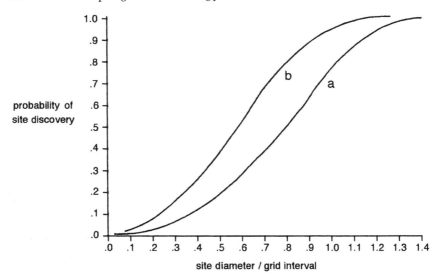

Fig. 4.8 The relationship between the ratio of site diameter to grid interval and the probability of discovering a site, using a square grid (a) and a staggered square grid (b) (Krakker *et al.* 1983, Fig. 2, reprinted with the permission of the *Journal of Field Archaeology* and the Trustees of Boston University).

second-stage sub-samples. This has implications for the aggregation of the survey results (see below).

Finally, both styles of survey could lend themselves well to the adaptive sampling approach (p. 34), which will be discussed in more detail in the following section.

### Selection of the sample

The primary decision is that of the appropriate sample size or sampling fraction (p. 22). It is preferable to think of the requirement as a sample of a particular size, and its implementation as the corresponding fraction (i.e. one in so many units). Ideally the sample size is calculated from the required precision (pp. 25, 210) and the variability of the population (p. 29 and below), modified if necessary by the finite population correction (p. 23). In practice it may be driven by other considerations, such as the amount that can be surveyed with the resources that are available. This approach is the less desirable, for two reasons:

(a) it may result in a sample that is too small, i.e. that is inadequate for the weight of analysis that will be placed upon it, or

(b) it may result in a sample that is too large, i.e. adequate results could have been obtained from a smaller sample.

In case (a), either the resources should be increased or the viability of the survey should be called into doubt. Case (b) will result in resources being diverted to the survey that could be better used elsewhere. It is hard to convince archaeologists that (b) is *ever* a possibility. It is not possible to tell whether a survey will be adequate simply on the grounds of either sample size or sampling fraction (especially not the latter), as it depends critically on the variability. In an extreme example, if sites were distributed uniformly in a region, we could estimate their density perfectly well from a sample of a single unit. The need for some knowledge of variability highlights the importance of a pilot survey (see below).

Another decision is whether the sample should be selected randomly or systematically (pp. 20–1). Archaeologists often seem to prefer systematic samples, partly because they appear to give 'better coverage' or an 'even spread' of a region, and partly because they are easier and quicker to select. These points should be weighed against the possibility of the sampling interval matching some regularity in the data. A possible compromise is the *stratified systematic unaligned* sample (e.g. Plog 1976, 137).

Statistical theory recommends the varying of sampling fractions between strata according to 'Neyman allocation', which maximises the precision for a given sample size (p. 30). This will be difficult if several parameters are to be estimated simultaneously, as each will give rise to its preferred allocation, and a compromise must be made. Archaeologists may decide that, what with this and the added complexity of the calculations (p. 212 and below), the game is not worth the candle, and opt for proportional allocation (p. 30).

The option of adaptive sampling (pp. 34–8) is a very recent one, and although it represents the sort of thing that archaeologists have long wished to do (but probably did not do, for fear of being 'told off' by nasty statisticians), there is little experience to guide the practitioner. For this reason, a simple worked example is given here. It is based on the Valdeflores Survey that was used as an example by Plog (1976, Fig. 5.5). It comprises an area of 5 by 11 km, i.e. 55 sq km, of which about 4.5 sq km is shown as 'unsurveyed mountain area', reducing the sampled population to 50.5 sq km. The total number of known sites in the area is 33. Plog took a nominal 10% sample of 24 units of 0.5 by 0.5 km, or 6 of 1 by 1 km.

A series of adaptive sampling experiments were undertaken to provide a comparison with Plog's results. All were based on units of 0.5 by 0.5 km, with the intention of providing final samples of 24 units, or slightly more on the grounds that the cost of sampling an adjacent unit would be less than that of sampling an unrelated one. For the first experiment, a neighbourhood (p. 34) was defined as the four units contiguous to a selected unit; it would be surveyed if one or more sites were located in the sample unit. On this basis, the area can be divided into networks (p. 34), which are shown on Fig. 4.9 and listed in Table 4.2.

Table 4.2 *Structure of networks for first adaptive sampling experiment.*

| network | | numbers of: | | | |
|---|---|---|---|---|---|
| | networks | units per network | sites per network | edge units | units surveyed |
| A | 1 | 12 | 3 | 13 | 25 |
| B | 1 | 7 | 3 | 8 | 15 |
| C | 1 | 12 | 11 | 14 | 26 |
| D | 1 | 5 | 2 | 8 | 13 |
| E | 1 | 2 | 1 | 6 | 8 |
| F | 4 | 2 | 2 | 6* | 8* |
| S(ingleton) | 5 | 1 | 1 | 4* | 5* |
| empty | 151 | 1 | – | – | 1 |
| total | 165 | 202 | 33 | n/a | n/a |

* = May be reduced if on edge of sample area

Table 4.3 *Outcome of first adaptive sampling experiment.*

| | min. | mean | max. | s.d. | target |
|---|---|---|---|---|---|
| estimated number of sites | 6.4 | 25.9 | 70.4 | 21.4 | 33 |
| number of units in final sample | 22 | 39.3 | 51 | – | 24 |
| number of sites located | 2 | 5.7 | 15 | – | ? |

One problem of adaptive sampling is that the final size of the sample varies from one 'run' to another, and is unknown in advance for any particular run (p. 34). The initial sample size needed to produce the required final sample must be estimated in some way. For a preliminary set of ten runs, an initial sample size of ten units was guessed. The outcome is shown in Table 4.3.

This is not satisfactory: the standard deviation of the estimated number of sites is high compared to Plog's values (1976, 149, Table 5.2), and the number of units surveyed is high, implying a costly but inefficient survey. The only benefits are that:

(a)　the actual number of sites located is also high, and
(b)　the edge effect discussed on p. 100 (the correction needed for sites that lie across a unit boundary) has been removed.

The poor performance appears to be due to the large sites located in networks A and B, which require a great deal of surveying but contribute relatively little to the number of sites. Various changes to the condition under which a neighbourhood would be surveyed were considered. The most satisfactory (experiment two) was 'survey the neighbourhood if one or more *complete* sites are located in a unit'. If only part of a site (or parts of sites) is (are) found in a unit, the neighbourhood is not surveyed. Since this restores the edge effect, it was combined with a rule for counting parts of a large site as fractions (p. 100):

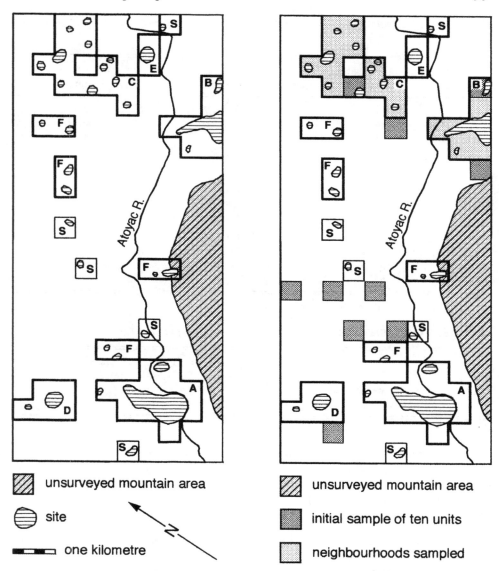

Fig. 4.9 (*Left*) Networks for first adaptive sampling experiment on Valdeflores data; (*right*) example of a sample of units (initial sample of ten units in dark tone, final sample in light tone) (based on Plog 1976, Fig. 5.5).

sites which on the basis of evidence from the initial sample are likely to occupy at least two units are scored $\frac{1}{2}$ for each sampled unit in which they occur; ones likely to occupy a least three are scored $\frac{1}{3}$ for each sampled unit in which they occur, and so on. This new rule breaks up the old networks A, B, C, D and E, as shown in Fig. 4.10 and Table 4.4.

Table 4.4 *Structure of networks for second and third adaptive sampling experiments.*

| network | | | numbers of: | | |
| --- | --- | --- | --- | --- | --- |
| | networks | units per network | sites per network | edge units | units surveyed |
| C' | 1 | 3 | 3 | 5 | 8 |
| F | 4 | 2 | 2 | 6* | 8* |
| G | 1 | 1 | 2 | 4 | 5 |
| P(artial) | 27 | 1 | see below | 0 | 1 |
| of which | | | | | |
| P2 | 12 | | 0.5 | | |
| P3 | 2 | | 0.33 | | |
| P4 | 9 | | 0.25 | | |
| P6 | 3 | | 0.17 | | |
| P7 | 1 | | 0.14 | | |
| S(ingleton) | 12 | 1 | 1 | 4* | 5* |
| empty | 151 | 1 | – | – | 1 |
| total | 165 | 202 | 33 | n/a | n/a |

* = May be reduced if on edge of sample area

Table 4.5 *Outcome of second adaptive sampling experiment.*

| | min. | mean | max. | s.d. | target |
| --- | --- | --- | --- | --- | --- |
| estimated number of sites | 5.1 | 25.9 | 61.1 | 20.1 | 33 |
| number of units in final sample | 10 | 14.6 | 24 | – | 24 |
| number of sites located | 1 | 3.0 | 6 | – | ? |

Table 4.6 *Outcome of third adaptive sampling experiment.*

| | min. | mean | max. | s.d. | target |
| --- | --- | --- | --- | --- | --- |
| estimated number of sites | 7.4 | 33.1 | 70.4 | 15.3 | 33 |
| number of units in final sample | 16 | 24.7 | 33 | – | 24 |
| number of sites located | 2 | 4.7 | 8 | – | - |

The outcome of this experiment is shown in Table 4.5.

This design is much more efficient than that of experiment one, with a slightly smaller s.d. on a sample less than 40% of the original final size. It is still inefficient in comparison to Plog's results, but it now has a smaller final sample than the target figure of 24 units. The next experiment, number three, was to increase the size of the initial sample from 10 to 16, while keeping the same neighbourhood and condition. This has the same neighbourhoods as experiment two (Fig. 4.10), but a different set of outcomes.

A preliminary set of ten runs gave samples that are on average the 'right' size, with a corresponding reduction in the s.d. A larger set of runs (25 in all) gave

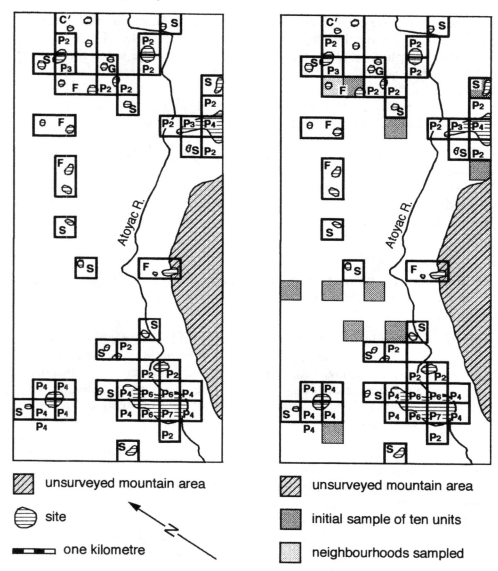

Fig. 4.10 (*Left*) Networks for second and subsequent adaptive sampling experiments on Valdeflores data; (*right*) example of a sample of units (same initial sample of ten units as in Fig. 4.9 in dark tone, final sample in light tone) (based on Plog 1976, Fig. 5.5).

the results shown in Table 4.6: the s.d. lies in the middle of those arising from Plog's experiments, being generally 'better' than large quadrat samples and 'worse' than small quadrat samples, which typically had a s.d. of about 13 to 14, compared to 15 in experiment three here. This is not at all a bad result, since:

(a)  the close correspondence between the average sample sizes prob-
     ably means that the adaptive samples are actually 'cheaper';
(b)  adaptive sampling shows to its best advantage when the 'objects'
     (sites) are highly clustered; in this example, the degree of clustering is
     relatively low;
(c)  the adaptive sample locates, on average, more sites per survey than
     the conventional method.

This experiment is sufficiently encouraging to suggest its use at other scales (see
chapter 5).

It should be clear by now that the actual selection of units may come as a
blessed relief to the archaeologist: a simple practical task, aided by a computer
program or a book of random numbers.

### The pre-test

As we have progressed through these stages, we have encountered many
different sorts of information that it would be useful to have before undertaking a survey. They can be grouped as:

(a)  knowledge of the spatial variability of the variables of interest,
(b)  knowledge of the relative costs of different activities: fieldwalking,
     test-pit digging, screening, locating sample points, transporting
     equipment, etc., and
(c)  knowledge of the ability of workers to cope with the recording
     system.

A good way to obtain some of this information is to carry out a small pilot
survey or pre-test. As well as straightforward information, useful for calculating sample sizes, etc., it may throw up all sorts of unexpected problems.
Instructions that seem perfectly clear in the office may suddenly become
ambiguous in the field, boxes on forms may be too small for the desirable
information, the lap-top's batteries may have a life of only half what you were
told, and so on. Anything that can go wrong is likely to do so, and a pilot
survey is the best place for it to happen. Then the archaeologist can 'go back to
the drawing board' and put it right before it really matters.

### Organisation of the fieldwork

It would be foolish to try to offer definite advice about how to carry out a
project, in ignorance of its location, size, duration, funding or any other
material factor. However, a general point that is always worth making is that
of ensuring that the workers know not only what they are supposed to do, but

why they are supposed to do it. Without at least a basic understanding of the principles of random sampling, strange things may happen when problems are encountered in the field. Time spent educating the workforce is rarely wasted.

### Summary and analysis of the data

As mentioned above (p. 85), it is important to know what analyses will be carried out, and what tables will be produced, before the survey is undertaken, with the proviso that any particularly uninformative ones can be suppressed. The methods of analysis must match the design of the sample; for example, the use of stratification with varying sampling fractions requires the results to be calculated separately for each stratum and then aggregated. The correct formulae must be used to estimate totals, means and standard deviations: estimates of site densities are likely to be ratio estimates (p. 38), and of site characteristics (e.g. size) are likely to be cluster estimates (p. 30).

More complicated spatial statistics, expressing (for example) the degree of clustering of sites, may with caution be calculated. Those based on counts in quadrats (Hodder and Orton 1976, 30–43), such as Morisita's Index (Rogge and Fuller 1977, 234; Shennan 1985, 15), are presumably robust when quadrats are sampled, but those based on point-to-point distances (e.g. nearest-neighbour analysis, Hodder and Orton 1976, 43–51) are very sensitive to *edge effects* (e.g. the possibility that a site's nearest-neighbour may be in an adjacent unsurveyed quadrat). A recent development has been the use of advanced computer graphics to display results, especially of landscape surveys (Boismier and Reilly 1988).

This might be a good place to mention the wider problem of *edge effects* in pedestrian survey (Schiffer *et al.* 1978, 11). With any sort of sampling unit, it is always possible that a site may lie across the boundary of two (or even more) units. For discovery, this is not a problem; in fact, it is an advantage. But for estimation, it can be a source of bias, likely to lead to over-estimation of the total number in a region. This can best be seen by imagining a 'total sample' (every unit of the population is sampled), in which the count of sites in each unit is simply added up. The total count will not be the same as the total number of sites, despite the 100% coverage, because some sites will have been counted twice. In statistical jargon, the estimator is not *consistent*, a serious fault. A simple way round this problem is to count any site that lies across the boundary of a sampling unit as 'half' instead of 'one', regardless of what proportion of it may lie outside the unit. If thought necessary, those right in the corner of a unit might be counted as 'one quarter', though this seems rather fussy. The total for each unit in the population will then add up to the true total.

*Information gained for future surveys*

Any survey is likely to generate much information that will be useful to future surveys, quite apart from the publishable 'results'. For example, there may be data on the time and cost of various forms of survey, estimates of the detectability of different types of site under different conditions, and accounts of problems encountered and how they were overcome. All are potentially valuable and should be kept in a project archive to be made available on request, with their presence and availability signalled in some way.

A ramification of the site/non-site discussion (p. 81) is the attempt to divide 'sites' into those that are *archaeologically* (or *culturally*) *significant*, and those that are not. Here we have yet another meaning to the overworked term *significance* (p. 24), applied this time to individual loci rather than to statistics derived from them. Clearly, the significance of a site is not an intrinsic or immutable characteristic; it depends on (at least) the existing state of knowledge, the condition both of the site itself and of other related ones, and the current research agenda, all of which can be expected to change over time. Many of the issues raised are beyond the scope of this book (see for example Tainter and Lucas 1983; Dunnell 1984; Leone and Potter 1992), but they impinge on it by creating the context in which regional sampling takes place. For example, they might suggest that the purpose of a survey is to obtain a representative sample of sites for future research (p. 78), which could 'at least theoretically permit any type of research to be carried out on the sample that could have been carried out on the original intact population' (Lipe 1974, 228). This in turn raises interesting questions of data redundancy (see e.g. King *et al.* 1977). The literature is mainly from the USA; the subject has also been considered in the UK, both nationally, for example in the context of the national Monuments Protection Programme for England (Darvill *et al.* 1987), and locally (Groube and Bowden 1982). A comprehensive annotated bibliography was provided by Briuer and Mathers (1996).

## Case studies

Finally, we look at three examples of how this theory has been put into practice on the ground, and how surveys may well contain experiments which not only help with the design of the current survey, but also provide information which may be useful in the planning of future surveys. The three examples chosen are all from England: this is not chauvinism, but a reluctance to comment on surveys carried out under conditions of which I have no personal experience. They have been chosen to represent a range of scales, from the very small (Shapwick Parish Survey) through the medium-sized (East Hampshire Survey) to the large national survey (Monuments at Risk Survey). These sizes are relative to the small and crowded English landscape. They will be examined in chronological order.

### East Hampshire

This project, undertaken in 1977/8, was a landmark in regional survey in Britain. It was on a larger scale than previous work, was based more rigorously on sampling principles, and included an unusually large and advanced element of statistical analysis. Its main aims lay in the areas of characterisation and analysis (p. 78). The survey area was chosen to encompass a range of ecological variation, leading to a need for an east–west dimension of 10 km; the north–south dimension was more arbitrarily chosen to be 15 km, giving a total survey area of 150 sq km (Fig. 4.11). In retrospect, this was probably too ambitious (Shennan 1985, 5). The survey was envisaged as the first part of a two-stage procedure:

    (a)   to search for sites at a minimal level of coverage,
    (b)   to examine some or all of them in detail to obtain more information about them (1985, 7).

The need to balance the resources available with the size of the region led to careful consideration of both the density of coverage and the level of detail of recording. The chosen survey method was line-walking; experiments in walking at intervals of 60, 30 and 3 paces ('saturation') indicated that a spacing of 30 paces would be adequate, reducing to 15 paces for inexperienced walkers (1985, 10–11). Since walkers were recruited through a Job Creation Scheme, the latter spacing was used most frequently (1985, 17). The definition of 'saturation' as 3-pace intervals suggests that the width of a walked strip was seen as 3 paces, so that the procedure could be interpreted as a 10% systematic transect sample (or 20% for inexperienced walkers). The unit of recording was taken to be each walked line within each field (1985, 8). Taking these factors together, it was thought that 30 sq km (20% of the total area) could be covered in the time available. Primary samples of systematic east–west transects, each 0.5 km wide, and staggered at their mid-point, were designated (1985, 12). Only part of the primary sample was actually available for fieldwalking (see Fig. 4.2); the rest was either too steep for settlement, or under permanent grass, woodland or urban development (although woodland was surveyed for earthworks).

In terms of the discovery of new 'sites', the survey could be seen as disappointing, with only one major discovery – the pagan Saxon cemetery at Alton (1985, 89). However, much was learnt about the distribution of material of different periods across the region, and the relationships between land use in different periods. Previous views about the nature and extent of Mesolithic activity were broadly supported by the results of the survey (1985, 49), but

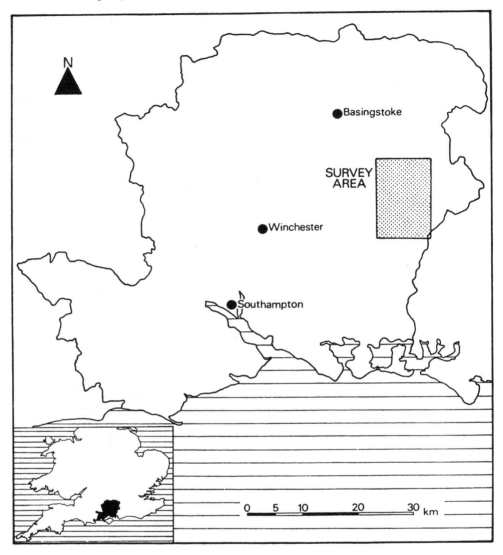

Fig. 4.11  East Hampshire Survey location map (Shennan 1985, Fig. 1.1).

there was a dramatic increase in the evidence from the Neolithic and Bronze Age (1985, 50). Continuity between the Iron Age and Roman periods was suggested, with intensification within the Roman period (1985, 85). It seemed more fruitful to compare periods with each other than to characterise each in detail (1985, 105–12). This would be in keeping with the overall aims of the survey. Shennan pointed out that the most important outcome was the development of methodology (1985, 2), which certainly strongly influenced the next generation of surveys (e.g. Shapwick, see below).

The statistical analyses are of great interest, and were copied in other surveys, e.g. Shapwick (Turner 1995) and Agro Pontino (Verhoeven 1991). The main technique used was multiple regression with dummy independent variables (O'Muircheartaigh and Francis 1981, 93); the logarithm of the dependent variable was taken after zero values had been removed. The dependent variables were the densities of post-medieval pottery, chipped stone and burnt flint, expressed as mean densities of finds per 100 m of walked line for each field (1985, 35). The main methodological aim was to try to assess how much of the variability in density was due to (a) environmental or topographical factors, (b) 'distorting' variables (e.g. weather conditions), and (c) inter-walker variability. The environmental variables 'explained' about 40% of the variation in density (but nearly 60% for burnt flint). Different factors influenced the density of different materials; geology was probably the most important overall, with the presence of Upper Greensand positively influencing post-medieval pottery and burnt flint, while the presence of Gault Clay negatively influenced chipped stone. In each case, the distorting variables 'explained' just under 20% of the variation, but also affected the relative importance of the environmental variables. Differences between walkers were examined after the effects of environmental and distorting variables had been removed. Although it was clear that some walkers were better than others at recognising particular classes of artefact (1985, 43), the contribution of walker effects to the overall variability appeared to be small.

### Shapwick

This project dealt specifically with the archaeology of a parish of some 13 sq km in the county of Somerset (Fig. 4.12). The main objectives were stated by Gerrard (1990, 21; see p. 78), and by Aston (1995, 5) as 'an attempt to test the hypothesis that the present village and the medieval field system were planned in the late Saxon period and had replaced an earlier, Saxon settlement of scattered farmsteads with individual fields'. The specific aim was thus embedded in a more general programme of characterisation, which would enable other questions to be tackled in the future. The chosen method of survey was large-scale fieldwalking, enhanced by selective geophysical and chemical survey, and very limited excavation. There was an initial assumption that 'the recovered material will be representative of the artefacts present in the topsoil but some deeper features may not be located, such as graves' (Gerrard 1990, 25).

The project started in 1989 with a pilot survey of 18,500 sq m (0.14% of the total area of the parish), which were walked in a total of 66 man-hours, excluding overheads such as travelling and setting up survey grids (1990, 25). It was noted that as much time again had to be allowed for cleaning, sorting and analysing the finds (1990, 25). An initial experiment in collecting material from

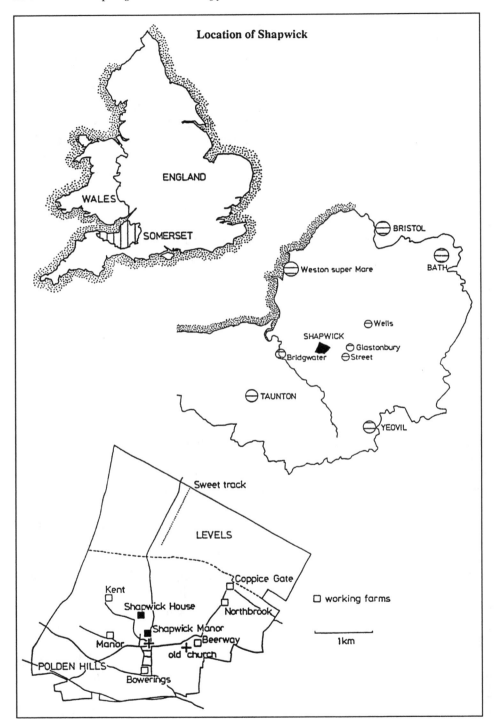

Fig. 4.12 Shapwick Parish Survey location map (Aston 1995, 4).

10 m by 10 m grids showed little fall-off in the rate of finds recovered per 5 minute 'stint' for the first 30 minutes of searching a square, but the proportion of 'waste' (e.g. stones) increased dramatically from an average of 17% in the first 15 minutes to up to 83% in the 25–30 minute stint, as if some walkers were trying to maintain their rate of collection, regardless of what they were collecting. Rates of collection for various walkers are shown in Fig. 4.13. This suggested that the optimum search time for a 100 sq m unit was 15 minutes; the survey allowed 20 minutes in subsequent practice. A second aspect of the experiment (1990, 29) showed that in 30 minutes an experienced walker could collect almost twice as many finds from his square as an inexperienced walker. The inexperienced walkers were thought to be 'unintentionally subjective', and to fail to collect pieces which they thought were small and unimportant. This may not be as worrying as it seems because, as Gerrard (1990) pointed out, total collection is less important than representative collection. This highlights the need for training – archaeologists cannot be expected to fieldwalk instinctively – and raised the possibility of 'inter-walker effects', which were examined in more detail in later years (see below). It also appears to have contributed to a decision (Gerrard 1995, 10) to collect all alien material, rather than to be material- or period-specific (as is more common), on the grounds that relatively inexperienced walkers may fail to recognise certain categories of material, and would therefore bias the results if they exercised selective collection.

By 1994 (i.e. in five years), some 300 ha (24% of the total area, or 38% of the 'potentially walkable area') had been fieldwalked (1995, 10). This shows that the sampled population, at around 800 ha, is only just over 60% of the total population, even in an area where accessibility is not a specific problem. Most of the survey had been undertaken by line-walking, with lines 25 m apart and collection points every 25 m, so that one collected unit represents 625 sq m. Areas of potential were rewalked in 10 m grids, as described above. The width of the scanned strips was taken to be 1.5 m (considerably narrower than in many others surveys, e.g. Bintliff 1985), so that the survey was actually a 6% systematic transect sample (1.5 m is 6% of 25 m) (Gerrard 1995, 13). The outcomes of some further experiments are probably the results of widest interest, at least until the publication of the final report. Rewalking some field in successive years indicated large variations in the amounts recovered and in their precise locations, but greater stability in the proportions of finds in different categories (1995, 46). Topsoil finds were not found to be a reliable guide to sub-surface remains, since much of the surface material seemed to have arrived by manuring or other forms of dumping (1995, 47) (sometimes known as 'dung cartefacts' (Rook, pers. comm.)). The importance of recognising that material can be 'ploughed-in' to a location, as well as 'ploughed-out' of underlying remains, was stressed. Concentrations are therefore difficult to interpret as 'sites'; they may represent other sorts of activities.

The data were examined further by Turner (1995), who closely followed

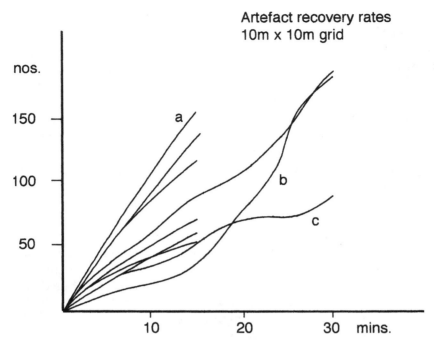

Fig. 4.13 Graph of rate of collection of artefacts by walkers in five-minute 'stints' (Gerrard 1990, 30, Fig. 18).

Shennan (1985; see above) in using multiple regression on the densities of four categories of artefact (tile, glass, metal, brick). Comparisons were made both between fields and between lines. He concluded that the environmental variables 'explained' about 40–50% of the variation in apparent density (except for brick, for which the figure was less than 30%); the most important of them was 'top of slope', i.e. fewer finds were made at the top of slopes, presumably reflecting the effects of erosion and down-slope movement (Turner 1995, 61). The distorting variables 'explained' about 30% of the variation (again, rather less for brick), rather more than in the East Hampshire Survey (see above). The most important appeared to be rain (finds were generally more visible in the rain), which was not among the variables used in East Hampshire. There were also complicated interactions between the two classes of variable. The conclusions about differences between walkers (1995, 64) were broadly the same as in East Hampshire. It has been suggested that such differences could be positively exploited, rather than regarded as a problem (Bradley *et al.* 1994).

Perhaps the biggest lesson from the very honest reports of this survey is the importance of standardised fieldwork and recording methods, and of a pilot survey for establishing what the parameters of the fieldwork should be. For example, if the rate of survey had not been standardised, the density of finds would simply have reflected the time taken to survey each area or field. It is interesting to see the intuitive use of what has since been called adaptive sampling (pp. 34 and 93), demonstrating a real archaeological need for this piece of statistical theory.

The statistical analyses of both these surveys may be less satisfactory; 'collected' data such as these are notoriously difficult to analyse in comparison to those that could be obtained from a designed experiment, because the effects of the various factors can easily be confused (*confounded*). Multiple regression can be unstable in the presence of correlated explanatory variables, so the results should be treated with caution. The need to take logarithms of the densities (presumably to reduce the effect of the rare very high values) had the unfortunate side-effect of necessitating the removal of zero values from the analyses. On the other hand, it is difficult to see what else could have been done; a 'controlled' experiment was out of the question, if only because the distorting variables (e.g. the weather) could not be controlled.

### *Monuments at Risk Survey (MARS)*

This is by far the biggest of our case studies, and also the most expensive – probably the most expensive archaeological survey in the UK to date. It arose from dissatisfaction with the Schedule of Ancient Monuments (a list of chosen monuments in Britain, membership of which gives some protection to a monument; see Darvill *et al.* 1987). The list had been started in the 1880s and by the 1980s had grown to about 13,000 (2%) of the 600,000 or so monuments estimated to exist in England alone. Fears were expressed that this 'sample' was in no way representative, and was inadequate for the purpose of managing this important archaeological resource (1987, 395).

MARS was therefore set up by English Heritage to remedy these defects, and specifically (Darvill and Wainwright 1994) to:

(a)  quantify systematically England's archaeological resource in terms of:
  (i)  changing knowledge of the scale and nature of the archaeological resources, including single monuments, ancient landscapes and historic urban areas;
  (ii)  the scale and rate of physical impact on monuments since 1945, and the reasons and causes for this;
  (iii)  the present condition and survival of the resource and future projection of these;
  (iv)  the effectiveness of measures introduced to improve monument management;
(b)  investigate the implications of decay for different classes of monument in terms of the information preserved at different states of survival;

(c)  publish a range of reports on the study in order to reach a wide audience.

Less formally, the Survey was described as 'the first ever national census of the condition and survival of archaeological sites in England', and as 'a sort of later 20th century Domesday Book' (1994). Following a pilot survey in one county (Wiltshire) in 1991, the Survey was scheduled to run from late 1994 to early 1996, with publication early in 1997 (Darvill and Wainwright 1994; Anon. 1994). The overall cost was given as £900,000 (Darvill and Wainwright 1994, 822), although much higher figures have been informally mentioned. Progress reports were published in June 1994 and April and November 1995 (Anon. 1994; 1995a; 1995b). The population was taken to be the entire ground surface of England, and the sampling units were blocks of land 5 km by 1 km, some running east–west and some north–south. A sample of 5% of such units (about 1300 in all) was chosen (Fig. 4.14), and all monuments in them (about 15,000 in all) were visited by one of six regional field survey teams. For each monument examined, some 26 key variables were recorded, ranging from monument form and class to survival and decay (Darvill and Wainwright 1994, 821). Novel variables are the measures of *survival* and *decay*, which were calculated as follows:

Survival is quantified by both *percentage area loss* (PAL), given by

PAL = 100*(projected original extent − area extent at time of survey)/(projected original extent),

and by *percentage height loss* (PHL), given by

PHL = 100*(projected original height − estimated average height at time of survey)/ (projected original height),

and more subjectively by the *percentage volume survival* (PVS), an estimate of the percentage of the volume of monument lost between the projected original extent and the point in time for which the gross survival estimate is being made (Anon. 1994).

Decay was measured as a decade factor (DDF), defined as the difference between PVS at the beginning and end of the decade in question.

It was estimated that the time taken to record one monument would be between half an hour and an hour. Additional information was to be provided from the County Sites and Monuments Records (SMRs), from aerial photographs of the sampled units, and from a small selective sample of case studies (three examples each of twelve classes of monument) (Anon. 1995a). Data were thus collected at three distinct levels: basic information from the SMRs (total coverage), detailed information from the field survey with comparative data from the aerial photographs (5% coverage), and very detailed information from the case studies (minute coverage). These three levels can in principle be combined to give a coherent national picture. The analytical procedures have been described by Bell and King (1996) and a summary report has been published (Darvill and Fulton 1998).

The Survey was unusual in archaeological terms in having a well-defined sampling frame – the County SMRs – that was nevertheless not used in the selection of the sample. Instead, the use of rectangular quadrats imposed a cluster sampling mode on the Survey, which may not be the most efficient, and should certainly complicate the calculations (p. 212). On the other hand, it presumably reduced travelling time and costs, which were considerable, perhaps around 5000 miles per county (Anon. 1995b). The sample itself has some odd features, such as the edge-effects that inevitably arise when sampling an irregular area by quadrats (p. 100); also, a higher proportion of the units than might be expected appear to be contiguous, and some even overlap (Fig. 4.14). The sampling fraction of 5% is apparently based on the (unpublished) results of the pilot survey. In the absence of any discussion of required levels of precision, it is difficult to see how this figure was arrived at; one hopes it was not simply transposed from a successful outcome of a 5% sample in Wiltshire. As a general point, the specification of a sample size as a percentage is often suspicious, since the fraction itself has little impact on the precision of results (p. 25). The variables *survival* and *decay* are likely to prove controversial. To many archaeologists they will simply be indefinable (how do we know the original extent, etc.?) and so meaningless; even to a sympathetic statistician they are likely to present severe problems of *reproducibility*: to what extent would different surveyors give the same values of these variables to the same monument? There is a great risk that comparisons may be between individuals or teams rather than (for example) between regions. It appears from the evidence so far available that the Survey suffers from severe deficiencies in planning and in the resources initially allocated to analysis, possibly to boost the field survey element. There is often a temptation to devote the lion's share of one's resources to the most visible element of a project; this is likely to lead to disappointing and even unreliable results.

### Summing up and looking ahead

The main conclusion of this chapter is that statistical sampling theory is a good deal more flexible and less restrictive than has been recognised by many archaeologists, and, with the advent of adaptive sampling in the 1990s, is converging towards the sorts of sampling that archaeologists would like to see. At the same time, archaeologists need to take on board the fact that statistical theory is not just about the mechanics of sample design and selection, but has much to say about the choice and quality of data, and indeed about the whole intellectual framework of a survey project. We also have Bayesian statistical

Fig. 4.14 Sample of 5 km by 1 km units selected for the Monuments at Risk Survey (Darvill and Wainwright 1994, Fig. 1).

theory waiting in the wings, ready to help assimilate past information into the design and analysis of future surveys, once archaeologists can master the necessary skills, particularly that of statistical modelling. An introductory example of what is possible will be given in the next chapter.

Once these theoretical advances have been assimilated (or even if they are not), short- and medium-term developments seen likely to be driven by advances in technology. The use of GIS is already bringing powerful new tools to bear on the analysis of spatial data, and will continue to do so in the area of sampled as well as 'total' data (p. 70). The imminent ability of 'personal data assistants' to link GIS with GPS in the field, to provide accurate and rapid spatial recording (p. 83), is set to transform data recording, and to provide a significant increase in the spatial resolution that can be achieved.

# 5

## WHAT'S IN A SITE?

### Introduction

In this chapter we move down a scale, from the region to the site, and look at problems that arise in sampling at this level, and some of the solutions that have been suggested. The problems are not simply those of the regional scale writ small (see Cherry *et al.* 1978, 151–7), although there is overlap, and indeed there is a continuum of scale from the small regional (e.g. parish) survey to the large site (e.g. Gaffney and Tingle 1985).

Even site survey is not a homogeneous topic, because the term 'site' itself has many meanings. Here we need to distinguish primarily between the development site – an area of land subject to some form of proposed commercial, agricultural or infrastructural development – and the archaeological site, already discussed in detail in chapter 4 (pp. 67–111). For the former, the broad aim is to detect the presence and extent of any significant archaeological remains on the site, with a view either to recording them before damage or destruction (*preservation by record*), or to mitigating the damage by redesign of the proposed development (*preservation in situ*). For the latter, the aim may simply be to determine the extent and character of a site (perhaps newly discovered in a regional survey), or there may be a more site-specific research design. The aims and methods may vary according to whether the site is largely invisible on the ground surface, or whether it has extensive visible remains, and also whether it is likely to be shallow or deeply stratified. These various circumstances raise different questions and to some extent require different approaches, so they will be looked at separately below.

### Historical overview

Although it has rightly been said that all archaeology is sampling (p. 1), explicit recognition of this fact seems to date only to the twentieth century. Informal sampling methods must inevitably have been practised in the surface collection of artefacts, and were reviewed by Kroeber (1916) and Spier (1917); slightly later Gladwin and Gladwin (1928, 1) proposed an informal way of achieving 'representative' samples in surface sherd collection. Excavation too is a process of sampling, and coincidentally at the same time Gifford (1916) reported the use of column sampling (p. 155) in the examination of shell mounds. The development of statistical theory (p. 14) was such that it would not be reasonable to expect more than an informal approach at these early dates.

Statistical analysis was used in the 1940s in two experiments in sampling from shell and other mounds (Cook and Treganza 1947; 1950; Treganza and Cook 1948), but the actual sampling was non-probabilistic. In the first, fourteen samples, each of 2 to 5 lb dry weight, were taken (Cook and Treganza 1947, 135), and in the second the mound was divided into thirty-five 5 ft squares and two samples taken from each, a 'random shovelful of mound material' and a column sample 4 in square from its north-west corner (Treganza and Cook 1948, 288). Worry was expressed that this procedure might bias the sample, because of the larger column samples taken from the deeper squares at the centre of the mound (1948, 290), but this aspect of the procedure seems valid, and the most likely source of bias is the uniform shovelful taken from each square regardless of its volume. The second experiment showed that small samples could give reasonable estimates of the percentage composition of a mound in terms of its main components (rock, bone, charcoal, shell), but the design of the sample was not really considered as an issue.

The first opportunity to review progress came in the 1970s, with the publication of the San Francisco Symposium (Mueller 1975b), the Southampton Conference (Cherry *et al.* 1978) and *The Early Mesoamerican Village* (Flannery 1976b). These reveal that intra-site sampling had then not been developed as extensively as regional sampling. In the USA, this may have been due to Binford's (1964) insistence on the primacy of the region as a unit of study, or to the fact that much of the earlier work had been carried out in areas of high visibility (p. 75), so that once a site had been located the next stage of sampling was from features (chapter 6 here) rather than from the site as such (e.g. Redman 1975, 148). In Britain, Cherry *et al.* (1978, 151) noted an antipathy towards sampling and that 'this anti-sampling stance has led to unhealthily dogmatic assertions (e.g. Barker 1977) that only totally excavated sites constitute fully valid samples, and a number of British excavators in recent years have attempted – unsuccessfully – to operationalise this philosophy'. Nevertheless, the issues were being discussed (Asch 1975; Morris 1975; Reid *et al.* 1975; Haselgrove 1978; Jones 1978; Wade 1978), not least the extra problems brought about by trying to sample a site in three dimensions (Brown 1975; Peacock 1978; see p. 146 below) rather than a region in two dimensions. The contrast between sampling deep and shallow sites was well brought out by Flannery (1976a) and Winter (1976). The need for sampling was beginning to be appreciated in other areas, e.g. marine archaeology (Muckelroy 1975), and computer programs to help in sample design and selection began to appear (e.g. Altman *et al.* 1982).

From this point on, various distinct trends can be distinguished. The need to monitor and assess the quality of small-scale CRM work, first in the USA (e.g. Dincauze *et al.* 1981) and later in England (English Heritage 1995; Darvill *et al.*

1995; Champion *et al.* 1995) led to the development of a sort of 'quality control' approach. Experiments in the resampling of areas that had already been extensively excavated or recorded, either empirically (Champion 1978; O'Neil 1993) or by computer simulation (Ammerman *et al.* 1978; Kintigh 1988), have repeatedly suggested that relatively large proportions of sites may have to be excavated if they are to be characterised adequately. This has been compared unfavourably with the low and apparently decreasing sampling fractions used in CRM site evaluations over the years (O'Neil 1993, 523–4). The problem with such experiments is that, although they raise very valid doubts about the adequacy of much recent and current sampling strategy at the site level, they are site-specific and cannot easily be generalised to fresh situations as they arise. Indeed, if they could, then they would probably contribute to the problem that they criticise: the unthinking transference of 'valid' sampling fractions from one situation to another. A more theoretical approach has therefore developed in parallel, in which the aim is to design a sampling procedure that will specify the probability that features above a certain size will be found, or that, if none is found, then none actually exists (Shott 1987; Whalen 1990; Orton forthcoming). Even more stringent demands have been made by theoretical considerations based on the need to detect rare categories of features or artefacts on a site (Nance 1981). None of such approaches seems to have yet significantly impacted on the world of the CRM practitioner, who still seems to prefer sampling fractions based on 'professional judgement' (Hinton, pers. comm.).

The continuing needs of regional surveys have not been overlooked. Chartkoff (1978) devised a procedure for estimating the size and boundaries of a site once it had been discovered. This approach was elaborated by Haigh (1981; 1982) who, with a background in physics, was not afraid to use polar coordinates, in contrast to the rectangular coordinates beloved by archaeologists.

Another continuing theme has been the study of shell mounds, perhaps because of the sheer density of information packed into them (Bailey 1975, 48). Moving on from earlier work (p. 112), which tended to treat mounds as single entities, Peacock (1978, 187) stressed the importance of variability within a mound, and of dividing samples into 'natural' strata wherever possible. Waselkov (1987, 150–3) went a step further by suggesting that each layer and/or feature within a mound constituted a separate population from which it would be desirable to sample, a position reinforced by Claassen (1991, 254). Work continues (e.g. Stein 1992). Both admit that this brings problems, in that the number of such populations may be in hundreds or even thousands, almost all of which are unknown before excavation starts. We shall return to this problem as a case study (p. 145).

Two important statistical developments that are 'waiting in the wings' – adaptive sampling and the use of Bayesian methods – will be discussed in the following sections on theory and practice.

## Theory and practice

In this section we shall follow through the three themes mentioned above: sampling in site evaluation (in particular, the question of assessing whether or not 'significant archaeological remains' exist on a site), sampling an 'invisible' site (e.g. one discovered by fieldwalking or sub-surface survey) and sampling a 'visible' site (e.g. a mound or an urban site). The first corresponds to Phase I Identification, the second and third to Phase II Evaluation in American terminology (Shott 1987, 360).

In each case, we shall look again at Cochran's twelve stages of a sample survey (pp. 27–9), emphasising where the themes differ from one another and from the practices of regional survey described in chapter 4 (pp. 67–111).

## Field evaluation

This section is based mainly on recent British experience, as recent surveys (English Heritage 1995; Darvill *et al.* 1995; Champion *et al.* 1995) have given a clear view of the present situation following the implementation of PPG 16 (Department of the Environment 1990; see p. 74), and its potential problems. The following new technical terms are introduced (English Heritage 1995, 17):

> *archaeological assessment*: the process by which the character, date, extent, condition and importance of archaeological remains are determined;
>
> *appraisal*: the process of checking planning applications or development proposals to identify, using local knowledge and experience, those with a potential archaeological dimension which needs further clarification;
>
> *detailed appraisal*: a thorough review of the SMR and other sources to determine whether there may or may not be an archaeological dimension to a development proposal;
>
> *desk-based assessment*: primarily a desk-top exercise commissioned to consolidate, examine and validate the recorded archaeological resources of an area potentially affected by development proposals;
>
> *field evaluation*: a systematic and problem-oriented programme of site investigation involving invasive and/or non-invasive fieldwork, designed to supplement and improve existing information to a level of confidence at which planning recommendations can be made;
>
> *mitigation strategy*: a plan for minimising the impact on archaeological remains from a proposed development. This may involve works to ensure *in situ* preservation, archaeological recording of

remains unavoidably threatened with destruction, or a combination of both approaches.

We can now move on to the twelve stages:

### Assimilation of existing knowledge

This stage starts as the appraisal of a site. If there is evidence (e.g. from the immediate vicinity of the site, or from aerial photographs) that there may be significant archaeological remains on the site, then a field evaluation may be the next step. If there is no such evidence, the archaeological involvement will end there. On the other hand, if there is enough evidence, of sufficient quality, fieldwork may not be necessary and the curator may proceed to a desk-based assessment of it. Particularly in urban areas, it is necessary to check on the likely current survival of any remains, as well as on their recorded existence at some date in the past. It may be that activities such as quarrying have destroyed remains recorded in the literature; this may not be immediately obvious if the area has since been reinstated. Conversely, in an urban situation, islands of archaeological stratigraphy may survive in an area that appears to have been completely 'cellared out'. Obviously, the more that is known the better; the existence of detailed information may make a field evaluation unnecessary, or reduce it to a check on the survival of known deposits. Often, old records are such that the exact location of recorded remains may not be known within a general area; they may have been surveyed relative to a landmark that has since disappeared, or be inaccurate in some other respect (e.g. orientation). For example, substantial remains of a Roman villa were excavated by Charles Darwin and others in 1887 near Abinger in Surrey, England. Despite the publication of a plan (Darwin 1904), the remains were 'lost' and not rediscovered until 1995 when trial excavations revealed substantial masonry walls and a mosaic floor. It is still not possible to relate them to the nineteenth-century plan. Problems of sampling in urban areas have also been discussed, e.g. by Wade 1978; Carver 1981.

The idea that existing knowledge can contribute to sample design suggests the possible use of a Bayesian statistical approach (p. 16). None such has, as far as I know, been implemented; even the suggestion has only been concretely made for the particularly simple situation when prior knowledge suggests the presence of significant archaeological remains, but not their location on the site (Orton forthcoming). Since this is just the situation considered in this section, we will examine the differences that a Bayesian approach might make, at each stage in the process.

### Objectives of the survey

The ultimate objective is to mitigate the effects of development upon the archaeological resource. This can be expressed as providing an assessment of

Fig. 5.1 Trial trenching at Hawkinge Aerodrome, near Folkestone, Kent, by the use of JCBs. Over 8 km of trenches were excavated, giving a 2% sample of the site. (Photo: Field Archaeology Unit.)

the site that provides sufficient information to meet the needs of the planning process. The aim is thus to obtain sufficient information about the existence, nature, extent and importance of archaeological remains on the site, given that there is already some evidence that there are likely to be such remains. We shall concentrate here mainly on the case where the existence of remains is inferred or suspected, and look at the problem of clarifying knowledge about a 'known' site in the following section.

### Population to be sampled

Unlike the case of the regional survey (p. 79), the archaeologist has no choice, since the area to be surveyed is determined by the specification of the planning application or development proposal.

### Data to be collected

The choice here is between surface and sub-surface data, i.e. between fieldwalking, trial excavation (trenches or test-pits, Figs. 5.1 and 5.2) or geophysical survey (David 1995), or a combination of two or more of these. It would seem logical to proceed in stages, with the extensive use of non-invasive methods being followed by intensive sampling of 'interesting' areas by invasive methods.

Fig. 5.2 Test-pitting on the route of the Brighton bypass, Sussex (photo: Field Archaeology Unit).

This seems to be fairly uncommon in practice, perhaps because it fits badly with the time constraints usually involved in this sort of work (Darvill *et al.* 1995, 33). The most common method seems to be the machine-dug trial trench, either purposive, i.e. targeted on possible features (identified from knowledge already available, e.g. aerial photographs), or probabilistic if little is known in advance about the site (1995, 35).

The definition of 'significant' remains is critical to the question of design, and impinges on the nature of the data to be collected. In some cases, *any* archaeological remains may be deemed 'significant', in others it may be features that are 'significant', but not unassociated artefacts, while in others the remains may have to occupy a specified total area, or a specified proportion of a development site, before they can be called 'significant'. This is an archaeological problem, depending on the period of any likely remains, the questions to be asked of them, and so on.

### Degree of precision required

Here, statistically speaking, we are in the realms of decision theory (Lindley 1985) rather than either estimation or hypothesis testing (p. 24, cf. p. 79) since the aim is to achieve a true outcome or 'diagnosis' (1985, 7–8). The situation can be summed up in a simple table (Table 5.1). Little is known about the

Table 5.1 *Summary of possible outcomes of an assessment exercise (after Darvill et al. 1995, Table 1).*

|  | correct diagnosis | incorrect diagnosis |
| --- | --- | --- |
| archaeological deposits present | true positive (present) | false negative (absent) |
| archaeological deposits absent | true negative (absent) | false positive (present) |

existence or otherwise of false positives; it seems possible that they might be created by some forms of non-invasive survey, but revealed in their true nature by trial excavation, whether trenches or pits. Since almost all evaluations include at least an element of excavation, false positives are not likely to be a serious problem. Far more serious is the possibility of false negatives, since they could result in the unrecorded destruction of significant archaeological remains. The aim should be to achieve a sample design that will guarantee, with a specified probability, the detection of significant archaeological remains if they exist on the site. Darvill *et al.* (1995, 7) suggest that achievement of a probability of 80% would be 'highly commendable'. The necessary theory has been developed through the 1980s and 1990s (e.g. Nance 1981; Krakker *et al.* 1983; Shott 1987; Kintigh 1988; Sundstrom 1993; see chapter 4, pp. 84–5). Read (1986, 484) and Shott (1987, 365) quote a standard statistical formula for the sample size that one needs to be confident of discovering at least one site (at a specified level of confidence) (5.1). This formula is intended for the situation where the sampling unit is larger than the site; it can also be applied to the problem of putting an upper limit to the proportion of an area that is occupied by archaeological remains, when none is in fact encountered in a sample (5.2). If this proportion is less than a value that archaeologists might consider 'significant', then they can say, with the prescribed level of confidence, that the area contains no 'significant archaeological remains' (here abbreviated to SAR).

The Bayesian approach is adapted from an analogous problem in marine biology (Nicholson and Barry 1995), which is itself based on a classical statistical approach to their problem (Barry and Nicholson 1993) that is remarkably similar to the archaeological approach described above. The prior knowledge that they assume is a belief about the likely values of the parameter that represents the proportion of the area that is occupied by SAR. If this belief is that the value of this proportion is likely to be 'small', then the sample size that is needed to achieve the specified level of confidence is less than it would be if there were no such belief: the stronger the belief, the smaller the sample need be (see Appendix, p. 217).

A more usual approach is to specify a minimum diameter of site that 'ought' to be detected by a sampling scheme. Detection depends on two factors: not only

(a)  the probability of *intersecting* a site of a certain size with a sampling unit, as above, but also
(b)  the probability of *detecting* the presence of the site in that unit (see 'the invisible site' below, and cf. p. 84).

The degree of precision needed to detect the scale of any patterning on a known site has been discussed by Rogers (1982).

### Method of measurement, see data to be collected

### The frame

If purposive sampling is used, the shape and size of the sampling units (trenches, pits, etc.) are likely to be determined by the nature of the visible evidence that points to their location. For probabilistic sampling, the choice in practice is usually between 2 m-wide machine-dug trenches, often 30 m long, and hand-dug test-pits, usually 1 m or 2 m square, although sizes up to 16 m square are known. Their relative merits have been discussed by Champion *et al.* (1995, 35–41). Briefly, trenches are flexible in design, cheap per area stripped, and good at detecting features, but are destructive and have a poor recovery rate for finds. Test-pits are almost the opposite: they are good at detecting finds and are relatively non-destructive, but are labour-intensive, and therefore expensive, and interpretation of features found in small pits can be difficult. To some extent the choice may depend on the period of the remains likely to be encountered; test-pits would be more appropriate for periods that generate scatters of finds (e.g. the Mesolithic), while trenches would be more appropriate for periods that generate large, and particularly linear, features. Statistical theory suggests that many small sampling units are preferable to fewer larger ones, but if the greater visibility (p. 75) of features in larger units is taken into account, the issue is not at all clear-cut. The case study below looks at some recent experiments that shed light on this.

It seems likely that adaptive sampling (p. 34) could have much to offer here; an example of its use is given in the following section (the 'invisible' site).

### Selection of the sample

The criteria discussed above are likely to lead to a systematic design of sampling, rather than a purely random one, if indeed a probabilistic sample is appropriate. The real issue is in the size of the sample. The first and crucial point to make is that the total size of the sample must be determined on an individual basis, and there is no rule of thumb that can be transferred from one site to another. Above all, there is *no statistical rationale whatever* for any particular sampling fraction, such as the 2% figure sometimes regarded as a 'standard' (Champion 1995, 36). The important parameter is the absolute size of the sample; the size needed will depend on the following factors: overall size of site, density of features on the site, size of feature that is required to be detected, the required probability of detection and the visibility of such features in the chosen sampling units. If a systematic sample of test-pits is used, simple geometric considerations (e.g. Kintigh 1988, 687–8; see also Shennan 1997, 393–8) show that the most efficient layout is a hexagonal one (see **4.1**) and that a spacing between the rows of pits equal to three-quarters of the required minimum diameter will ensure that sites of this size, or larger, will be intersected by at least one pit. The test-pit size selected will be the minimum size which gives a suitable probability of detecting the site when intersected; this in turn depends on the density and statistical distribution of features and/or finds on the site. One solution is to plot a graph of the detection probability against the size of pit, and choose a size at which the gain from any further increase in size appears to be diminishing (Champion *et al.* 1995, 40). For example, Fig. 5.4 shows such a graph for the Newbury Sewage Works site (1995, Fig. 8); the chosen test-pit size was then 2.4 m squares.

Cost is clearly a factor, but if archaeologically reasonable criteria cannot be met at a cost that is regarded as reasonable in planning terms, there is clearly a serious problem which should not be avoided. It is perhaps the failure to raise this issue explicitly that has caused the greatest disquiet about the process of evaluation.

### *The pre-test*

It is unlikely that in the situation of a field evaluation there will be either the time or the resources for any pilot work. Since it is important to 'get it right first time', the experience and design skills of those responsible are of crucial importance.

### *Organisation of the fieldwork*

As at the regional level, it would be foolish to attempt to offer general advice in ignorance of particular circumstances. It is worth noting that, because of the smaller sizes of the areas of study, the cost of travel between units does not have to be taken into account, and the cost of locating units is relatively lower.

### *Summary and analyses of the data*

What is needed here is not so much a statistical summary of the data collected (cf. the regional survey, p. 99), but statements primarily about the existence (or not) of significant archaeological remains, and secondarily about their likely extent, nature and importance. It is unlikely that the scale of the investigation will allow statistically reliable estimates to be made of parameters such as densities of features or of artefacts across a site, nor is that its purpose.

### Information gained for future surveys

It is however important that the information that is obtained should be made widely and readily available. As we saw in the first stage, evidence from nearby is an important factor in the decision whether or not to call for an evaluation of a particular site, and evidence from the current site may in turn play this role for a future site. This is especially important when neighbouring sites may be evaluated by different organisations, since the existence of 'local knowledge' may then not be relied on. Apart from this, there are of course overall academic and social reasons for placing such information in the public domain, which need not be elaborated on here.

### Case study

There has been much discussion as to whether the process of site evaluation actually 'works', i.e. achieves its stated aims (p. 118) (e.g. McCracken and Phillpotts 1995; Phillpotts 1997). The question can be divided into two parts:

(a)  Are the 'right' sites being selected for field evaluation?
(b)  When a site is selected, is the 'right' diagnosis achieved?

The first is by its very nature difficult to assess; its resolution requires the undertaking of experiments in which a sample of sites rejected by a curator for field evaluation is actually evaluated (presumably funded by someone other than the developer). But being part of an experiment might well influence the curator's decisions, causing further problems. The second requires the total, or at least the larger-scale, excavation of sites that have already been evaluated, and a comparison of the outcomes of the two procedures. Such experiments, recently undertaken by Champion *et al.* (1995, 43–63), are used here as a case study.

Champion *et al.* (1995) considered six areas in the counties of Berkshire (B) and Hampshire (H), which had been subjected to field evaluation and subsequent larger (though not total) excavation: Grange Road, Gosport (H); Charnham Lane, Hungerford (B); West Lower Farm, Greenham (B); Park Farm, Binfield (B); Dunston Park, Thatcham (B); Newbury Sewage Works, Thatcham (B). The sites ranged in area from 0.375 ha to 85 ha, and the proportion excavated in the evaluation from 3.7% of the smallest to 0.14% of the second largest (50.9 ha) and 0.72% of the largest. Champion *et al.* found that the types of finds that were most common across the sites as a whole were over-represented in the evaluation (probably because the samples were, at least

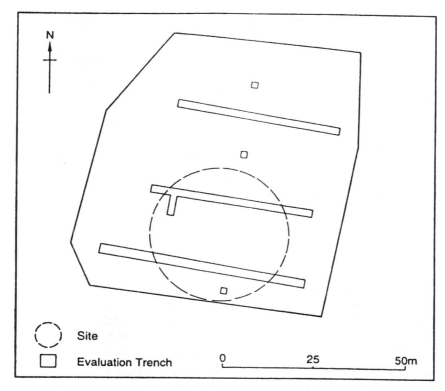

Fig. 5.3 Newbury Sewage Works, Thatcham, Berkshire: schematic plan of evaluation (Champion *et al.* 1995, Fig. 7).

in part, purposive in design), while the *ranges* of feature and find types were consistently under-estimated (1995, 48–9). This clearly relates to the general tendency for rarer types to be less well represented in small samples (see p. 63). They further discovered (1995, 49) that although the evaluations successfully identified the *periods* of on-site activity, they were notably less successful in determining both the *nature* and the *extent* of that activity. In other words, 'most of the resources of the evaluations had to be expended in detecting the main centres of activity on site, leaving little for the further investigation of such centres' (1995, 50). The need that this highlighted for efficient sample design prompted a further series of experiments, of which two were reported in detail: Newbury Sewage Works and Charnham Lane.

### Newbury Sewage Works

Here a large Mesolithic site was later found to occupy almost half the development area (Fig. 5.3), but the remains were thinly scattered, so that a test-pit that intersected the site could easily fail to detect it. A test-pitting strategy designed

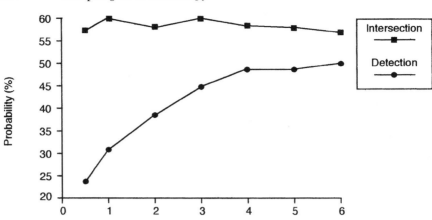

Fig. 5.4  Newbury Sewage Works, site intersection and detection probabilities for a range of test-pit sizes (Champion *et al.* 1995, Fig. 8).

to locate prehistoric sites larger than 48 m diameter consisted of nine 2.4 m by 2.4 m (about 6 sq m) pits in a hexagonal pattern (1995, 56). Application of the Kintigh formula (p. 90) showed that, although the probability of a single test-pit intersecting the site was about 60%, the probability of detecting the site in such a pit was low, because of the low density of the finds (Fig. 5.4). It was therefore not sufficient to guarantee that at least one test-pit should intersect the site; two were needed, and even then the probability of detection was only 74% (1995, 54), still below Darvill's 'highly commendable' figure of 80% (p. 119). This increased the required sampling fraction from 0.43% to 1.44% (1995, 54).

### Charnham Lane

Attention was drawn to this area by its potential for medieval activity. The evaluation revealed two medieval and three prehistoric sites (Fig. 5.5); further investigation of these areas showed them to be two sites of medieval settlement, one possible early Bronze Age occupation site, and one Mesolithic and one Palaeolithic flint scatter (1995, 44). A test-pitting strategy designed to locate prehistoric, Roman, Saxon and medieval sites larger than 25 m diameter consisted of 334 test-pits, each 3.9 m by 3.9 m (i.e. about 15 sq m), in a hexagonal pattern (1995, 55). Application of the Kintigh formula showed this had about a 90% probability of detecting any one site (Fig. 5.6). In the experiment, all five sites were 'discovered', although the probability of doing so was only about 55% (Fig. 5.7).

These experiments appear to show the success of the test-pitting strategies, but they are limited to the information obtained from excavation of the known sites. But, as the authors point out, 'as the subsequent excavations did not

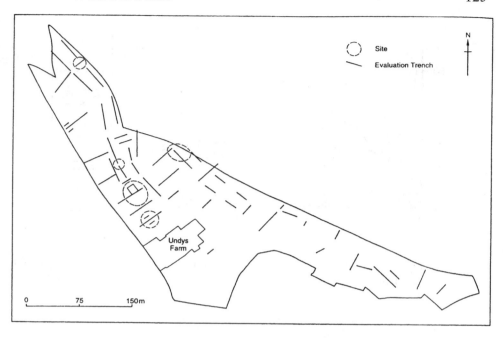

Fig. 5.5 Charnham Lane, Hungerford, Berkshire: schematic plan of evaluation (Champion *et al.* 1995, Fig. 3).

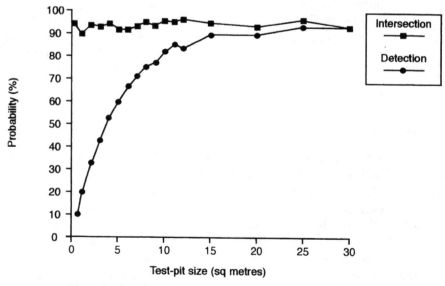

Fig. 5.6 Charnham Lane, Hungerford, Berkshire, site intersection and detection probabilities for a range of test-pit sizes (Champion *et al.* 1995, Fig. 9).

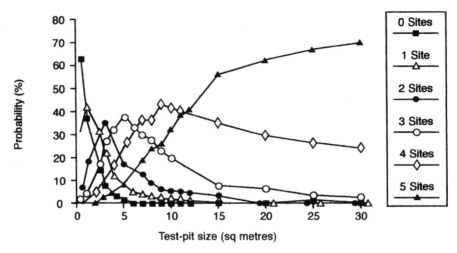

Fig. 5.7 Charnham Lane, Hungerford, Berkshire, the probability of detecting 0, 1, 2, 3, 4 and 5 sites for a range of test-pit sizes (Champion *et al.* 1995, Fig. 10).

address areas believed not to be of interest as a result of the evaluation, there is no means of testing whether the evaluations were correct in believing such areas to be empty' (1995, 58). More than a desk-top study of existing information would be needed to assess the success of the evaluations; it would require further fieldwork based on a carefully designed strategy, or analysis of development areas that have subsequently been totally excavated.

What the experiments did show was that a two-stage strategy, of using test-pits to locate sites and trenching to explore them, produced gains in information over conventional strategies as practised in the real evaluations, in terms of the nature and the extent of the sites that had been discovered. This aspect will be explore more fully in the next section.

### The 'invisible' site

We now move on to the situation in which evidence for a site has been discovered, perhaps in the course of a regional survey (chapter 4) or of a site evaluation (pp. 115–16). We look first at the situation where there are few, if any, surface indications as to the extent or the nature of the site, except perhaps artefact scatters. We are thus in the realm of intra-site sampling, associated by Nance (1981, 151) with 'the most perplexing archaeological sampling problems'. These arise not only from the variability of archaeological sites (in terms of their extent – both areal and in depth, degree of survival and/or depth of overburden, nature of remains, etc.), but also from variation on the archaeologist's research aims and mental template of what a 'site' is (see p. 67). In some cases, a site will be envisaged as a contiguous spread of artefacts (for example, as implicit in Kintigh's (1988) simulation program), in others, as a series of discrete features (e.g. Brzezinski *et al.* 1984; Shott 1987; Whalen 1990; Odell 1992; Hoffman 1993). Aims include the recovery of the frequency and relationships of features, and the recovery of statistically adequate samples of artefacts and ecofacts (see also chapter 6); the balance between the two may vary according to the period and type of site, and the questions asked of it. It should be clear that, as Nance (1981, 152) said, 'valid generalizations about site sampling are few and difficult to come by'. Nevertheless, careful consideration of Cochran's stages (p. 27) can guide the archaeologist through this intellectual minefield.

### Assimilation of existing knowledge

Existing knowledge is likely to be general, rather than specific, in this case, and to find its expression in the archaeologist's research questions and field expectations. By definition, very little is likely to be known about the site itself. There may be some expectation of the nature of 'typical' sites in the area, but while this can guide the design of this stage, it should not control it to the extent of becoming self-fulfilling. For example, if a test-pit encounters a patch of gravel that looks like part of a Roman road, extending it to a trench whose length corresponds to the expected width of a road can make it look much *more* like a road (this appears to have been the case of the London end of the supposed West Wickham–London road (Davis 1935, 68–9)). If available, the results of geophysical prospection should be included as existing knowledge, as they can contribute greatly to the planning of fieldwork (Lyall and Powlesland 1996).

### Objectives of the survey

These are probably as many and varied as archaeologists themselves. Common ones are likely to include:

(a) to define the extent or boundaries of the site,
(b) to determine the period(s) of the site, and
(c) to characterise the site in terms of the main activities that appear to have taken place there.

The first raises interesting statistical questions about the determining of edges, sometimes referred to as *change-point analysis* (Buck *et al.* 1988; 1996, 258–75). The second and third relate to the question of diversity and its estimation (see pp. 171–6), since some periods and/or activities may leave fewer or less obvious traces than others, and the sample size must be adequate to ensure that the less frequent categories, whether of features or of finds, are actually represented.

*Population to be sampled*

This is difficult, since it requires the delimitation of some sort of boundary, which may well be just what the archaeologist is looking for. Brzezinski *et al.* (1984, 378) suggest that the first stage is to approximate to the borders of a site, and then seek to characterise it, but this may often not be possible or practicable. If the point of discovery is a sampling unit of some larger survey, then the boundary must lie between that unit and the adjacent sampling units, unless they also intersect the site, in which case it must lie between them and their adjacent units, unless . . . and so on. Eventually a zone can be built up which contains the site and a swathe of surrounding 'non-site', and which can form a population for the purposes of statistical sampling. It would still make sense to attempt to delimit the boundary before characterising the site, if only to make the population as small as possible.

*Data to be collected*

This depends very much on the assumed defining characteristics of the site. The need may be for artefact collections from the surface or sub-surface, or for recognition of features, possibly as soil colour changes (Whalen 1990; Hoffman 1993) or chemical changes, e.g. in phosphate (Bjelajac *et al.* 1996). Decisions will need to be made about the definition of the edge of a site, e.g. in terms of the density of finds (see discussion on p. 67).

*Degree of precision required*

We may wish to estimate a total (e.g. total number of houses on a site, see Winter 1976, or total number of features, see Shott 1987), or a proportion (e.g. proportion of a particular species in a faunal assemblage, see Ammerman *et al.* 1978, or the proportion of a particular class of artefact in an assemblage, see Nance 1981, 160–4). The choice of the required degree of precision is an archaeological, not a statistical, one. Since it is likely to be based on a need to compare data (e.g. whether there are more houses than the 'typical' number on this site, or whether there are more cattle on site A than on site B), the decision should be based on what is considered to be an 'archaeologically significant difference'. For example, if a difference of 10% in the proportion between a site and a 'standard' is considered significant, then it would be reasonable to specify a precision of 10% at, say, 95% confidence level (see p. 26). If the comparison were between two sites, the precision would have to be reduced to about 7% to allow for the two sources of error.

The estimation procedure will usually be based on cluster sampling, which requires its own formula for the calculation of standard deviations (see p. 25, Appendix p. 210). Sometimes this complexity is avoided by dividing the sampling units into 'feature' units (which intersect a feature) and 'non-feature' units (which do not), and estimating the proportion of feature units (e.g. Shott 1987, 363–4). This makes the estimation easier, since simple binomial formulae (**2.4, 2.5**) can be used, but I suspect it may slightly overstate the precision in terms of number of features discovered, although this is probably not crucial, given all the other approximations that must be made. An additional complication is that the use of these formulae implies a rough knowledge of the proportions that we are trying to estimate. For example, a margin of 5% on a proportion of 50% requires a smaller sample than the same margin on a proportion of 20%. Fortunately, this is not likely to be upset by a small discrepancy, and if in doubt we can 'err on the side of caution' by assuming the smallest likely proportion.

In some circumstances, particularly on short-lived but well-dated sites such as occur in the historical period in the USA (South 1978), there may be an interest in characterising a site by looking at the proportions of particular classes of artefact, and matching them to defined 'types' of site (e.g. South's *Brunswick pattern, Carolina pattern* and *frontier pattern* (1978, 39–43)). In such cases the estimates must be precise enough to support the assignment of a site to one type rather than to another – the sampling errors must not be so large that a site of one type could appear to belong to another.

So far, we have been in what has been called the 'statistical precision' mode (Nance 1981; Shott 1987); we also need to consider the 'discovery' mode. The root of the problem is that the presence of relatively rare classes of object, whether features or artefact types, may be important to the interpretation of the site, but may easily be missed if a small sampling fraction is used, giving rise to a false negative for that class. Nance showed statistically what had long been experienced archaeologically, that items present in only a small proportion of sampling units require very large samples for us to be reasonably sure of their detection (Nance 1981, 156–8) (Figs. 5.8, 5.9). The formulae (**5.3, 5.4**) are in the Appendix. He further examined empirically the probability of detecting several classes of items that may be present. Again, the conclusion was that the sample sizes needed for reliable results are far in excess of those usually employed, e.g. in evaluations.

Although methods for estimating boundaries have been suggested (p. 127), the question of the precision of such estimates does not seem to have been posed. One relatively simple approach might be to see this as a question of estimating the area of a site, a figure to which acceptable limits could reasonably be attached. However, even an acceptable estimate of area could exclude a significant proportion of a site, and include a significant area of 'non-site'. This is a topic which has received little attention and could do with more.

Finally, we have to admit that precision may not always be an appropriate criterion. If we are looking at the adequacy of the characterisation of a sampled spatial pattern, it is hard to define relevant parameters and to put acceptable

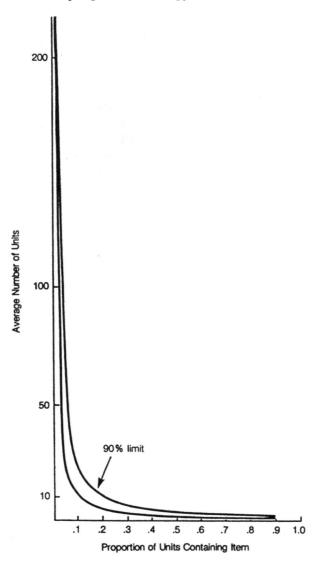

Fig. 5.8 Average number of sampling units required for 'discovery' of item classes in 'small sites' sampling as derived from the Negative Hypergeometric distribution. The 90% confidence limit is a Geometric approximation. Sampling units are assumed to be randomly selected from a grid of $N = 625$ units. (Nance 1981, Fig. 1, reprinted with the permission of the *Journal of Field Archaeology* and the Trustees of Boston University.)

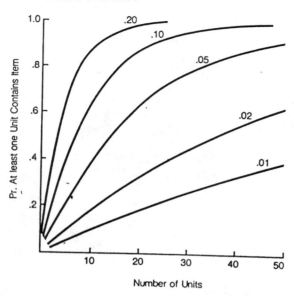

Fig. 5.9 Probability of at least one unit containing the item class of interest for various sample sizes, where the item class occurs in 1, 2, 5, 10 and 20% of the sampling units in the population, for a grid of 625 units (Nance 1981, Fig. 2, reprinted with the permission of the *Journal of Field Archaeology* and the Trustees of Boston University).

limits on them. A more subjective and visual approach may be needed, as used to good effect by Lock in a re-examination of data from the Danebury hillfort (Lock 1995, 110–17).

### Method of measurement, see data to be collected

### The frame

There may well already be a sampling frame in existence (e.g. of grid squares) and sampling at this level may just be a continuation of its use. Alternatively, larger or smaller units may be used to help delimit and characterise a site once it has been detected. Champion *et al.* (1995, 51–63) suggested the use of machine-dug trenches at this stage, while at the other extreme, Hoffman (1993) suggested the use of close-interval coring and Whalen (1990) suggested the use of augering (Fig. 5.10) at the same interval (2 m spacing).

A radically different approach, in effect setting up a separate local frame for each site, was suggested by Haigh (1981; 1982) in conjunction with the use of polar sampling. Here the location of sampling units was fixed by their angle and distance from a central point of the site, the distance being measured as a fraction of the distance from the centre to the edge of the site. An example, showing the circular sampling frame, the outline of the site and a selection of

Fig. 5.10 Augering to establish the extent of peat deposits at Shinewater, near Eastbourne, Sussex (photo: Field Archaeology Unit).

units, is shown as Fig. 5.11. As Haigh noted (1982, 65), this results in compression of the sampling units in the directions in which the distance from centre to perimeter is least. This is a potential source of bias, since some parts of the site are more likely to be selected than others, but can be corrected for by weighting (1982, 66). Accurate definition of the centre and perimeter of the site is essential for accurate estimates (e.g. of total sherd numbers).

Many of the criteria for the use of adaptive sampling (clustered or ag-

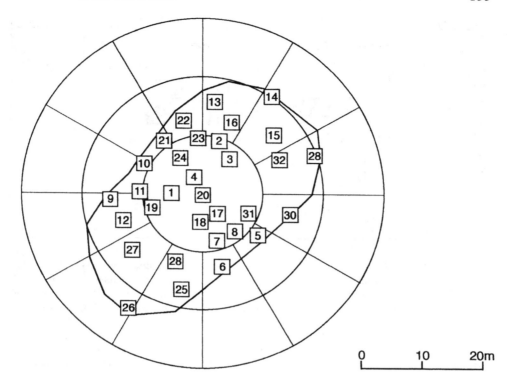

Fig. 5.11 Polar sample of thirty-two units, selected according to angle and 'distance' from the centre of the site (redrawn from Haigh 1981, Fig. 4).

gregated populations of rare or sparse items, see p. 37) seem likely to apply here, so an experiment in its use will follow.

### Selection of the sample

A systematic sample, rather than a purely random one, seems likely to be most useful here, although some have advocated simple random sampling (e.g. Haigh 1981), and there is a slight risk than the interval between systematic samples might coincide with some regularity in patterning on the site (see p. 22). An example of the use of adaptive sampling, based on the Lasley Vore site (Odell 1992), is given here.

The modified site comprises an area of 120 m by 120 m, divided into 576 quadrats, each 5 m by 5 m. Of these quadrats, 55 contain archaeological features, with a total of 82 features in all. A neighbourhood (p. 34) is defined as the four units contiguous to a selected unit; it is excavated if one or more features are located in the sample unit. The division of the site into networks is shown on Fig. 5.12 and listed in Table 5.2.

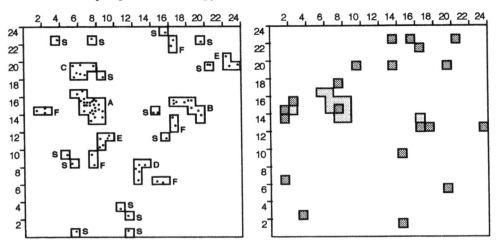

Fig. 5.12 (*Left*) Networks for adaptive sampling experiment on Lasley Vore data; (*right*) example of a sample of units (initial sample of twenty units in dark tone, final sample in light tone) (based on Odell 1992, Fig. 3, and reproduced by permission of the Society for American Archaeology from *American Antiquity* vol. 57, no. 4, 1992).

Table 5.2 *Structure of networks for adaptive sampling experiment.*

| network | networks | units per network | numbers of: features per network | edge units | units surveyed |
|---------|----------|-------------------|----------------------------------|-----------|----------------|
| A | 1 | 10 | 26 | 13 | 23 |
| B | 1 | 6 | 9 | 11 | 17 |
| C | 1 | 5 | 7 | 9 | 14 |
| D | 1 | 4 | 5 | 9 | 13 |
| E1 | 1 | 3 | 5 | 7 | 10 |
| E2 | 1 | 3 | 3 | 6 | 9 |
| F1 | 1 | 2 | 3 | 6 | 8 |
| F2 | 4 | 2 | 2 | 6 | 8 |
| S(ingleton)1 | 2 | 1 | 2 | 4 | 5 |
| S2 | 12 | 1 | 1 | 4* | 5* |
| empty | 521 | 1 | – | – | 1 |
| total | 546 | 576 | 82 | n/a | n/a |

* = May be reduced if on edge of sample area

An initial sample size of 20 units was chosen, and a set of 200 such samples was taken. The outcome is shown in Table 5.3. As Lasley Vore had not been sampled by random quadrats, a direct comparison is not possible. Instead, a set of 80 simple random samples of quadrats was selected, with the sample size (40) being chosen to approximate to the average number of quadrats actually

Table 5.3 *Outcome of adaptive sampling experiment, compared with simple random sampling.*

| | adaptive sample (n = 20) | | | | simple random sample (n = 40) | | | |
|---|---|---|---|---|---|---|---|---|
| | min. | mean | max. | s.d. | min. | mean | max. | s.d. |
| estimated number of features | 0 | 80.5 | 279.6 | 57.2 | 0 | 82.3 | 230.4 | 51.5 |
| number of units in final sample | 20 | 39.2 | 81 | – | 40 | 40 | 40 | - |
| number of features located | 0 | 13.4 | 45 | – | 0 | 5.7 | 16 | - |

selected (39.2, see Table 5.3). The adaptive sample is slightly less efficient than the corresponding simple random sample, with a standard deviation of about 57.2 against 51.5 (i.e. about 11% greater). This implies that a simple random sample of about 32 or 33 units should have the same s.d. as an adaptive sample of 20 initial units.

This outcome appears disappointing, in that an adaptive sampling strategy with an average sample size of 39 units has proved to be as efficient as a simple random sampling strategy with a sample size of 32 or 33 units. However, the comparison is not as bad as it seems, because the degree of clustering of the features is not high, the actual work involved is probably not very different, and the adaptive sampling strategy locates, on average, far more of the features than the simple random sampling strategy.

Two further points follow:

(a)  The adaptive strategy, because of its smaller initial sample size, has a much greater chance of failing to detect any features than the simple random strategy. In this example, the empirical probabilities were 0.11 and 0.012 respectively; the long-term average probabilities can be calculated to be 0.134 and 0.018 (**5.5**). The former might be thought to be unacceptably high, indicating a need for a larger initial sample; this is not likely seriously to affect the relative efficiencies of the two strategies.

(b)  One drawback of adaptive sampling is that the final sample is open-ended. In this example, although the average is less than 40 units, the maximum obtained is over 80, so that the resources needed cannot be closely predicted. One way to overcome this is to introduce a 'stopping rule', e.g. 'stop sampling after 40 units, even if there are more to be done'. This would require development in the theory to make it feasible; this is the subject of current research.

*The pre-test*

As above (p. 121), it is unlikely that there will be time or resources for pilot work on a particular site. On the other hand, there may be a wealth of experience that has built up on similar sites in the area, and this should of course be drawn upon.

*Organisation of the field work, see above (p. 121)*

*Information gained for future surveys*

In this case the information that will be useful for future work is likely to be general and methodological, rather than the archaeological specifics of a particular site. This implies that the successes and (in particular) the failures of approaches and techniques should be reported alongside the actual archaeological results, if only to prevent future workers making the same mistakes and 'reinventing the wheel'.

### Case study

'What if' is a good game to play, and archaeologists have joined in enthusiastically, especially since computer simulation programs became widely available in the 1970s, enabling them to re-excavate a site hypothetically according to many different strategies, by varying the shape and size of sampling units, and the sampling fraction. Here we shall look briefly at three examples from different parts of the world – England, Kenya, and the south-west USA – and discuss the value of computer simulation in assessing the relative merits of competing strategies.

(a) We first look at Champion's re-examination of the early Saxon settlement site at Chalton, Hampshire (Addyman *et al.* 1972; Addyman and Leigh 1973). The site was excavated by

(i)   mechanical removal of the topsoil and examination of all subsoil (chalk-cut) features,

(ii)  excavation in large open areas,

(iii) continuation of this technique until the whole site had been explored (Champion 1978, 211).

This favoured the recovery of structures at the expense of artefactual or ecofactual evidence (1978, 214). In his retrospective study, Champion considered the types of sampling that would be needed to recover different types of evidence; here we shall look only at the more quantitative aspects, i.e. the numbers of structures on the site. Champion argued for the use of a random sample of 8 m by 8 m quadrats, since smaller units might fail to detect structures for which the only evidence was widely spaced post-holes. A single desk-based experiment was reported: a simple random sample of 68 such quadrats (about 20% of the total site area) was 'excavated', and extended to uncover the whole of any structures revealed in the sample (1978, 222–3) (an

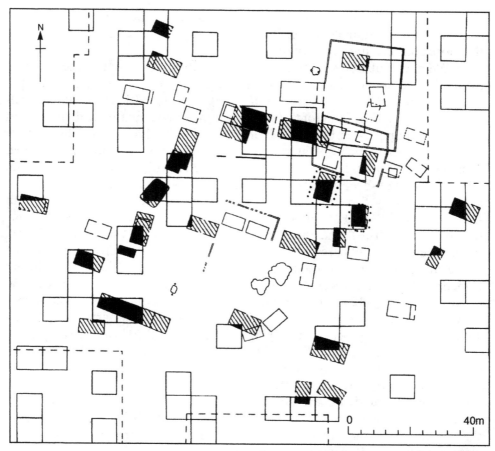

Fig. 5.13 Specimen 20% random sampling of Chalton site using 8 m by 8 m quadrats: buildings located are in light tone, parts within the sampling units are in dark tone (Champion 1978, Fig. 14.5).

early intuitive form of adaptive sampling). The outcome is shown as Fig. 5.13. Of the 57 buildings known to be on the site, this strategy located 30 and estimated the total number to be 61 (1978, 222–3).

This study provides an interesting insight into what would have been known if the alternative strategy had been followed; archaeologists must judge its adequacy for themselves in terms of the sorts of questions they would like to see answered. From a statistical point of view, its weakness is that we have no way of telling how typical the results are: is this sample a particularly 'good' one, or a 'bad' one, or just average? The statistician would be more interested in the long-run behaviour of the sampling process, rather than the fortuitous outcome of a single event, and without enormous work this can only be achieved by computer simulation (Freeman 1988). Such an approach would also enable the comparison of different sizes of units, and different strategies (e.g. quadrats vs. transects) (see Lock 1995). Such comparisons are relatively common at the regional scale (p. 70) but less so at the intra-site scale, reflecting the more complex internal structure of a site.

(b) We next look at a situation where computer simulation has been used to create hypothetical excavations of an ethnoarchaeological site in Kenya (Ammerman *et al.* 1978; Voorrips *et al.* 1978). The site 2001 is a small pastoralist settlement, and the aim (of the simulation) was to estimate the composition of the site's faunal assemblage (Ammerman *et al.* 1978, 124). Some 734 pieces of bone (sheep/goat or cattle), as well as other cultural material, were recorded from within or immediately outside an enclosed area of about 4000 sq m (1978, 126). The ratio of sheep/goat to cattle overall was 50:50. In the first experiment, a grid of 5 m by 5 m quadrats was laid over the site, and simple random samples of 1, 2, . . ., 125 units (50% of the total area) were taken; this was repeated for 20 'runs' and the proportion of sheep/goat was estimated each time. When the results are plotted (Fig. 5.14a), they show a clear tendency for the results to converge to the true value as the sample size increases, with no evidence of bias. However, the margins of error remain wide; even with 30 quadrats samples (12% of the total area), only 75% of the results lie within 10% of the true value. This can best be seen in a 'gain histogram' (Fig. 5.15), which shows the numbers of runs lying within 10% and 20% as the sample size increases; it indicates that 'diminishing returns' set in quite quickly, and that only modest improvements are made once the sample exceeds 15 or 20% (1978, 128). The apparently erratic nature of the gains probably reflects the low number of runs made at each stage. When the experiment was repeated with 2.5 m by 2.5 m quadrats, the convergence was stronger (Fig. 5.14b), indicating that (in this case) the smaller units were more efficient (more precise results were obtained for the same excavated area).

A further experiment (called 'Prior knowledge' in Fig. 5.14c) sampled quadrats in descending order of abundance of faunal remains, based on the assumption that a 10% sample of the assemblage in each quadrat was visible on the surface (1978, 130). Not surprisingly, this improves the precision of the estimates considerably, but at the expense of introducing a bias, which appears to be worse when the sample is small (Fig 5.14c). This seems to arise because the quadrats with fewest bones appear to have the lowest proportion of sheep/goat bones (1978, 131), though why this should be so is not clear.

In one sense, computer simulation may merely confirm what statistical theory has already predicted, but it is encouraging to know that our site 'follows the rules'. The surprises are often more interesting – for example, what is the unexpected bias trying to tell us about the co-distribution of bones of the two species? One drawback is that results cannot (and should not) be transferred uncritically from one site to another. They are all unique, and the best that can be hoped for is to shed some light on general principles and shared problems.

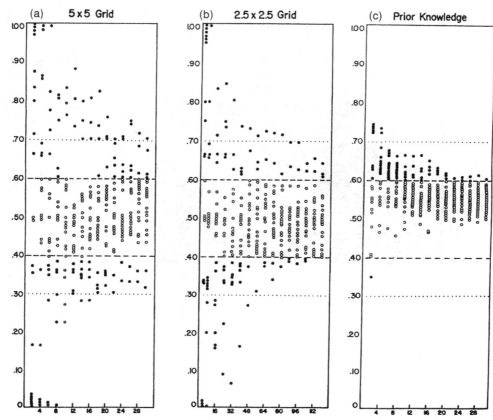

Fig. 5.14 Plot of the estimates of the relative proportion of sheep/goat in the faunal assemblage at site 2001, obtained by simulated excavations. The true value is 50%. The numbers of squares sampled is indicated along the horizontal axis. (a) random samples of 5 m by 5 m squares, (b) random samples of 2.5 m by 2.5 m squares, (c) 5 m by 5 m squares sampled by 'prior knowledge'. (Ammerman *et al.* 1978, Fig. 2.)

(c) The final case study concerns the exploration of a site which is largely covered by wind-blown sand (Whalen 1990). Although an area of almost 30,000 sq m could be delimited as a site on the basis of artefact scatters, evidence for features was hard to come by, and test-pitting was almost fruitless (1990, 324). It was therefore decided to use a bucket soil auger to excavate columns 7.5 cm in diameter down to the top of the subsoil, in units of 10 cm depth. The spacing between holes was set at 4 m in a square grid, as this would give about an 80% chance of intersecting an average-sized pit-house of 4 m diameter, and a 50% chance for smaller structures, e.g. 3 m diameter. Features were identified by means of soil colour changes (1990, 326) as artefact distributions could not be relied upon in such small samples.

Of the 1480 holes drilled initially, 108 located moderately or heavily stained deposits at least 10 cm thick (1990, 328). About 1000 more holes were drilled at

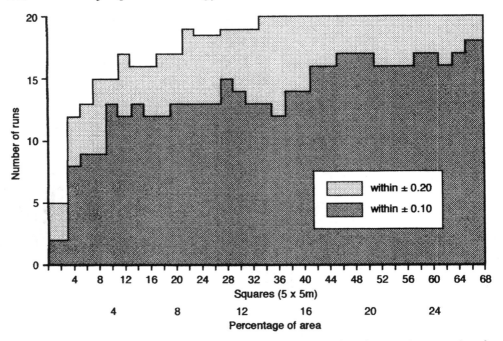

Fig. 5.15 Gain histogram for twenty simulated runs based on random samples of 5 m by 5 m squares. The numbers of runs lying within (a) 10% and (b) 20% of the true value are indicated by dark tone and light tone respectively. (Redrawn from Ammerman *et al.* 1978, Fig. 3.)

2 m intervals around these; the two sets were used to define sub-surface features, which were checked by 1 m by 1 m test-pits. The existence of the features was confirmed, but not clarified, by this procedure, so transects were augered at 1 m intervals through the centres of buried deposits (1990, 329). On this basis, four types of feature were defined in terms of their size and shape. Excavation of features in subsequent seasons revealed that the interpretations made on the basis of the augering were correct in every case (1990, 330).

This study shows several interesting characteristics. Use of the bucket auger clearly depends on the presence of a relatively easily workable and stone-free topsoil, which is readily distinguishable from the subsoil, and the use of colour in feature identification depends on the characteristics of this type of site. Statistically, we can see a sequential procedure, with successive 'homing in' on interesting areas. Once again, this can be seen as an intuitive expression of the adaptive principle.

### The visible site

Finally, we turn to the issues involved when at least some structural aspects of a site are clearly visible without the need for sub-surface survey. Many urban sites fall into this category, especially if they have been deserted and not re-occupied or built over. Sampling in the latter case can be extremely problematic, because it will be driven by the needs of urban renewal and development, not archaeological research needs (see Wade 1978; views that would be echoed by many urban archaeologists). The point made by Redman (1987, Fig. 5), that as one learns more about a site the proportion of probability sampling decreases and that of judgement sampling increases, is relevant here, as our initial knowledge of a visible site is, almost by definition, likely to exceed that of an invisible one.

We shall also in this section return to the question of shell mounds and middens (p. 112): upstanding and highly visible sites that may have a far more complex structure than could be guessed at from their spatial outline.

As in earlier sections, we shall see how Cochran's stages apply to this new situation, but as we have now been through this procedure twice in the context of site sampling, I will only highlight those stages where there are significant differences from previous sections.

### Assimilation of existing knowledge

In this situation, there may be much specific knowledge available. Conventional survey may give us information on the outline of a site (town walls, etc.) and aspects of its internal structure (roads, major public buildings, and even more). This may be augmented by aerial photography and satellite imagery (Scollar *et al.* 1989) which may extend our definition of 'visible' by using wavebands other than visible light. One might argue further that modern methods of geophysical prospection may, under suitable conditions, render much detail of a site 'visible', as in the Wroxeter Survey (Gaffney *et al.* 1998). An essential first step is to integrate all this information, which may not be as straightforward as it sounds. Much detailed adjustment of spatial data may be needed (e.g. rectification of aerial photographs (Scollar *et al.* 1989, 207–306), and the filtering out of evidence of modern activity (Perkins 1996)) before the different sources of data can be brought into a coherent state. Modern GIS technology is of great assistance.

### Objectives of the survey

The greater prior knowledge permits the possibility of far more specific research objectives. Given that our knowledge is likely to be mainly two-dimensional, priority may be given to establishing three-dimensional parameters of a site (chronology, expansion and contraction, etc.), for example through establishing the depth of archaeological deposits across the site (e.g. Biddle *et al.* 1973; Yanin 1992, 5). This has some similarities to the exploratory technique known as *kriging* (Zubrow and Harbaugh 1978; Clark 1979), but it is clearly an over-simplification to regard a site as analogous to a geological deposit (e.g. of coal), except perhaps in the very initial stages. More specific questions will follow, and are likely to lead to more purposive sampling.

### Population to be sampled

The visibility of a site should make it easier to define its boundary, but the possible existence of (for example) extra-mural settlement should not be ignored, and if parts of a site have been destroyed by later development they will have to be 'defined out' of the population.

### Degree of precision required

Just as probability sampling tends to become less relevant in this situation, so may one of its justifications, the need to attach measures of precision to estimates. The question of estimating parameters of archaeological features (e.g. proportional breakdowns of various sorts of assemblages) will be dealt with in chapter 6.

### The frame

There may well be an opportunity to exercise more flexibility and creativity here, in two respects. First, the use of statistical stratification may be both more useful and more feasible here than in the other situations we have examined. A site may be divisible into zones (e.g. defences, administrative/religious, industrial, domestic), which can be demarcated as statistical strata and sampled from at different rates according to the nature of the research questions.

Second, there is far more scope in the choice of sampling units. If plots, buildings or even rooms can be distinguished in advance, it makes little sense to impose an arbitrary grid of quadrats over them as a sampling frame (see for example Redman 1987, 254 as an example where this would have been inappropriate). If at all possible, it is preferable to define 'natural' sampling units relating to the structure of the site as known (cf. p. 87), and use more flexible sampling techniques such as the *pps* method (p. 34). Sometimes there is insufficient evidence for this to be possible (e.g. Keay *et al.* 1991), but even then alignment of the sampling frame along any major alignment visible in the site could well be beneficial (cf. 1991, Figs. 3 and 4).

### Selection of the sample

As we have already seen, purposive rather than probability sampling may be required, although there may be circumstances in which some element of random sampling is needed. The use of adaptive sampling (p. 34) should be considered as a possibility, although as far as I know it has not yet been used in such circumstances. Indicators for its use include sampling for activities that are likely to be both clustered and spatially restricted, for example antisocial activities like metal-smelting and tanning.

### Information gained for future surveys

It is worth making the very obvious point that the locations of all sampled units should be recorded and made generally available. This has not always been the case in the past, and indeed in some surveys the first stage has had to be the mapping of all previous archaeological interventions on the site (e.g. P. Barker 1975, 112).

### Case study

Our first case study contrasts three different approaches to three 'urban' sites, presented and discussed by Redman (1987) – Shoofly Village, Pueblo de los Muertos and Qsar es-Seghir (see also Redman *et al.* 1979). At the first, a very simple stratification was adopted, the area inside the enclosure wall being sampled at four times the intensity of the area immediately outside (Fig. 5.16). Inside, the area was divided into 20 m by 20 m blocks, and one 1 m by 1 m test-pit was dug in each, giving an unaligned systematic sample (stage 1) (see p. 93). Stage 2 consisted of the excavation of randomly selected structures, while stage 3 consisted of purposive sampling designed to answer specific questions. We see here a natural progression of decreasing randomness and increasing purposiveness as knowledge grows from one stage to the next. One might question the rigidity of the first-stage design; many of the blocks (twenty-eight out of fifty-three) appear to lie across the enclosure wall, thus creating edge-effects that might be serious if estimation were the purpose of this stage. As the aim appears to be an initial and general characterisation of the site, this statistical worry is not a serious one. Nevertheless, division of the site into 'natural' units (some of which would be structures and others the spaces between the structures), and selection of squares from those units, would give a more flexible and balanced approach and avoid any potential problems.

The second example demonstrates a more flexible initial approach. The room block area was divided into twenty strata, four along each side and one in each corner (Fig. 5.17). A sample described as 25% (Redman *et al.* 1979, 255), but apparently rather more on the plan (two corners and one stratum on each side) was 'wall-cleared' to provide a detailed architectural map. On this basis, a random sample of seven rooms was selected for excavation, together with seven adjoining rooms (1979, 255). This approach makes best use of the information available at each stage, and ensures that the sample is geared

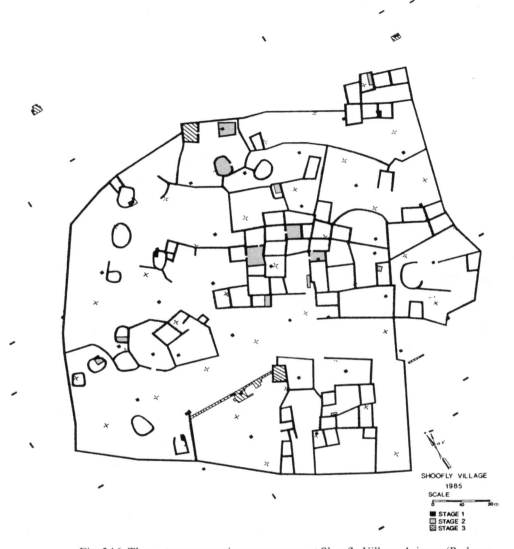

Fig. 5.16  Three-stage excavation programme at Shoofly Village, Arizona (Redman 1987, Fig. 2, reproduced by permission of the Society for American Archaeology from *American Antiquity* vol. 52, no. 2, 1987).

towards specific questions of intra-site variability and relationships between adjoining rooms.

Qsar es-Seghir was initially less 'visible' than the others two examples, being covered in pine forest (1979, 256). A preliminary step was to define the site by checking the location of the fortifications. Once this had been done, sampling of the interior proceeded in stages, the first being a stratified systematic unaligned sample of nineteen squares, each 9 m by 9 m, selected from a block of

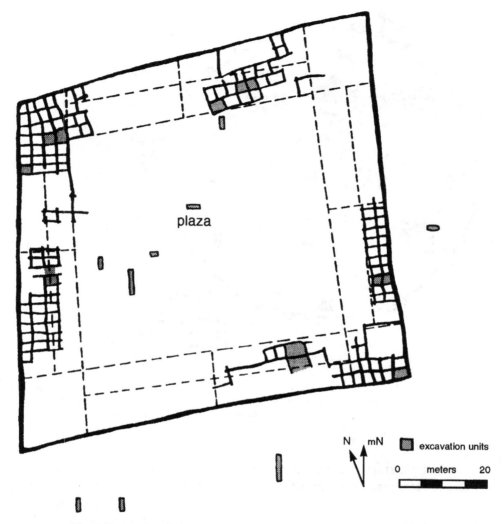

Fig. 5.17 Results of wall clearing (strata outlined by dashed lines) and location of excavations at Pueblo de los Muertos, New Mexico (Redman 1987, Fig. 3, reproduced by permission of the Society for American Archaeology from *American Antiquity* vol. 52, no. 2, 1987).

40 m by 40 m (Fig. 5.18). Further sampling consisted of the expansion and linking of the original squares to complete the exposure of buildings that had been partially revealed, and to answer specific questions (1979, 257). Once again, existing knowledge played an increasing part in the sample design as it gradually accumulated. The initial design, like that at Shoofly, carried potential edge-effects, but as at Shoofly, they do not seem to be serious archaeologically.

Finally, we return to the question of sampling from shell and other mounds,

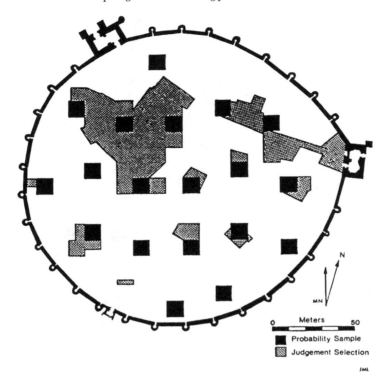

Fig. 5.18 Location of excavations selected by a probability sample (dark tone) and by judgement (light tone) at Qsar es-Seghir, Morocco (Redman 1987, Fig. 4, reproduced by permission of the Society for American Archaeology from *American Antiquity* vol. 52, no. 2, 1987).

with which we started this chapter (pp. 112–13). We have seen how ideas have developed from treating a mound as a single entity to a realisation that it may have a complex internal structure and consist, not of one 'population', but of many. The problems were well stated by Peacock (1978) in an account of the sampling of the site of Cnoc Coig on the Isle of Oronsay (Hebrides), and more mathematically by Bellhouse (1980; see also Bellhouse and Finlayson 1979); they are of such complexity that little progress has been made since. The root problem is that this is a three-dimensional site, and that the location, and indeed the existence, of many of the 'populations' was unknown before excavation started, and therefore could not be taken into account in the sample design. The design itself must be 'global' (i.e. relating to the mound as a whole) and two-dimensional, since one cannot excavate below areas that have not themselves been excavated. This raises the problem of the possible lack of independence between the samples taken from different archaeological strata by means of the same spatial unit (Peacock 1978, 185–6). The extent to which this is a real, and not just a hypothetical, problem, and how it can be dealt with, remain unknown. In the event, a twofold approach was adopted: a wide-area approach, with large judgement samples aimed at elucidating questions of site structure and history, and much smaller probabilistic samples directed towards obtaining representative samples of midden constituents, such as bones, shells and artefacts (1978, 182).

In a sense, this problem is a microcosm of a fundamental problem of archaeological excavation, that of obtaining representative samples from a deeply stratified site (Brown 1975). It may appear more pressing in this case, simply because mounds are such obvious, visible and apparently (but misleadingly) simple structures that one feels that there 'ought' to be a solution. In the case of other deeply stratified sites, one might not even pose the question in this way. The only solution may be to disaggregate the problem, that is to treat the site as a series of distinct features, and to seek to achieve representative samples from such features as we consider relevant to our research aims. To this question we shall turn in chapter 6.

# 6

---

# THE ANSWER LIES IN THE SOIL

### Introduction

We now move a step further down in scale, to sampling from archaeological deposits, done with the intention of recovering artefactual or ecofactual material, or geoarchaeological material for the characterisation of the deposit itself. The necessity for sampling is immediately apparent; every deposit potentially contains very many 'objects' (embracing all the above categories), some of which may be visible to the eye of the excavator, but a high proportion of which are invisible, either because of their size or because of other characteristics, such as colour or texture (see, for example, Keighley 1973), which make them indistinguishable from their soil matrix. It is simply not feasible to retrieve them all, not only because of the resources needed for retrieval itself, but also because of the resource implications for the subsequent stages of sorting, identification, recording and analysis, and the problem of storage. Nor indeed is total retrieval necessary, since the amount of data that could potentially be extracted is likely to be far in excess of what would be required for any conceivable analysis.

Given that sampling is a necessity, what particular issues are involved at this scale, and how do they differ from those at other scales? First, the issue of *bias* is ever present, both in the sampling process and in the associated literature, because the material exists across a wide spectrum of sizes, and there is no practical way of recovering it 'all' (whatever that might mean). Sample size raises interesting problems, because what is sampled is in effect 'space' (Gamble 1978, 326), but what is wanted is a certain quantity of objects (bones, seeds, etc.), and the relationship between the two (i.e. the *density* of objects per unit volume) is only apparent *after* the sample has been taken. This leads to the possibilities that a sample may be either too small (a well-recognised problem) or too large (less well-recognised, but just as much a problem), to which we will return. There is also much concern about the efficiency of the process of extracting samples of objects from their matrix, in terms of (for example) litres processed per person-day; in view of the enormous resources that this process can soak up, the concern is well justified. An issue which also occurs at the site level, but which is particularly important here, is that of *diversity*, that is the representation (or not) in a sample of types of object that are rare in the parent population. This is of such importance that it deserves a separate section to itself (pp. 171–6). A statistical issue that does not arise to the same extent at other levels is the possibility of lack of independence between observations. This arises whenever broken material (e.g. bone, pottery) is encountered, since fragments from the same original object are not independent of one another (in the statistical sense), and therefore simply counting fragments may overstate levels of statistical significance, as well as biasing the apparent compositions of assemblages. The same might be said of some types of seeds, when vast numbers may be produced from the same seed head. This issue too will be treated as a special topic (pp. 51–7). By contrast, the discussion of the design of samples is less well developed at this scale than at others, often being reminiscent of a Mrs Beeton recipe ('take twelve litres of soil . . .').

It may sometimes happen that, because of the difficulty in predicting the size of assemblage that will be recovered from a given volume of soil, sub-sampling from such an assemblage may be necessary or desirable, to reduce the workload and prevent the accumulation of redundant data. This poses one of the easier sampling problems in archaeology, since for once we have a well-defined population securely in hand.

### History

The study of archaeological faunal and floral remains goes back to at least the mid-nineteenth century. As early as 1848, Steenstrup was working on bird and mammal bones from Danish mounds (Steenstrup 1857), while in the 1850s and 1860s examination of lake-dwellings in Lake Zurich led to reports on the plants and seeds (and, in passing, insects) by Heer (1866; extracted from Heer 1865), and on the animal remains by Rütimeyer (1866). Heer (1866, 336) commented that the remains were 'by no means spread regularly over the bottom, but are found frequently in patches', thus anticipating one of the sampling problems of recent years. He also commented (1866, 337) on the problem of contamination by modern seeds, a problem to which archaeologists have relatively recently returned (e.g. Keepax 1977). Rütimeyer (1866, 355) commented that 'It was to be expected that the smaller animals – the birds, the fishes and the little mammalia – would form the chief addition to our earlier list of animals [see Rütimeyer 1861]', an interest to which archaeologists would return a century later (p. 150). Bones as small as mouse were recovered (Rütimeyer 1866, 356). Lee (1866) described a special tool devised for excavating trenches in the mud of the lake bed.

At the turn of the century, sieving was employed by Schmidt at Anau (Turkestan) to retrieve animal bones, cultivated grains and small objects (Pumpelly 1908). The use of boring for the specific retrieval of faunal and floral material from deposits is known as early as the 1920s (Moorehead 1929). Yarnell (1969, 217) listed reports on American archaeological plant remains from the decade 1876–85 onwards, with a sharp increase around 1916, although he claims that the first significant report was not published until 1931 (1969, 218). Interestingly, 1916 was also the year in which Gifford reported experiments in sieving material from shell mounds (see p. 112). Despite some early interest, there was little discussion of methodological problems, perhaps because the interests were mainly qualitative (which species were present) or metrical (comparing dimensions in different examples of the same species) rather than quantitative (e.g. proportions of species in assemblages). As late as the 1950s it was possible to say 'Recovery of bone from a site presents no great problem to the excavator' and 'Complete sampling . . . is most desirable' (Meighan *et al.* 1958, 6).

The picture began to change in the 1960s, perhaps under the impact of the 'New Archaeology', with its greater emphasis on quantitative analysis. Struever (1968) reported experiments carried out in 1960 that showed that sieving on a $\frac{1}{4}$ in mesh did not recover small bones, let alone smaller material like seeds. His response to the problem was to devise a technique of water-separation, which made use of the differential settling rates of different materials in a sample, when agitated in water, in order to separate them into a *light fraction* (bone, plant remains) and a *heavy fraction* (stone, pottery, etc.). Further separation of the light fraction into bone and plant remains by chemical flotation was suggested. At about the same time, Thomas (1969) reported the results of experiments on the differential recovery of bones of animals of different sizes on sieves of different meshes. Building on work by Ziegler, he suggested the use of correction factors that could be used to adjust the numbers of bones of animals of different weights from those found on a $\frac{1}{8}$ in screen to those that would have been found on a $\frac{1}{16}$ in screen. Such factors were seen as site-specific, not universal; therefore, each excavation would have to determine its own from a test unit. Although this approach seems to have been little used, it created a greater awareness of the problems of differential recovery that influenced much subsequent work.

In the UK, a similar function seems to have been fulfilled by the British Academy Major Research Project in the Early History of Agriculture, directed by E. S. Higgs, and in particular by the work reported by Payne (1972a and b). He first showed conclusively that conventional excavation techniques yield biased samples, even for materials like flint and pottery. He quoted the example of the Upper Magdalenian site of La Gare de Couze (France), where successive excavations employing conventional excavation, dry-sieving and wet-sieving yielded increasing proportions of *outillage lamellaire* and of geometric microliths (Fitte and Sonneville-Bordes 1962; Bordes and Fitte 1964). In experiments with animal bones, he reported that sieving increased the numbers of bones from cattle, pigs and sheep/goats by factors of 2, 10 and 20 respectively (Payne 1972a, 59–60), but that these factors could vary greatly depending on the site and excavation conditions. His conclusion was that far more is missed in excavation than is generally realised. In his second paper

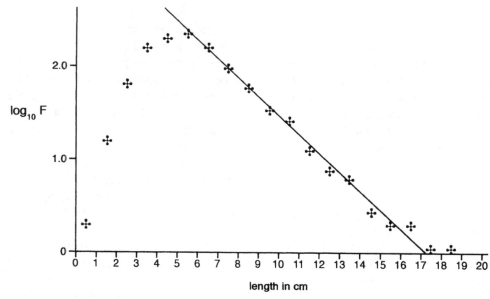

Fig. 6.1 Graph showing the logarithm of the frequency of bones of different lengths plotted against the length. The straight line represents the formula (**6.1**). Note that it breaks down at a 'critical value' (here, about 6 cm) and at a 'maximum value' (here, about 17 cm) which depends on the sample size. The slope of the line is roughly the same for all sites examined by Watson. (Graph based on undiagnostic bone fragments from Nea Nikomedia, see Watson 1972, Fig. 2.)

(1972b) he looked at the implications of the first for site strategy, concluding that 'total recovery' could not be justified, and that sampling should be determined by the specific aims of the excavation. In the interests of comparability, it was important that the means of excavation and recovery should be carefully reported. The botanical side of the project probably had less influence: Jarman *et al.* (1972) described the use of mechanical devices (e.g. froth-flotation) to increase the throughput of processing soil samples, although they noted (1972, 47) that total soil processing was still not feasible, or might generate more material than could be sorted. The tone of regret is worrying. Dennell (1972) reported on sieving experiments with modern barley, wheat, and weed seeds, suggesting that differences between samples from the site of Chevdar (Bulgaria) could best be explained in terms of prehistoric sieving as part of crop processing.

    Another aspect that received attention at this time was that of the fragmentation of animal bones (Watson 1972). Watson showed that the frequency of bone fragments could be expressed as a simple formula (**6.1**, see Fig. 6.1) related to the length of the fragments and the size of the sample, together with a parameter which, although it varied from site to site, seemed to lie within reasonably close limits. The formula broke down below a certain 'critical' length, partly because of failure to recover fragments smaller than that length, but also because of failure to identify such small fragments (1972, 224). The critical length depended on species as well as on the particular bone element; it was found to be smaller for sheep or goat than for cattle or pig, for example. He suggested that scaling factors (**6.2**), based on sieved samples, could be used to adjust figures obtained from unsieved samples and make them comparable with sieved samples. Although this suggestion was not widely adopted, this work had a significant influence in highlighting yet another problem in the search for methods to ensure comparability between sites.

A period of experimentation and discussion followed (e.g. Jacobsen 1974; Limp 1974; G. Barker 1975; Cherry 1975; Payne 1975; Casteel 1976; Clason and Prummel 1977; Keeley 1978; Diamant 1979). The San Francisco Symposium of 1973 (Mueller 1975b) was perhaps just too early to reflect this (but see Benfer 1975). However, the Southampton Conference of 1977 (Cherry *et al.* 1978) was well timed to receive some very thoughtful contributions on the subject (Cherry 1978; Fasham and Monk 1978; Gamble 1978; Torrence 1978; Wilson 1978). Cherry (1978) stressed the importance of *efficiency* as an argument for sampling, making the familiar point that sampling errors only decrease as the square root of the sample size increases (e.g. a fourfold increase in sample size only halves the sampling errors). He also made the less familiar point that as sampling errors decrease, they become a smaller part of the total error (the rest being *non-sampling error*), so that very little may be gained by decreasing them beyond a certain point (1978, 306; see also Nance 1987). He raised the question of the *integration* of sampling designs for different classes of remains: how does one design a sampling scheme to provide adequate (but not excessive) samples of the different categories of remains in which one is interested? Gamble (1978) and Wilson (1978) both stressed the importance of the spatial element in sampling; spatial variation is likely to be encountered (indeed, it may be a prime topic for study) and this must be allowed for in sample design. Gamble also made the point that soil samples are, strictly speaking, cluster samples (1978, 306, 333) and that this has implications for statistical analysis (p. 166 below), and contrasted this complexity with the relative simplicity of sub-sampling from already collected samples (1978, 335–8). Torrence (1978) showed that similar considerations can be applied to artefacts as well as ecofacts. Slightly later, Bradley (1984) showed how soil sampling could recover the location of features such as mounds and ditches that had been completely levelled.

A relative latecomer to the scene is the topic of *micro-artefacts*, defined as being between 0.25 mm and 2 mm in size (Dunnell and Stein 1989, 34–5), which seem to have been first recognised as a distinct category by Hassan (1978) and individually studied by Fladmark (1982). The size limits are said to correspond to shifts in archaeologists' ability to sample and identify, with and without the aid of low-power microscopes (Dunnell and Stein 1989, 35).

They can be useful in spatial analysis as they are less likely than larger artefacts to be moved horizontally by site formation processes, e.g. ploughing (Lewarch and O'Brien 1981; Dunnell and Stein 1989, 38; Sherwood *et al.* 1995, 429–30), but their advocacy on the grounds that they can provide large samples even on sparse sites (Sherwood and Ousely 1995, 423) is worrying, because it seems to imply that we could increase information retrieval by breaking artefact samples into smaller fragments. Specific sampling procedures were described by Sherwood *et al.* (1995, 440). The approach seems to have emerged from an interest in sampling and characterising soil itself as an aid to interpreting stratigraphy and formation processes (e.g. Stein and Teltser 1989). Archaeological sediments themselves (in contrast to the artefacts and ecofacts that they may contain) can be studied through *soil micromorphology* (Courty *et al.* 1989). The topic was introduced into archaeology in the 1950s (Cornwall 1958), but its use has only recently become widespread. Samples of about 10 cm by 10 cm by 6 cm are taken from an archaeological section by use of a *Kubiena box* (Courty *et al.* 1989, 42–3). A thin-section is taken from an impregnated sample (1989, 57–62) and studied in broadly similar ways to ceramic thin-sections (p. 184).

Even more recent is the suggestion that field sampling should take into account the possibility of extracting DNA from samples (Spigelman 1996).

The method of taking samples in general has received growing attention from the 1970s onwards. Three particular topics are: column vs. whole-unit sampling (Casteel 1976); cumulative sampling (Fasham and Monk 1978; Veen and Fieller 1982; Miksicek 1987, 235); bulk vs. scatter sampling (Lennstrom and Hastorf 1992). The issues centre on problems of specifying the volume of soil needed to yield an assemblage of a required size, highlighted since at least the 1960s (Greenwood 1961, 417), and the problem of within-context variability (which goes right back to Heer, see p. 149), both of which relate to the essential point that we are dealing with cluster samples. Casteel (1976) compared the procedure of taking column samples from the walls of excavation units, and processing them in the laboratory, with that of dry-sieving all excavated material on site, and forwarding the recovered material to the laboratory. Perhaps not surprisingly, the former proved superior, not only in the reduction of bias and the increased range of species represented, but also in the effort involved, achieving about a tenfold reduction. Veen and Fieller (1982) examined the procedure of *cumulative sampling*, that is, of taking relatively small incremental sub-samples until the total sample meets some criterion (see p. 157 below). Lennstrom and Hastorf (1992), in a wide-ranging experiment on botanical remains from Pancán (Peru), compared results from bulk samples (taken from a single location within a context or *locus*) with those from scatter samples (taken from several small 'pinches' of soil throughout a locus), a technique borrowed from palynology. They concluded that:

(a)   scatter samples were more homogeneous in terms of density of remains (1992, 209);

(b)   botanical remains were not distributed homogeneously throughout a locus (1992, 210);

(c)   the conventional view, that small loci are best represented by bulk samples and large ones by scatter samples, was not supported (1992, 220);

(d)   scatter samples are more representative than single bulk samples, but less so than multiple bulk samples (1992, 226).

The implications of these findings for theory and practice will be discussed below.

The concern that large-scale sampling might produce samples that were too large to sort and analyse economically was voiced by Gamble (1978). Levitan (1983), faced with samples totalling over 230,000 bones from Uley (Gloucestershire), experimented with sub-sampling to reduce the workload. This provoked worries about the potential loss of information (Turner 1984). Nevertheless the principle of analysing 'no more material than necessary' (Veen and Fieller 1982, 293) is a sound one and must be faced. The issue can only be resolved on a case-by-case basis, depending on the nature of the site and the questions asked of it. Long-term storage was also noted as a potential problem (Diamant 1979, 216).

There is a large literature on various mechanical devices for separating artefacts and ecofacts from their matrix, based around the principles of dry-sieving, wet-sieving and flotation (Figs. 6.2 and 6.3), but also including air-blowing (Ramenofsky *et al.* 1986). The need to integrate them into an overall work programme, and to choose the appropriate technique for the particular problem, has been faced in many places, for example the Environmental Archaeology Unit of the University of York, responsible for work on the very large number of samples from the long-term programme of excavations in the city of York (Jones 1983; O'Connor 1989; Dobney *et al.* 1992). In parallel are many studies of the costs of different techniques, usually in terms of the time taken to process given volumes of soil, noting that the sorting and analysis stages are probably the most costly (Koloseike 1970; Keeley 1978). The efficiency of various devices in extracting material has also been tested, often by experiments on known quantities of modern material (e.g. Wagner 1982; Pendleton 1983; Shaffer 1992; Shaffer and Sanchez 1994; Muckle 1994).

Finally, there has been a need to make specialist information available to excavators and others, in order to faciliate communication between sub-disciplines. This can be done at two levels: overview papers to spread awareness of the possibilities and problems (e.g. Veen 1985; Lennstrom and Hastorf 1995), and practical manuals to ensure that samples taken in the field are actually of value to the specialist (e.g. Payne 1992; Murphy and Wiltshire 1994).

Fig. 6.2 Wet-sieving at Bignor Roman villa, Sussex (photo: Field Archaeology Unit).

## Theory and practice

In this section we shall once again examine how the general principles of sampling (see pp. 27–9 and Fig. 2.2) can be implemented in practice in the specific situation of sampling from features for artefactual and ecofactual material. As far as possible, principles will be applied to all types of material; comments specific to a particular type (e.g. animal bone) will be as few as possible. In previous chapters the same principles were applied to different scales of survey and sampling. To do this we need to use an appropriate terminology, referred to above as the 'language of sampling' (pp. 17–27), augmented by some terms which are more restricted in their scope:

> *Bulk sample*: a sample taken from a single location within a feature, context or locus, consisting of a contiguous 'block' of soil or other matrix (see Lennstrom and Hastorf 1992, 206). They are usually from about 15 to 60 litres in volume, and are processed by bulk sieving or flotation using a fine (e.g. 0.5 mm) mesh (Murphy and Wiltshire 1994, 5).
>
> *Column sample*: a series of samples, of small cross-section and greater depth, taken one above another from the side of an excavation unit (Fig. 6.4), or, less frequently, by direct coring of deposits (Casteel 1970; 1976). If they are taken to study vertical

Fig. 6.3  Flotation tank in use at Pevensey, Sussex (photo: Field Archaeology Unit).

Fig. 6.4 Column sampling for pollen analysis at Shinewater, near Eastbourne, Sussex (photo: Field Archaeology Unit).

variation, they may include sub-samples from several layers within a feature.

*Composition of an assemblage*: a description of an assemblage in terms of the proportions of different types of objects in it, e.g. percentages of different species in an assemblage of seeds.

*Cumulative sampling*: the process of sorting and analysing incremental sub-samples from an assemblage. As each sub-sample is taken, its data are added to those of all the previous sub-samples. The procedure stops when the sample size is judged to be adequate, usually when the results (e.g. proportions of different species in the sample) do not fluctuate appreciably from one accumulated sample to the next (see Fig. 6.5) (Fasham and Monk 1978; Veen and Fieller 1982; Miksicek 1987, 235).

*Hand-collected sample*: samples of large objects, e.g. artefacts, wood or large bones, collected by hand without any mechanical aids (Murphy and Wiltshire 1994, 6).

*Monolith sample*: a block of deposit removed from the side of an excavation unit using a special container called a *monolith box* (Murphy and Wiltshire 1994, 3 and Fig. 3), thus a particular example of a *column sample*.

*Scatter sample*: a sample consisting of several small samples taken from different parts of a feature, context or locus, and then

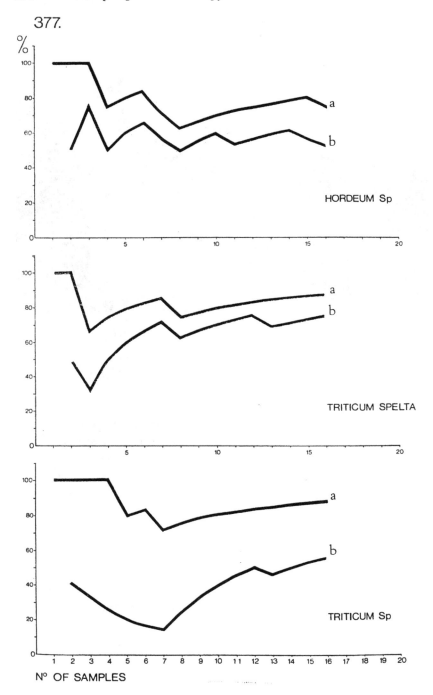

Fig. 6.5 Proportions of different species obtained by cumulative sampling (Fasham and Monk 1978, Fig. 22.2).

aggregated for purposes of sorting and analysis (see Lennstrom and Hastorf 1992, 206).

*Site-riddled sample*: a very large sample (commonly 100–200 litres) which is processed on site, by dry- or wet-sieving on a coarse (e.g. 4 mm) mesh (Murphy and Wiltshire 1994, 5–6).

*Spot sample*: a small sample taken from (for example) a stony deposit when a monolith box cannot be inserted (Murphy and Wiltshire 1994, 4).

We can now turn once again to Cochran's twelve stages.

### Assimilation of existing knowledge

Since it is very unlikely (but not impossible) that one would excavate the same feature twice, the question of specific prior knowledge (i.e. about a particular feature) will normally not arise. However, there may be much useful background information available, perhaps better called experience, for example about the likely density of material in features of different types, and thus the size of sample likely to be needed. Experience may also suggest the likely level of spatial homogeneity within a feature or deposit of a particular type, and thus what steps need to be taken to ensure that a sample is likely to be representative.

Knowledge about the operating characteristics of the equipment it is proposed to use is essential. If sieving is to be employed, what mesh size is needed for the type of remains that are to be retrieved? What is the expected throughput of the equipment, and can it cope with the demands that may be put on it? The logistics of the whole sampling operation must be carefully thought through, and such basic information is obviously a prerequisite.

### Objectives of the survey

As has been stressed by many writers, the objective of sampling at any scale is to obtain information, not to accumulate vast collections of material, or even large quantities of data (see especially Cherry 1978, 294). This is particularly true at this scale, where the risks of *over-sampling* (collecting more data than are needed to meet one's objectives) are higher than at other scales. A good summary of the objectives of sampling faunal assemblages was given by Payne (1972b). In general, the objectives are most likely to be either

(a) to estimate the proportions of various species in the relevant populations, with a chosen level of precision, or

(b) to assess the number of different species in the populations, and hence their *diversity* (pp. 171–6).

These objectives correspond to the 'statistical precision' and 'discovery' modes of site survey (p. 129). The first is relatively straightforward; the approach has been well discussed (Veen and Fieller 1982; Veen 1985; see **2.4–2.6**) and can lead to specifications of required sample sizes (although there are complications, see p. 166). Derivation of required sample sizes in the second case is less obvious, and does not seem to have been discussed in the 'applied' literature. One approach, using the analogy with site and regional survey, would be to specify the probability that a species that forms $x\%$ of a population ($x$ being a small number) should be represented in the corresponding sample. The same arguments as were used at the other scales (pp. 84, 118–20) could be used to suggest an appropriate sample size.

Other possible objectives might concern measurements made on objects (e.g. does the length of a specific bone element change between one population and another?), or the presence and nature of evidence for human activity, e.g. butchery marks on animal bones. In the first case, one might specify a 'critical value', i.e. the smallest difference that we would consider to be significant in *practical* terms, and calculate the sample size that would be needed to achieve a chosen probability (e.g. 90%) of detecting such a difference (**6.3**). This calculation requires a knowledge of the variability of the measurement in the assemblage; this might be obtained from a small pilot sample or from prior knowledge of similar assemblages. The second case depends on whether such marks are likely to be common or rare. Most likely, it will involve estimating proportions, as in the breakdown into species, but the total may be smaller if not all examples show such marks.

### Population to be sampled

Frequently, defining a population will just mean defining the boundary of the feature to be sampled, although in some cases the boundary may not be clear, and for extensive layers it may be arbitrary. A more difficult question is the choice of which features or layers to sample from. Almost by tradition, or intuition, excavators have tended to sample from cut features (for faunal remains) or from 'dark' or 'ashy' deposits for botanical remains, presumably in the belief that such deposits are likely to be the most productive. This approach has been criticised on several grounds (see Lennstrom and Hastorf 1995): it makes the mistake (see p. 153) of assuming that the need is for large samples, it tells us nothing about what might be present elsewhere on the site, and it can be self-fulfilling. It may not even be true; although botanical remains are most likely to be preserved when carbonised (Hally 1981), hearths and other obviously burnt areas may not be the best places for this to occur. In contrast to earlier advice to concentrate on selected deposits (e.g. G. Barker 1975; Veen 1985), Lennstrom and Hastorf (1995, 702) strongly recommended 'blanket sampling', i.e. the collection of samples from all deposits. They make the point that the contents of features should be compared to those of neighbouring deposits, at least the one above and the one below (1995, 705), to distinguish between what is specific to a particular feature and what is merely 'background'. This has obvious implications for the workload over a whole site, and strengthens the case for ensuring that samples from individual deposits should be no larger than is necessary.

It must also be appreciated that a population can only be specified in terms of a given volume of soil or deposit, not in terms of an (as yet unknown) population assemblage of artefacts and ecofacts. This means that we are firmly in the realm of cluster sampling (p. 30), which in turn has serious implications for both the design of the sample and the analysis of the data from it (p. 166). The situation is not appreciably different if we are sub-sampling from an assemblage that was itself originally a cluster sample. If we treat it as a population and use the statistical techniques appropriate to that situation, our inferences will be limited to statements about that assemblage, not about the population from which it was taken.

### Data to be collected

At the simplest level, the data will comprise just counts of objects of different types in each sample (e.g. seeds of different species, bones of different anatomical elements and species, sherds of different fabrics, etc.). The range of materials that can yield different sorts of information is shown in Table 6.1.

A second level of data may consist of measurements or characteristics of the objects. Both levels are much complicated by the sad but universal fact that much archaeological material is both broken and incomplete when found, and the best way of 'counting' fragmentary material is not self-evident. The theory of this problem is discussed elsewhere (pp. 51–7); here we note that it is an issue that must be resolved before material is recorded and data are analysed. A second effect of the fragmentary nature of archaeological material is the high proportion of 'missing data' – either dimensions where all we can say is 'greater than . . .' because part is missing, or absences (e.g. of decoration on a pot) which may be real or may just be because the relevant part of the object is missing. Refitting studies may help, but although they provide valuable information in many ways (see, for example, Moorhouse 1986, 88–100) they rarely seem to reduce the total number of objects appreciably.

There is also a need for ancillary data, so that the sample can be located within its feature and within its site. The volume of bulk samples should also be recorded (so that densities can be calculated) and the total context volume should be measured or estimated (to give an idea of the sampling fraction) (Murphy and Wiltshire 1994, 7).

Table 6.1 *The different sorts of information that can be obtained from the analysis of different sorts of material obtained from soil-sampling (based on Murphy and Wiltshire 1994, Table 1).*

| Analysis | Category of material | Potential information |
|---|---|---|
| microfossils | diatoms | salinity/acidity of depositional environment |
| | | level of eutrophication (e.g. pollution) |
| | pollen, plant spores, etc. | local and regional vegetational history |
| | | changes in local hydrology and climate |
| | | nature of local soils |
| | | function of features |
| | | effects of human activity on landscape |
| | | crop husbandry |
| | | plant resources |
| | foraminifera | salinity and elevation of inter-tidal and sub-tidal |
| | | depositional environments |
| | parasitic worm eggs | pathology |
| macrofossils | fruits/seeds | local vegetation |
| | | plant food collection; agriculture |
| | wood/charcoal | local woodland composition |
| | | exploitation and management |
| | charred cereals | crop production, processing and storage |
| | | local palaeoenvironments and land use |
| | insects | local landscape |
| | | structure of woodland |
| | | food storage pests |
| | | plant pests |
| | molluscs (water) | salinity etc. of depositional environments |
| | | shellfish collection and/or consumption |
| | molluscs (land) | local vegetation structure |
| | bird bones | hunting/wildfowling |
| | | stock management |
| | | domestication studies |
| | fish bones | marine/freshwater fisheries |
| | | fish processing, consumption, etc. |
| | small mammal bones | local palaeoenvironments |
| | | faunal population studies |
| | large mammal bones | hunting |
| | | stock management |
| | | domestication studies |
| | | animal pathology |
| soils/sediment | micromorphology | pedogenesis |
| | | soil structure and human impact |
| | | nature of husbandry |
| | | function of features |
| | | alluviation |
| | | deposit taphonomy |
| | chemistry | pedogenesis and climatic impact |
| | | nutritional status and acidity of palaeosols |
| | | impact of arable and pastoral husbandry |
| | | evidence of human occupation |
| | particle size | sedimentary sequences |
| | | impact of high/low energy water flow, etc. |

### Degree of precision required

As we have seen (p. 25), this may be expressed as a permitted margin of error on a proportion (e.g. 5% with 95% probability), as the chosen probability of detecting a species that comprises less than a certain small proportion of the population, or as the critical difference between a measurement in two samples (again, with a probability value attached, since we can never be certain that we will detect a difference of a specified size). The first has been discussed for seeds by Veen and Fieller (1982), in the context of the implications of such decisions for sample size. The archaeological rationale for the choice of a 'significant' value, or difference, and the probability value that should be attached to it, are rarely discussed, and many archaeologists find it difficult to think about. One way into it may be to carry out an imaginary dialogue with oneself (or a real one with a colleague) on the lines of 'Would it matter to you if the proportion of . . . in two features differed by 1%? No. By 20%? Yes. By 10%? Probably' and so on until a critical value is reached. As always, there are cost considerations. If the sizes of samples implied by the degree of precision one requires cannot be afforded, then one must either reconsider one's objectives and widen the limits, or, in the worst case, abandon the question. There is no point in collecting inadequate data which cannot answer questions to some useful level of precision.

### Method of measurement

For once, there is a real issue here – the question of the quantification of fragmentary material – already mentioned under *data to be collected*, and fully discussed elsewhere (pp. 51–7). Even when dealing with complete objects, e.g. seeds, this issue can arise; for example, should they be weighed or counted? There is no hard-and-fast rule in such cases; the choice depends on the questions being asked, as well as on practical considerations such as the time or difficulty involved in each method. The choice must not obscure points of interest; for example, if one is particularly interested in variations in the proportions of (light) weed seeds between assemblages, weighing would make little sense because the differences might scarcely show up in the weights, while they might be very obvious in terms of counts.

### The frame

There is no obvious 'natural' basis for the creation of a sampling frame, which must therefore be seen as the outcome of a series of arbitrary decisions. The most important are

(a)  the division of the feature or deposit into spatial units from which a sample can be selected, and

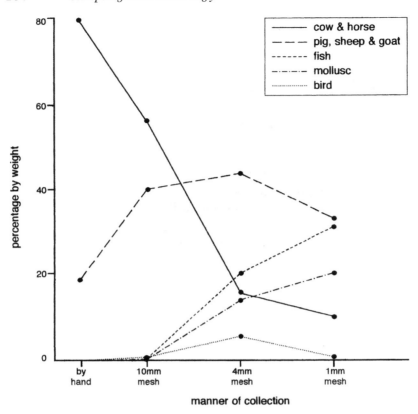

Fig. 6.6 Graph showing proportions of different classes of bones retrieved on meshes of various sizes (based on data taken from Clason and Prummel 1977, Table 1).

(b)   the choice of method of extraction of archaeological material from its matrix – hand collection, site riddling, bulk sampling, column sampling, monolith sampling, etc. – and the corresponding choice of mesh size if sieving is to be used.

These decisions correspond to the choice of sampling unit (e.g. quadrats, transects) and their size, and the intensity of survey (e.g. the spacing between the lines in fieldwalking) at the larger scales (chapters 4 and 5).

(a) This may be determined for us by the tools used to extract the sample. For example, use of a *monolith box* (p. 157) implies that the sampling units are the same size as the dimensions of the box. If the requirements specify a bulk sample of 'so many litres' (perhaps in terms of buckets-full), then the size of the unit is fixed, and its shape should suit the general method of excavation and the tools used. The choice is more complex than at larger scales because we are working in three dimensions rather than two. This has the secondary effect of

Table 6.2 *Percentages by weight of different type of faunal remains retrieved on meshes of various sizes at early medieval Dorestad (from Clason and Prummel 1977, Table 1).*

|  | hand-collected | 10 mm mesh | 4 mm mesh | 1 mm mesh |
|---|---|---|---|---|
| cattle, horse | 80.2 | 56.1 | 15.5 | 11.1 |
| pig, sheep, goat | 18.6 | 40.4 | 46.3 | 33.2 |
| fishes | ... | 0.6 | 19.3 | 31.6 |
| birds | 0.1 | 1.3 | 3.1 | 1.1 |
| molluscs | 0.2 | 0.9 | 14.0 | 21.1 |

making *edge effects* (see p. 100) relatively more important, partly because an irregular shape in three dimensions has more 'edge' to it than one in two dimensions, but also because each sampling unit is a relatively greater proportion of the population (i.e. of the feature or deposit) at this scale. There seems to have been little, if any, discussion of this problem, and it is difficult to judge how serious it might be in practice. *A priori*, one might imagine that the edge of a feature (e.g. of a pit) might contain a rather different assemblage to the bulk of its fill, but this is an area where practical experimentation is needed.

(b) Bias due to the intensity of sampling is an inescapable fact of archaeological life (e.g. Struever 1968; Thomas 1969; Payne 1972a; Clason and Prummel 1977; O'Connor 1989; Shaffer 1992; Gordon 1993; Shaffer and Sanchez 1994; Muckle 1994) (Fig. 6.6; Table 6.2). We cannot possibly retain, sort, identify and record literally 'everything' from a sampled unit of soil or deposit, so to pursue absolute freedom from bias is futile. More important is freedom from relative bias. Usually, our aim is to compare assemblages (e.g. in terms of their *compositions*), rather than to study the details of an individual assemblage in isolation. It then matters not so much that the assemblages are biased, but that they should have the same bias, and so can reasonably be compared. If two features are sampled to the same intensity (*not* the same sample size or sampling fraction) then, other things being equal, it is reasonable to compare (for example) their compositions. It is very easy to create differences between assemblages simply by sampling them to different intensities. If, for special reasons, one has to be sampled to a higher intensity (e.g. a finer mesh), it may be necessary to sample it at a lower intensity as well for the sake of comparability (for example by use of a column of sieves, as is often done in practice (e.g. Diamant 1979)). Overall, there is a powerful case for standardisation and detailed documentation of processing methods.

A further problem is that 'other things' are not always equal, chief among them being fragmentation rates (Watson 1972). If one assemblage is more fragmented than another, then if both are sampled at the same intensity, a smaller proportion of the first would be recovered. This in itself might not be too serious, provided that the proportions of different species (or bone elements, or whatever) could still be compared. But such a comparison would rely on an assumption (possibly implicit) that the fragmentation affects all the species (or whatever) equally, and there is no reason *a priori* why this should be so. As a simple example, heavy fragmentation may reduce small mammal bones to a size at which they are not recovered (e.g. by wet-sieving), while even fragmentary large mammal bones may still be in large enough pieces to be recovered. The situation may be compounded by differences in *identifiability* if, for example, small fragments of bones of one species are easier to identify than fragments of a similar size from another species (Stallibrass 1985). What can be done? One possibility would be to establish a measure of the brokenness of an assemblage (as has been done for pottery, see Orton 1993), and only to compare assemblages with roughly comparable levels of this measure. Otherwise, there is always the possibility that what we are comparing is differences in post-depositional history rather than in the original assemblages (see chapter 3).

### Selection of the sample

As usual, sample design and sample size are the main issues here, and the main problem is that we are almost always dealing with cluster samples. The only practical exception is if we are sub-sampling from an assemblage that was itself originally a cluster sample. Even then, the theoretical situation is not appreciably different; if we treat it as a population and use the statistical techniques appropriate to that situation, our inferences will be limited to statements about that assemblage, not about the population from which it was taken. The primary implication is that a single soil sample, however large (in term of volume), and however many 'objects' it contains, is from a statistical point of view a sample of size one. This means that it is not legitimate to calculate standard deviations and confidence intervals, or to undertake hypothesis tests (p. 24), on data from such a sample. Of course, it is perfectly possible to 'go through the motions' and carry out the calculations appropriate to a binomial distribution (p. 211), and many archaeologists have done just that (see Veen and Fieller 1982). But from a statistical point of view such calculations are meaningless, because they are based on the assumption that we have a random sample of all the objects in a feature, which is simply not the case. This point has long been appreciated intuitively by archaeologists when they comment on the lack of homogeneity within features (p. 154), but they have generally failed to think through the implications. A noteworthy exception was Nance (1987, 249), who approached this problem through the concept of reliability (p. 75). Does this mean that there is no basis for measuring variability, and so no basis for confidence intervals, tests for significant differences between assemblages, calculations for required sample size, etc.? Fortunately not; but what it means is that such calculations must be based on a sample of several sampling units from within the feature. In practice, this mean that several small samples from the same feature are preferable to one large one, not only to enable such calculations to be carried out validly (p. 32), but also to ensure a more representative spread across the feature. It should go without saying that such samples should be sorted and analysed separately, and not amalgamated into one 'bulk' sample. There are further implications for the way the calculations are done, which will be explained in the appropriate section below (p. 168). In turn, this point makes it very difficult to predict the size of the sample (in either volume or numerical terms) that will be needed to yield the required degree of precision, since it will vary according to the internal variability of the feature, about which we have no direct advance knowledge. The traditional statistical response is to recommend a pilot sample (p. 168); it is possible that experience of samples from similar features may prove useful (p. 159), provided that they have been treated as cluster samples.

Does all this really matter, the archaeologist might ask? The calculations might not be technically valid, but would their outcome be very different from those of the 'proper' calculations? The short answer is that we don't know, but that the answer may be different for each feature. Some may have been so homogenised that the contents of a single sample can be regarded as a random sample from all the objects in the feature. Others may be very variable internally, so that a single sampling unit may be quite misleading, both in terms of variability and in terms of actual composition. In the short term, then, the problem does matter, because we simply do not know where we stand. In the longer term, it might be possible to build up a body of 'case law' to suggest the difference that internal variability might create between the 'actual' and 'effective' sample sizes (p. 169 below), for various classes of feature.

The actual layout of the sampling units needs to be considered. Stratification is not likely to be an option (if it were, the feature should probably be divided stratigraphically). The choice is likely to be between simple random and systematic sampling (p. 21), and the latter has a practical appeal. The problem of designing a systematic sample in three dimensions is not a trivial one; the important point is to ensure that each element of volume in the feature has the same chance of selection. For example, a bias could be introduced into column sampling by taking the whole of a shallow column but only a sub-sample of a deep one (Fig. 6.7).

The actual mechanics of taking samples has been well discussed in the literature (e.g. Murphy and Wiltshire 1994) and there is no need to repeat it here.

### The pre-test

The previous discussion has brought the issue of a pre-test, or pilot sample, into a prominence that it rarely possesses at this scale. There is a clear logistical

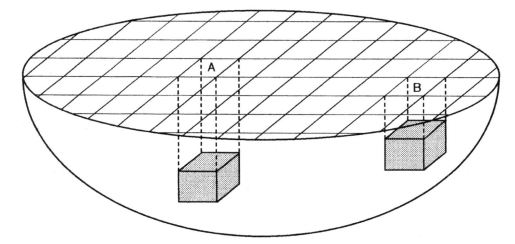

Fig. 6.7 Illustration of the creation of bias by sampling at different rates from different parts of an irregular feature. If samples of the same volume are taken from column A and from column B (e.g. the shaded blocks), then any part of column A has less chance of being selected than any part of column B.

problem here: how can one organise an excavation so that it is possible to take a pilot sample, and process, sort and analyse it in time to determine the size of the sample that is needed, before the whole feature is excavated? One answer might be to take far more samples than are likely to be needed, to make a pilot study of a few to determine the number needed, and then to jettison the rest. It seems likely that a period of experimentation will be needed to develop procedures for properly coming to terms with cluster sampling.

### *Organisation of the fieldwork*

There has been much work done and published, over the last thirty years or so, on the time taken to collect, process, sort and identify samples, using various levels of mechanical assistance (see a summary by Cherry (1978, Table 19.1)); space (for storage) needs to be taken into account alongside labour costs.

### *Summary and analysis of the data*

Cluster samples require a more complex form of analysis than simple random samples. In general, *ratio estimation* (pp. 38, 214) is the appropriate technique to use, and gives the 'correct' values of standard deviations, etc. Different formulae for the estimate are possible; the best is likely to be the *ratio to size estimate* (p. 38, **2.12**), while the *mean of the unit means* (p. 213) is to be avoided. Frequently, there is likely to be a need to estimate the proportion of a particular type of object in a feature; there is a special case of ratio estimation for this situation. As we have seen above, the use of the binomial formulae (**2.4, 2.5**) is not appropriate. Comparison of compositions of different features may be more difficult than it seems, because the conventional approach, the chi-squared test, is a generalisation from the binomial distribution for individual types. One solution, which would need experimental validation, is to calculate for each feature a hypothetical sample size which would give (using the binomial formula) the same standard deviations of the proportions of each type as were obtained using ratio estimates on the actual sample (see **2.13**). This figure, which could be called the *effective sample size*, is analogous to the 'pseudo-total' of pottery statistics (Orton and Tyers 1990; Orton 1993). The ratio of effective sample size to actual sample size would give a measure of the internal homogeneity of a feature: a value of 1 would indicate a random mixture of object types; smaller values would indicate increasing internal variability (or decreasing homogeneity); larger values would indicate the unlikely situation of a mixture on the homogeneous or uniform side of random. If the data were scaled to sum to the effective sample size for each feature, classical comparative techniques such as the chi-squared test could then be used.

The display of large amounts of data, e.g. of compositions of many assemblages, can give difficulty. Multiple bar charts and pie charts have been used (e.g. Lennstrom and Hastorf 1995); if the aim is to show the relationships between features in terms of their different compositions, or indeed the relationships between different classes of object in terms of the different features in which they occur, then correspondence analysis (Greenacre 1984; 1993) is a very effective tool (compare Fig. 6.8 with Table 3.1).

### Information gained for future surveys

Since excavation is usually a one-off exercise, it might seem that there would be little scope for information gained from sampling a feature to be useful in the future. This is so in the direct sense that we are unlikely ever to sample from the same feature again, but it ignores the point that we are likely to sample from similar features in the future. Experience, and knowledge gained about the densities, levels of variability, etc., of different types of object in different types of feature, can be very useful in planning future work. For this reason, such information should be published alongside the more conventional archaeological 'results'.

### Special topic

If the pattern of previous chapters were followed, there would here be one or more case studies to show some of the ways in which the principles of the *theory and practice* section have been employed in the field. However, in the

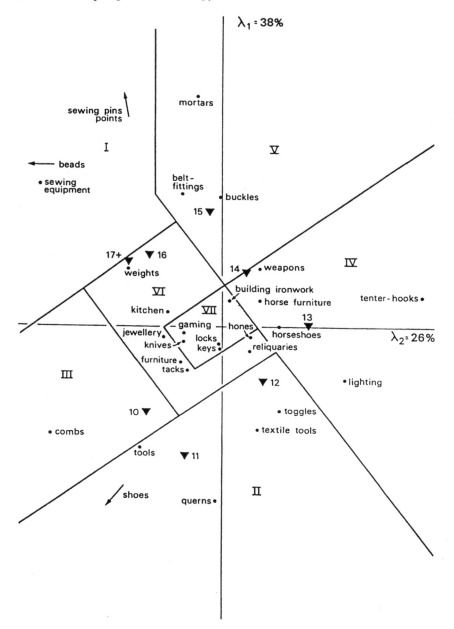

Fig. 6.8 Comparison of correspondence analysis (ca) plot of Winchester small finds by centuries with multiple pie charts of the same data (Table 3.1). Key to artefact types: b buckles, bi building ironwork, h hones, hs horseshoes, k keys, kn knives, p points, sp sewing pins, sh shoes, tt textile tools, t tools. (ca plot from Barclay *et al.* 1990, Fig. 7, by permission of Oxford University Press.)

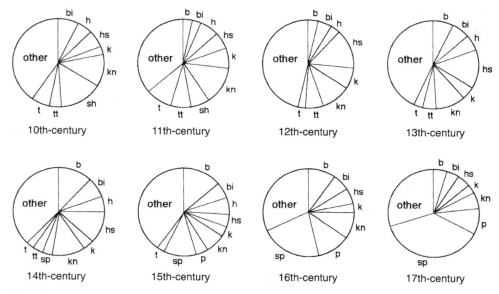

Fig. 6.8 *continued*

light of the discussion in that section, it does not seem appropriate to select any particular applications for special presentation. The practical methods of sampling are remarkably similar, making it invidious to choose one rather than another, while the universal problem of the failure to recognise the implications of cluster sampling (p. 166) means that any chosen example would be subjected to unfair criticism.

Instead, we will look at a special topic, diversity, which, although present at every scale of research, has made most impact on archaeological thought at this scale, where it appears to answer some of the questions archaeologists are asking.

### Diversity

Diversity is a rather late example of the 'Great Borrowing' of techniques by archaeologists from other disciplines (Aldenderfer 1987, 90), in this case from ecology. The formal concept goes back at least to the 1920s (Arrhenius 1923), and much work was done from the 1940s onwards (e.g. Fisher *et al.* 1943); by the 1970s it had become a fully fledged sub-discipline (Pielou 1975; Grassle *et al.* 1979). The general idea, expressed in informal terms, can be found in archaeology in the early twentieth century (e.g. Holmes 1919, quoted by Jones and Leonard 1989, 2). Explicit archaeological uses blossomed in the 1980s (e.g. Conkey 1980; Jones *et al.* 1983; Grayson 1984, 138–49; Kintigh 1984), applied to a wide variety of materials, both artefactual and ecofactual. A collection of work done in the 1980s was published at the end of the decade (Leonard and

Jones 1989). The 1990s have seen various developments on the basic ideas (e.g. McCartney and Glass 1990; Meltzer *et al.* 1992; Plog and Hegman 1993; Kaufman 1998), together with a very useful review of the topic (Ringrose 1993b).

Most archaeologists have an intuitive idea of what they mean by 'diversity', and the concept plays an important part in anthropology (Shott 1989b, 283–4). Nevertheless, it is a difficult concept to define formally. The term in itself is vague, and can be broken down into two aspects, *richness* and *evenness* (Cruz-Uribe 1988; Kintigh 1989), and possibly a third, *heterogeneity* (McCartney and Glass 1990, 522).

The simplest of them is *richness*, which is just the number of classes of object present in a sample; the more classes, the more diverse the sample. Even this is not as simple as it seems (Kintigh 1989, 26), because there may be problems of different levels of definition, e.g. in a seed sample, when some can be identified to *species* level but others only to *family* level. There is also a related *richness index* (**6.4**; Cruz-Uribe 1988, 180).

*Evenness* reflects the feeling that an assemblage in which all classes are equally represented is in some sense more diverse than one in which some are well represented and others are poorly represented. Many indices have been proposed to measure this; the most commonly used one is the *Shannon index of diversity* (**6.5**; Cruz-Uribe 1988; Shott 1989b; McCartney and Glass 1990), also known as the *Shannon-Wiener* (or *Weaver*) *information function* (or *index*); the next most common is *Simpson's* (or *Gini's*) *index of concentration* (the opposite of diversity) (**6.6**). Both have been criticised for being heavily dependent on the most abundant species (Ringrose 1993b, 281). A measure of heterogeneity suggested by McCartney and Glass (1990) is the *niche width* (**6.7**; Hardesty 1975, 77), though this does not appear to have been used in archaeology.

One major problem with all of these indices is that they appear, *a priori*, to depend on sample size (Grayson 1981). The most obvious dependency is that of richness: it is a widespread experience that the larger the sample, the more classes are likely to be present, and that one cannot argue from the absence of 'rare' classes from small samples. Clearly, this dependency cannot continue indefinitely, since there is only a finite number of classes in the population, and sooner or later the curve of number of classes against sample size must reach a plateau (Fig. 6.9). The question is – how soon? Other indices are algebraically related to richness, and so apparently to sample size, though the empirical relationship is less clear. Cruz-Uribe (1988, 182–3) argued that a plateau was reached above a sample size of 25, but this has been disputed (Meltzer *et al.* 1992) and the existence of a simple 'magic number' seems intrinsically unlikely. The only definite agreement appears to be that 'The relationship between sample size and diversity and richness should be investigated prior to any interpretation' (Cruz-Uribe 1988, 194; quoted in Meltzer *et al.* 1992, 385).

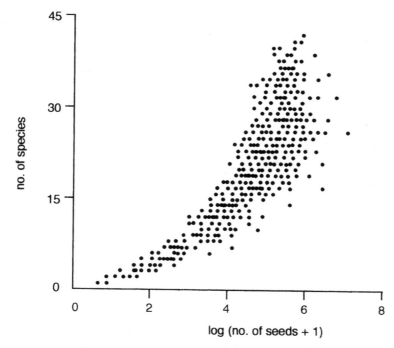

Fig. 6.9 Graph showing number of species identified as sample sizes increase (redrawn from Lange 1990, Fig. 4.3).

So what can be done? Is it possible to compare the richness of samples from two or more populations, or will any possible differences between the populations be confused by differences in sample size? There have been four main approaches to this question:

(a) sampling to redundancy (Lyman 1995, 370),
(b) computer simulation (Kintigh 1984; 1989),
(c) the regression approach (Jones *et al.* 1983), and
(d) rarefaction analysis (Birks and Line 1992), also known as the *expected species index* (Ringrose 1993b, 282).

*Sampling to redundancy*: This is just the procedure of taking incremental or cumulative samples until the statistic of interest (in this case, the number of classes of objects) 'settles down' (p. 157). It can result in very large samples (McCartney and Glass 1990, 523), and may not always be practical, for logistical reasons.

*Computer simulation*: This approach asks the question 'how many classes would we expect in a sample of a certain size?' The answer clearly depends heavily on the proportions of classes in the population, so the procedure is to

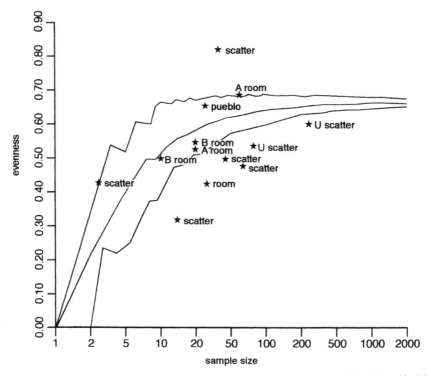

Fig. 6.10 Computer simulation of number of types of object identified in samples of increasing size, compared to site data (redrawn from Kintigh 1989, Fig. 4.12).

  (i)   estimate these proportions by pooling all relevant available data,

 (ii)   use computer simulation to select large numbers of samples of the required size with these parameters,

(iii)   calculate the means and confidence intervals of these,

(iv)   plot them all as a graph of expected richness against sample size (Fig. 6.10),

 (v)   compare the individual assemblages against this curve to see which are 'more diverse than expected' and which are less.

This approach has been criticised by Rhode (1988) and Ringrose (1993b) for being heavily dependent on good estimates of the proportions in the population, and because the pooling creates a dataset that may not look like any of the original datasets (Ringrose 1993b, 283). Further, simulation is not necessary because the curve can be calculated directly (1993b, 283).

*Regression approach*: This more straightforward approach is simply to calculate the regression line of the number of classes against the sample size, and classify assemblages as more or less diverse as they lie above or below the line. This is likely to indicate whether or not a sample size effect exists, but is of little use for comparing sites.

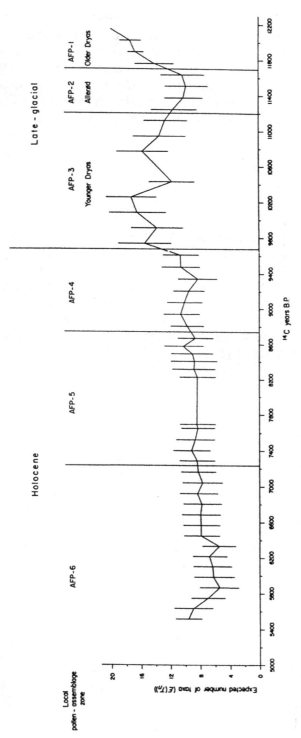

Fig. 6.11 Example of rarefaction analysis (Birks and Line 1992, Fig. 2).

*Rarefaction analysis*: This is in a sense an opposite approach to the others. The idea is to achieve comparability by artificially reducing the size of all the samples to a common value, that of the smallest one. Samples can then be compared without fear that sample size will distort the comparison. The way this is done is to use statistical theory to estimate how many classes would be present if a sub-sample of the size of the smallest were drawn randomly from each of the larger samples in turn (**6.8, 6.9**; Raup 1975; Birks and Line 1992, 3) (Fig. 6.11). This seems to be the best of the approaches suggested to date, though it clearly does not make full use of all the information available; this could be serious if the samples were of widely differing sizes.

Thus considerable effort has been devoted to attempts to remove the 'sample size effect' from comparisons of the richness of samples of many different sorts of archaeological material – pollen, seeds, bones, artefacts – some more successfully than others. It has also been pointed out that sample size itself can be an important factor, which should not always be automatically 'removed' (Plog and Hegman 1993; but see Leonard 1997; Plog and Hegman 1997), and that examination of the size:diversity relationship can be a useful interpretative tool (Shott 1989b). The problem of assessing when rare species are really not present, as opposed to just apparently not present because they do not appear in samples, has recently been raised (Lyman 1995). This relates closely to the issues considered earlier, in the case of site evaluations (p. 119).

# 7

## 'BUT MANY SANGUINE PEOPLE HOPE, TO SEE THEM THROUGH A MICROSCOPE'

### Introduction

In this chapter we consider the smallest of the scales at which sampling is undertaken in archaeology – that of sampling from artefacts or ecofacts for 'scientific' analysis, such as chemical, physical or textural analysis (p. 184). This process usually divides into two stages:

(a)  the selection of objects (whether artefacts or ecofacts) from an assemblage,
(b)  the selection of samples from the chosen objects themselves.

The aim is usually to estimate parameters, such as chemical compositions, isotopic ratios or grain size distributions, which will help to characterise the assemblage in some way, for example in determining its provenance(s), in dating it, or in providing information about manufacturing techniques.

The first stage is needed because assemblages can be very large, and the scientific techniques can be very expensive, or very time-consuming. A few examples may therefore have to represent a very large collection, for example in the characterisation of the products of a pottery production site, but the issues involved in ensuring that the sample is truly representative are rarely discussed, and often taken for granted. Even the question of sample size seems often to be determined by financial or time constraints rather than by any archaeological or statistical consideration. Frequently, it seems that inferences have to be drawn from very small samples about very large populations, which must make one very concerned about the cavalier or unthinking attitude that is sometimes taken towards the selection of such samples.

The need to sample from each selected object may arise for a variety of reasons. There may be a need to cause as little damage to the object as possible, particularly if it is valuable or wanted for display. Alternatively, the analytical equipment may place requirements on the amount of material submitted for analysis, such as the six to twelve 30 mm by 30 mm by 10 mm samples required for TL dating (Aitken 1990, 155), or may specify the nature of the sample, such as ceramic thin-section, which is a highly specialised form of sample. Sometimes the analytical procedure may involve an inherent sampling process, such as the counting and identification or measuring of grains in heavy mineral and textural analyses (p. 184), when the counting of all grains would be an expensive and unnecessary luxury.

177

In some cases, particularly in the field of dating, the object or assemblage itself is not the ultimate target, but only a way of providing information about the context, or about the event that produced that context. Especial care is then needed to ensure that the sample is actually related to the event – for example, that the piece of charcoal is likely to be contemporary with the feature within which it was found, and which it has been used to date. Such issues have been widely discussed, and will not be pursued further here.

### Historical background

The uses of scientific analyses in archaeology go back at least to well into the nineteenth century (e.g. Brongniart 1844; Bastelaar 1877; Bamps 1883). At this early date, of course, statistical sampling theory was not well enough developed to make a useful contribution (p. 14). The great increase in techniques, and their widespread application, started in the 1950s following the success of radiocarbon dating as one of the first widely acknowledged valuable contributions of science to archaeology. There is now a wide and growing range of dating techniques (Aitken 1990) and archaeometric techniques available to the archaeologist. Many require equipment which is beyond the reach of all but a few fortunate archaeologists (such as Neutron Activation Analysis, which requires the use of a nuclear reactor (Sayre and Dobson 1957)). This led to a need for more 'low-tech' approaches, which would be more accessible and so could be used by more archaeologists on more material.

This need was met in the case of pottery (probably the material most heavily studied by scientific analyses) by the adoption of techniques from sedimentary petrology. Thin-sectioning and the identification of characteristic mineral inclusions have been widely used since the 1930s (Liddell 1932; Obenauer 1936; Gladwin 1937; Shepard 1942), but are of little use in the parts of the world (such as south-east England) where the mineral inclusions consist mainly or totally of sand (quartz) grains. A breakthrough came in the 1960s, when Peacock used some traditional parameters of sedimentary petrology – percentage of inclusions in the matrix, roundness and sphericity of the grains, and in particular the size distribution of the grains – to describe and compare Roman pottery from excavations at Portchester, Hampshire (Peacock 1971). He may not have been the first to use such methods, as Wagner (1933–8) apparently used the sizes of grains in bricks to distinguish between Carolingian and post-Carolingian churches in Germany (see Parsons 1977, 186), but he established a developing school. Peacock's approach, which was subsequently simplified and became known as *textural analysis*, was extended to Roman tiles (Darvill 1979) and medieval pottery (Streeten 1982). A period of experimentation (e.g. Darvill and Timby 1982; Wandibba 1982; Leese 1983) was followed by a definitive review (Middleton *et al.* 1985), which resolved many of the practical sampling issues (p. 186). Although cheaper than 'high-tech' methods, such approaches can be very time-consuming (p. 185), and thus contain considerable 'hidden costs'. A major advance was made by Fieller and Nicholson (1991), who pointed out the unreliability and other weaknesses of current methods of characterising grain size distributions, and suggested the use of an explicit statistical model, in this case the truncated skew log Laplace distribution (1991; Patel *et al.* 1976, 139). Much of this work appears to have gone relatively unnoticed outside the UK; for example, it was still possible to refer to it as 'new' in the USA in the late 1980s (Stoltman 1989).

It should not be thought that statistics and sampling apply only to ceramics. Although less developed, they have been discussed in the context of studies of bone (Grupe 1988), timber (Morgan 1975) and metals (Merkel 1997).

### Theory and practice

There is remarkably little theory about the selection of samples at any stage, except perhaps in the case of textural analysis, which will be dealt with as a case study. Nevertheless, it is still worth seeing how Cochran's twelve stages (p. 27) would apply in these situations; indeed, the lack of theory may make it even more necessary to take this approach.

#### *Assimilation of existing knowledge*

It is not likely that there will be any information relating directly to the material currently being studied. With so much material available, and relatively speaking so few resources, the likelihood of repeated sampling on the same material is low. However, useful background information may be available, for example on the expected level of natural variation within a supposedly 'homogeneous' body of material, like the waste material from a production site (Streeten 1982). For some materials, the units of sampling may not be the same as the units about which inferences are required, in which case information about the variability between the sampling units within 'inferential' units is essential. For example, Charters *et al.* (1993, 216) showed that there was great variation in the level of organic residues (lipid concentrations) between different parts of the same ceramic vessel, as well as between different forms. This means that samples from individual sherds, particularly if they cannot be assigned to a particular part of a particular vessel form, give unreliable estimates of concentrations in whole vessels, and thus of their possible function. Similarly, Grupe (1988) showed large variation in concentration between compact and trabecular bone within the same medieval human skeletons, over a wide range of elements, suggesting that the common practice of sampling from rib bones (1988, 124) is unlikely to produce reliable results on a 'whole skeleton' basis. Forewarned is forearmed.

*Objectives of the survey*

The objectives of a sampling programme are likely to vary, according to whether the material is from a production site or a consumption site. For the former, the aim is likely to be a descriptive characterisation in terms of estimates of relevant parameters, such as proportions of major and/or minor (trace) elements or isotopes, or (for pottery) proportions of different classes of inclusions, or the distribution of grain sizes, together with a measure of their inherent variability. This will enable comparisons to be made with material from consumption sites; ideally, a 'bank' or 'library' of data from production sources should gradually be built up. At a consumption site, a primary aim might be to establish the homogeneity of the material: is it all likely to have come from one source, or two, or several? Attempts can be made to link the various groups detected with material from production centres, which hopefully will already have been characterised.

Some types of sample, e.g. ceramic thin-sections, can be used to obtain information about processes of production, for example whether a pot was coiled or thrown. Such questions may influence the way in which thin-sections are taken, e.g. radially or tangentially (Hodges 1962), and therefore need to be asked before samples are taken.

As always, then, careful definition of objectives is needed if full benefit of a sampling programme is to be achieved. With the high cost of such programmes (whether financial or in terms of time), it is important not to waste resources by either over- or under-sampling.

*Population to be sampled*

In one sense, this is a very straightforward issue. We have a collection of objects (sherds, coins, bones, etc.) from which we are able to select a sample. So surely that collection constitutes our population? While that is true in a practical sense, there is a problem in that the collection may well not be the population about which we wish to make inferences from our sample. There are two reasons for this:

(a)   the units to be sampled may not be the units about which we wish to make inferences (this is the problem of sherds and pots, or of bones and skeletons, discussed above (p. 51));

(b)   the collection is itself some sort of a sample (not necessarily a random or representative one) from the population that we are really interested in, having been 'selected' by all sorts of site-formation processes (Schiffer 1987).

The latter is the problem of 'sampled populations' and 'target populations', discussed at length in chapter 3, which is perhaps more acute here than at other scales (chapters 4–6, 8). There is no need to repeat that discussion here, but we do need to remind ourselves of the dilemma – is our population, for example, the collection of sherds retrieved from a pottery production site, or is it the actual production of pots from that site? The answer may affect how we approach the question of assessing whether or not a pot found at a consumption site was produced at a particular centre.

### Data to be collected

Again, this may not be quite as straightforward as it seems. On the face of it, the choice of data is determined by our research questions and the capabilities of the equipment to which we have access. But there is a snag that, with equipment that produces multivariate data, such as elemental analyses, too many data, in the sense of too many variables, may actually obscure the patterns we are seeking. Suppose, for example, that the products of two centres differ in their proportions of elements A, B and C, but that we collect data on elements A, B, C . . . H. Then random fluctuations in elements D . . . H will tend to obscure the patterns of elements A, B, C, whereas if we had only measured A, B, C, the pattern would be clear. This will be particularly problematic if we try to assign other material to one or other of the centres (Baxter 1994, 72–7). This is an example of the dangers of the 'collect everything and see what happens' approach to archaeological data collection and analysis.

### Degree of precision required

This may be difficult to determine in advance, without some knowledge of the inherent variability of our material, both within and between sources. If sources are radically different, e.g. in their elemental compositions or in their grain size distributions, relatively imprecise estimates will show such differences, but if those differences are more subtle, greater precision will be needed. This in turn affects the size of sample that will be needed, and highlights the need to have as much background information as possible (p. 179) before starting an analytical programme.

Another problem is the level of precision of the equipment used. It is tempting to believe that if a figure comes from a piece of expensive equipment, probably *via* a computer, it must be 'true'. This is not so – such equipment is always subject to random errors and possibly to systematic ones too (p. 23) – and much scientific effort is spent in controlling them. A particular problem comes from very low measurements (e.g. very rare elements). A very low percentage may be rounded to zero, or may appear as 'trace' in the output (i.e. present in a proportion smaller than the lowest limit that can be recorded). This in itself is difficulty enough, but the limit may depend on the calibration of the equipment, and may vary from one model to another, and certainly from one technique to another. Close liaison with the specialists involved, and an understanding of their problems, is important for successful analysis.

### Method of measurement

In many cases, there will be no choice here, as it will be determined by the availability of analytical equipment. But there are some areas in which choice is possible, particularly in the study of thin-sections. Even an apparently simple task such as counting grains can be done in different ways, which may lead to different results (p. 187). It is important to ask what we hope these data will show before deciding how to collect or measure them.

### The frame

The lack of a sampling frame, or indeed of the recognition of a need for one, is one of the most worrying aspects of sampling as it is practised at this scale, especially in stage (a) (p. 177). The difficulty, if not the impossibility, of selecting a small representative sample from a large collection of sherds, bones or whatever is rarely admitted, although it should force archaeologists towards imposing some structure on the collection before selecting a sample. A quite simple experiment can demonstrate just how difficult it is to select by eye a sample that is representative, even of a variable that can be observed. For example, lay out a collection of sherds (or flints, or pebbles, etc.) on a table and try to take a 'representative' sample of say five or ten of them. Then compare their lengths with those of the whole collection. Even if the mean is estimated accurately, it is very likely that the overall variability will be understated; an observer tends to select 'average' examples rather than representative ones.

So what can we do if we want a sample that is representative in terms of variables, such as trace elements, that we can not even see? This is perhaps the major problem in the application of analytical techniques in archaeology, and one that has received surprisingly little attention. The most fruitful statistical approach seems to be stratification (p. 30), based on observable macroscopic characteristics, such as textural parameters (p. 178). Whatever is chosen will have to be quick and simple enough to be applied to the whole sampled collection, or it will be self-defeating. If it is necessary to reduce the size of the collection first, then Cowgill's advice (1964, in reply to Willey 1961) is sound, that it is best to sample all the material from selected contexts, rather than some from each context. Further sampling from the unselected contexts is recommended if it is necessary to increase the sample size for rare categories (Cowgill 1964, 471). This discussion was in the context of the retention or disposal of material, which is a much wider debate. It goes without saying that any such decisions should be fully documented.

### Selection of the sample

Given that some structure has now been imposed on the collection, systematic sampling (p. 21) is probably the best way to proceed at stage (a), using the same sampling fraction in each stratum for the sake of simplicity, unless there are very good reasons to do otherwise. This removes the need to number each object individually, but does require that they can be put into an unambiguous order (p. 200). At stage (b), the requirements are probably laid down as part of the analytical procedures. For example, when sampling from ceramics for chemical analysis, a minimum amount of material is needed to even out the differences between the inclusions and the clay matrix (Bromund *et al.* 1976). When counting or measuring grains in a thin-section, the use of a graticule imposes a spatial systematic sample.

We have already seen (p. 177) that sample size may be imposed by constraints of money or time. Even within such constraints, a balance must be struck between the intensities of sampling at different stages. For elemental analyses, is it better to take one sample each from a relatively large number of objects, or two or more from each of a smaller number? For grain counting in thin-sections, is the extra precision obtained by counting (say) 100 grains per section rather than 50 worth the extra thin-sections that must be foregone for lack of time? There are no general answers, as they depend on the variability of particular materials and specimens; the general principles are those of two-stage sampling (pp. 33, 197, 222).

### The pre-test

The need for as much background information as possible has been stressed throughout this section. If it is not available, then a pilot sample is essential, to give an idea of the likely levels of variability. It can also be expected to highlight any problems that may arise in practice, and to indicate the time needed for the main sampling programme, though it should be noted that the speed that can be achieved in a short burst (e.g. of grain counting) may not be sustainable in the longer term.

### Organisation of the fieldwork

This is probably laid down as part of laboratory procedures. Stage (a) work is best done over as short a period as possible, to ensure consistency.

### Summary and analysis of the data

One of the differences between this and other scales is that the data are often multivariate, consisting of measurements of several interrelated variables (e.g.

elements). Large amounts of data are therefore produced, which it may not be feasible to publish *in toto*; if they are published, they may be in the form of large indigestible tables. Such tables can be so impenetrable, and any patterns in them so difficult to see, that it may be better not to publish them as such, but to make them freely available on request, and to publish graphical summaries of them. The most useful such summaries are probably scatter-plots based on the techniques of *principal components analysis* (pca) or *correspondence analysis* (ca) (Baxter 1994, 48–139), depending on the nature of the data, or the *biplot* (1994, 66–71) as an alternative to pca. There has recently been controversy (Tangri and Wright 1993; Baxter 1993) about the analysis of *compositional data* (i.e. data which add up to a fixed total, for example percentages), but overall the techniques seem to be well established.

As we saw in chapter 6, some samples are cluster samples (p. 30), not simple random samples (p. 20), and must be treated as such. A good example at this scale would be a thin-section, or a count of grains extracted from a sherd in some way. Since we first take a sample and then count the grains in it, rather than take all the grains and sample from them (which is hopelessly impractical), each unit is a sample of size 1, regardless of how many grains it contains. This means that, strictly speaking, the binomial distribution (p. 211) cannot be used to attach standard deviations ($\pm$s) to the proportions of (for example) different minerals among the grains. The statistically correct approach is to take several samples from the same unit and estimate the standard deviations by comparing the proportions in each. This is probably not as serious a problem as it was in chapter 6, since the inclusions in a ceramic fabric are likely to be more homogeneous than (for example) in bones or seeds in a pit, but empirical studies are needed to check this point.

### Information gained for future surveys

Just as background information can make a valuable contribution to a sampling programme, so the results of one programme may provide a springboard for the next, whether it is one's own or someone else's. Full documentation should therefore always be kept and made available on request (or, these days, put on the Internet so that it can be downloaded).

### Case study: textural and related analyses

Here we look at the statistical, and in particular the sampling, issues that have arisen in attempts to study ceramics through the inclusions visible in a thin-section. Heavy mineral analysis aims to characterise and compare thin-sections in terms of the proportions of different minerals present among the inclusions. It appears to have been originated by Oakley (1933) and was popularised by Peacock (1967). A good example of an application was given by

Williams (1977), who counted and analysed the numbers of grains of each of ten non-opaque minerals in samples of 150–200 grains from each of 300 ceramic samples. Nevertheless, this approach has not 'caught on' as a quantitative technique (although widely practised qualitatively), perhaps because of its time requirements. For example, Stoltman (1989, 148) estimated that together with grain size counting it took over twice as long as the size analysis alone (2 hours vs. 45 minutes per slide).

A less demanding approach is to estimate the ratio of inclusions to clay matrix (Hodder 1974), perhaps with the aid of percentage inclusion estimation charts (Mathew *et al.* 1991). It has been found to be inadequate for linking material from consumption sites with that from production sites (Streeten 1982, 124).

As we have seen (p. 178), textural analysis concerns mainly the distribution of the sizes of inclusions in ceramic thin-sections to describe and compare ceramic products in terms of their possible sources. It is time-consuming (but less so than heavy mineral analysis) and a qualitative analysis of mineral inclusions is preferable if it is possible (Darvill and Timby 1982, 173).

Some important statistical sampling issues that arise are:

(a)   the size of the sample (number of grains counted per section),
(b)   the method of counting the grains (*area-*, *line-*, *point-*, *or ribbon-counting*, see Middleton *et al.* 1985),
(c)   the characterisation of the grain size distribution,
(d)   the levels of variability between sherds from the same vessel, and between different observers.

(a) The conventional wisdom (Peacock 1971), taken from sedimentary petrology, is that a sample of 50 grains per section is adequate for statistical purposes (Pye 1943, reacting against the then petrological standard of 300 grains). Later experiments suggested that, while this number is adequate for estimating the mean size (Middleton *et al.* 1985, 72), larger samples are needed if other parameters are required. Leese (1983, 49) suggested 150 grains per section for mean and standard deviation, or, if the shape of the distribution itself is to be estimated, Streeten (1982, 128) and Fieller and Nicholson (1991, 78 and 88) independently suggested 150–200 grains for quite different statistical approaches. The time factor too must be taken into account: Fieller and Nicholson (1991, 79 and 88) and Stoltman (1989, 149) agreed on 45 minutes per slide of 150–200 grains, in contrast to Streeten (1982, 127) and Leese (1983, 47), who respectively suggest 20 and 15 minutes per slide of 150 grains.

(b) The four main methods of counting grains are (see Fig. 7.1):

(i)   *Area counting*: All grains lying completely within the study area of the section are measured (those lying only partly within cannot be measured because their size is not known).

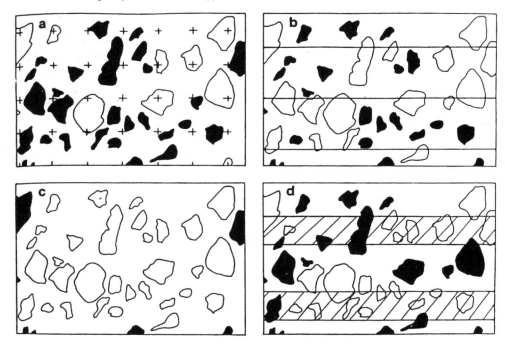

Fig. 7.1 Comparison of (a) point-, (b) line-, (c) area-, and (d) ribbon-counting, showing which grains would be selected by each method (Middleton *et al.* 1985, Fig. 3).

(ii)   *Line-counting*: All grains intersected by lines across the section, conventionally spaced at intervals approximately equal to the diameter of the largest particle, are measured.

(iii)  *Point-counting*: A regular grid is established, and every grain which falls under a grid point is measured. There are at least three variants (see Middleton *et al.* 1985, 66–8):

    1  each 'hit' by a point on a grain is counted (e.g. if a grain lies under two grid points, its measurement is counted twice) – the *multiple intercept* approach;

    2  no grain is counted more than once – the *single intercept* approach;

    3  if a grid point does not intersect a grain, then the nearest grain is measured – the *nearest grain* approach (Darvill and Timby 1982, 74; Streeten 1982, 126).

(iv)  *Ribbon-counting*: This is similar to line-counting, but all grains with their lowest point within a series of ribbons ( = transects) across the section are measured (Betts 1982).

There are major theoretical differences, as well as the obvious practical ones, between these approaches. There is a fundamental difference between area-

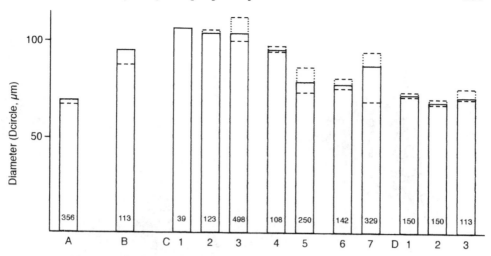

Fig. 7.2 Bar chart showing mean diameters (solid horizontal lines) and ranges of means for subsets (dashed lines) when using various grain selection techniques.
A. area-counting
B. line-counting
C. point-counting

| C.1 | multiple intercepts: | large interval |
| C.2 | | medium interval |
| C.3 | | small interval |
| C.4 | single intercepts: | medium interval |
| C.5 | | small interval |
| C.6 | nearest grain: | large interval |
| C.7 | | medium interval |

D. ribbon-counting
D.1    broad ribbon
D.2    medium ribbon
D.3    narrow ribbon

The figure within each bar gives the number of grain measurments by that method. (Redrawn from Middleton *et al.* 1985, Fig. 4.)

counting and point-counting: the former estimates the proportions of numbers of grains in each size group, while the latter estimates the proportion of the *area* of the section occupied by grains of each size group. Neither is 'better' than the other – the choice depends on one's aims – but if a possible difference between fabrics is the addition of larger grains to one of them (e.g. as deliberate temper), then point-counting is definitely preferable. Of the options within point-counting, multiple intercepts is best, since it gives an unbiased estimate of area (the other methods favour smaller grains). The other counts tend to give a mean grain size between those produced by area-counting and point-counting, with some variation depending on the width and/or spacing of lines or transects (Fig. 7.2). It is thus important that comparisons should only be made between samples that have been subject to the same method (otherwise

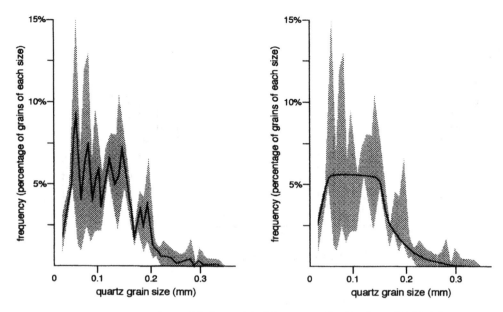

Fig. 7.3 Comparison of (*left*) empirical frequency distribution with (*right*) a corresponding smoothed frequency distribution. The shaded zone shows one standard deviation, based on a sample of 150 grains from each of five sherds. (Redrawn from Streeten 1982, Fig. 14.4.)

we may be comparing methods rather than samples), and that the method as well as the results is fully documented.

(c) The traditional method of characterising the grain size distribution goes back to sedimentary petrology, and is basically a graphical method of estimating the 'moments' of the distribution – its mean, standard deviation, skewness and kurtosis (Folk and Ward 1957). It is a cumbersome and unreliable approach. Today it would be better to use either a model-based approach, such as that advocated by Fieller and Nicholson (1991) (see p. 179); this makes use of the interesting statistic $N_{crit}$ defined as the 'smallest sample size at which the fit of the distribution would be declared unsatisfactory by a chi-squared goodness-of-fit test at the five percent level of significance' (1991, 75–6; see p. 44). Alternatively, one could use a more exploratory technique that makes fewer assumptions, such as *kernel density estimation* (*kde*) (Beardah and Baxter 1996). The idea of simply plotting the grain size distribution and comparing different samples visually can be seen in Streeten (1982), but his plots suffer from sampling variation and appear very 'spiky', making them difficult to compare; some form of smoothing is needed (Fig. 7.3). Today *kde*, which estimates the shape of the underlying distribution, is probably the best way to do this.

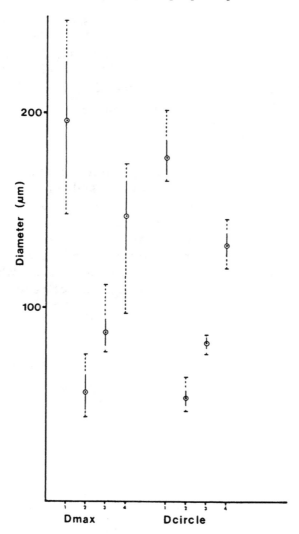

Fig. 7.4  Reproducibility of repeated measurements of grains using $D_{max}$ and $D_{circle}$ (redrawn from Middleton *et al.* 1985, Fig. 2).

(d) Inevitably, there will be variation between sherds from the same vessel, between samples from the same sherd, and between observers. The aim should be to minimise the last, and to check that the other sources of variation are not large enough to upset our conclusions. One aspect where inter-observer variation is important is in the measurement of grain size; Middleton *et al.* (1985, 65–6) showed that, if an image analyser is used, the diameter $D_{circle}$ (the diameter of the circle with the same area as the grain) is more precisely measured than $D_{max}$ (the maximum diameter of the grain) (see Fig. 7.4).

Streeten (1982, 128) took repeated samples from the same sherd, obtaining results that were 'remarkably consistent'. Stoltman (1989) took four sherds per vessel and point-counted each twice, distinguishing between 'sampling error' (i.e. between sherds) and 'counting error' (i.e. between repeated counts of the same section), and concluded that 'a single sherd is capable of reliably representing the vessel with an error factor [in mean grain size] of 3.5%'.

### Conclusion

There are some interesting parallels between sampling at this scale and sampling at the regional or site level. There are similar choices about sampling strategies – quadrats (areas), transects (ribbons) or counts, and about the spacing of the sampling units. One important difference is that at this scale the main aim is likely to be estimation, rather than discovery. Samples at this scale are likely to be much 'larger', in terms of numbers of objects found in them, and there are not likely to be such problems of visibility (p. 75). Nevertheless, what unites is perhaps more than what divides, and experience at one scale may well suggest fruitful lines of approach at the other.

**8**

# 'IN ITS DEPTHS, WHAT TREASURES'

### Introduction

Having looked at sampling at a wide range of scales, from the regional to the microscopic, we now turn to our final topic – the sampling of objects from museum stores. This may seem to be an unusual topic for a book on archaeology, but there are several good reasons for including it:

(a) since the museum store is the ultimate destination of most archaeological finds, we as archaeologists have a legitimate interest in their care there;

(b) the museum store makes an excellent vehicle for demonstrating some of the approaches described in chapter 2;

(c) the application of some approaches is particularly clear here, since some of the problems typically associated with sampling in the field may be avoided;

(d) techniques have been developed for repeated sampling (p. 201), which have potential for use at other scales, but have not yet been applied there;

(e) I have had a long personal involvement and interest in this topic.

### Historical background

In the UK, statistical interest in the care of museum collections was stimulated by the publication of a report from the National Audit Office (1987–8), although of course the care of collections has always been a recognised duty of museums. The first survey intended to establish the overall condition of an entire collection seems to have been one undertaken by the Horniman Museum (London) in the late 1980s (Walker and Bacon 1987). When, shortly after, the Museum of London decided to undertake similar surveys (Keene 1991), the immense amount of work that would have been involved in surveying a complete collection meant that sampling was an obvious, indeed a necessary, option, and I was asked to advise on the statistical aspects. The nearest parallels were on work that had been done on library collections in the 1980s (Anon. 1984; 1985), but it seemed more appropriate to define the problems and design the surveys from first principles. Funding was obtained from the Office of Arts and Libraries for a series of short surveys of various of the Museum of London collections; preliminary reports (Keene 1990a and b) were followed by a more detailed one (Keene 1991), and the statistical aspects were described shortly after (Keene and Orton 1992).

At about this time, the Horniman Museum expressed interest in resurveying its collections to assess the scale of any changes that had taken place since 1987, as part of a planned programme of routine assessment. Some design work was undertaken, but for various reasons the survey itself was delayed and it was therefore decided to publish the design by itself as an aid to others who might be thinking in the same direction (Orton 1996). So far, the only expression of interest in the methodology has come from the MARS project (p. 107). Parallel work at the British Museum (Leese and Bradley 1995) concentrated on other important aspects, such as inter-observer consistency, rather than on sampling issues as such.

I would not like to suggest that interest in collection condition surveys, as they have become known, exists only in the UK. There is clear international recognition of the importance of such exercises (e.g. Craft and Jones 1981; Anon. 1991); what is not so clear is the extent to which sampling is used in them. It may well be that such work has gone on unreported.

### Theory and practice

Although this is a relatively new topic, a coherent methodological framework seems to be developing. This may be because the issues are more clear-cut, giving less scope for variation in practice, or because the work has been undertaken under the auspices of a Working Party (Keene 1991), which has ensured a certain consistency of approach. Whatever the reason, it certainly makes it easier to describe the approach that has been followed, and again we use Cochran's twelve stages (p. 27) to structure the description.

#### Assimilation of existing knowledge

Two radically different situations can be envisaged:

(a)    a collection on which no such survey has previously been done,
(b)    a collection which has already been surveyed (or censused), as at the Horniman Museum.

(a) Although there is no knowledge relating directly to the objects in the collection, there may be much information about its organisation within the store – boxes, shelves, bays, etc. – which will be useful in designing a sampling frame (p. 197). Sometimes the size of the collection (the number of objects) may be known or estimated; this may not be as useful as it seems, because (i) the actual size of the sample is more important than the sampling fraction (p. 22), and (ii) such a figure often turns out to have been an over-estimate when the collection is surveyed. Collections seem rarely to be as large as their curators believe.

(b) A previous census or survey, by contrast, provides a great deal of information. Provided the data are in the same format as that proposed for the present survey, this is just the sort of information needed to design an efficient sample, if the questions to be asked are of a 'snap-shot' type (see *objectives* below). If, however, the questions are about *change* since the previous census or survey, the relationship between condition at a point in time and subsequent changes is more problematic, and may need one or more repeated surveys to clarify it (p. 201).

### Objectives of the survey

As we have already seen, surveys can be divided into the *static* and the *dynamic* – those whose aim is to provide a 'snap-shot' of the condition of a collection at a point in time, and those that are concerned with monitoring changes in condition over time, perhaps at regular intervals such as every year or every three years. A further distinction can be made between *condition surveys* and *conservation surveys*: the former are designed to characterise a complete collection, while the latter are carried out with a view to identifying the conservation status of all the objects in the collection (Leese and Bradley 1995, 82).

More detailed objectives can be specified than just the overall condition of a collection or its trend over time. Variations between the locations within a store may highlight problems of environment that require remedial action, while variations between similar objects that received different conservation treatments in the past may provide information on the effectiveness of those treatments (Keene and Orton 1985; Suenson-Taylor *et al.* 1999). An important objective of a static survey may be an assessment of the work needed to bring a collection up to an acceptable overall condition (Keene 1991, 5); while a dynamic survey can show whether progress is being made towards this end, or whether the collection is in fact deteriorating. More dramatic and overtly political aims may be met by producing statistics such as the 'half-life' of a collection – the time taken for half a collection to decay unless remedial action is taken – although in standard Risk Assessment theory objects would have to be weighted according to some measure of their value (Orton 1996, 150).

### Population to be sampled

It is useful to define a few terms at this stage.

> *Collection*: an administrative unit within the overall collection. There can be collections within collections. They can be divided into three types:

(a) *well organised*: neatly arranged in store, with all objects inven-
    toried, and total number of objects (population size) known;
(b) *partly organised*: well arranged in store, well described generally,
    but incomplete inventory and little idea of population size;
(c) *unorganised*: dispersed or disorganised in store, few or no objects
    inventoried, no factual estimate of population size.

*Store*: a self-contained room in which collections are kept.

*Storage location*: an important concept, on which the survey design
    rests. The smallest identifiable grouping of objects within a store,
    e.g. a shelf, a box on a shelf, a group on the floor, etc.

*Object*: the unit to which an individual observation relates. An
    object made up of component parts is counted as a single object
    (Keene and Orton 1992, 163).

The definition of a population thus does not normally cause problems, as it is
likely to coincide with a particular collection. If a collection is divided between
several areas (e.g. floors of a building, or even different buildings), the areas can
be thought of as sub-populations, or perhaps as separate *strata* (p. 30) within
the population. Minor problems of definition may be encountered in a dynamic survey. For example, objects may be lent out for exhibition, and new
ones may be acquired. At what point do they become, or cease to be, part of the
population?

### Data to be collected

As a minimum, the data to be collected are the identification of the object (e.g.
accession number) and a measure of its condition, usually as a point on a scale,
for example a four-point scale as used at the Museum of London:

> *urgent*: object at serious risk of further deterioration,
> *high*: object needs remedial treatment to prevent further deteriora-
>     tion,
> *low*: seriously disfigured but not deteriorating; treat before display,
> *little*: no work needed, or superficial cleaning only.

Usable definitions of the points must be provided to ensure, as far as possible,
consistency both within and between surveyors. Experiments have shown that
staff of different institutions differ in their view of the proportion of objects
requiring conservation, perhaps because of differing views as to the extent to
which the 'value' of an object should enter into the consideration (Newey *et al.*
1993; Leese and Bradley 1995, 82).

It should be remembered that, even if one surveyor or one team can examine
the whole of a sampled collection on one occasion, someone else may be
required to do so on another occasion, and the aim is to study variation over

time, not variation between surveyors. Recently, work has been done to attempt to create *criterion-anchored rating scales* (CARS, see Suenson-Taylor *et al.* 1999). As well as seeking to remove ambiguities of definition, it is claimed that these enable the data to be treated as *interval* rather than just *ordinal* data (p. 18), thus allowing a wider range of statistical techiques to be used.

Other data may be collected on the nature of the damage (if any), for example:

> major structural damage
> minor structural damage
> surface damage
> disfigurement
> chemical deterioration
> biological attack
> bad old repairs
> accretions
> (Keene 1991, 15).

If other data are available, e.g. on past treatments of the objects, they can be extremely useful, although the extent to which they can be used may depend on the compatibility of the various recording systems that may have been used.

### Degree of precision required

We start with a static survey, for which the aim is to estimate the proportion of objects in a certain condition category, with a chosen level of precision or for a chosen 'cost'. Since there are usually four such categories, there are four variables (the proportion in each category) for which we could in principle seek to optimise the design. In fact, there are more, because we could create a new variable by combining two original ones. In practice, it seems likely that it is the proportion in the *urgent*, or 'worst', category, or perhaps the total of the *urgent* and *high* categories, which we should seek to estimate most precisely. As usual, we have the choice of specifying the required level of precision (i.e. the standard deviation that we would like to see attached to the estimate of this proportion), and calculating the sample size and design needed to achieve it, or of specifying the resources that can be devoted to the survey, and then seeking a design to give the most precise results possible. The second is probably the more likely situation here; even so, it is worth having some idea of what an acceptable margin of error would be, since if the resources available cannot produce an acceptable margin, there is little point in undertaking the survey, except as a pilot survey.

Before we can look at the question of precision in a dynamic survey, we need to know what we are trying to estimate, and this requires some simple modelling. The chosen model is the *Markov chain* (Orton 1996), in which each

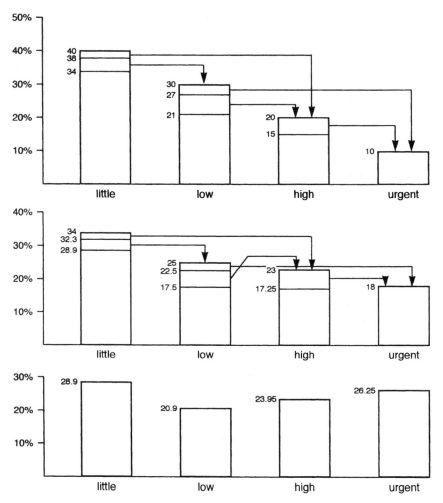

Fig. 8.1 Schematic representation of a Markov chain and its transition probabilities. Suppose that initially the percentages of objects in the four priorities (*little*, *low*, *high* and *urgent*) are 40, 30, 20 and 10 respectively (*top chart*), and that the transition probabilities over one year are:

*little* to *low*, 0.10; *little* to *high*, 0.05; *little* to *urgent*, 0;
*low* to *high*, 0.20; *low* to *urgent*, 0.10;
*high* to *urgent*, 0.25.

In this first year,   4% (i.e. 40% × 0.10) move from *little* to *low*,
               2% (i.e. 40% × 0.05) move from *little* to *high*,
               6% (i.e. 30% × 0.20) move from *low* to *high*,
               3% (i.e. 30% × 0.10) move from *low* to *urgent*,
               5% (i.e. 20% × 0.25) move from *little* to *low*,
so that at the end of the year the percentages in the four priorities are 34, 25, 23 and 18 respectively (*middle chart*).

object is in a certain 'state' at each survey (we have just four states here – the priority categories *urgent*, *high*, *low* and *little*), and may move from one state to another (or stay in the same state) from one survey to the next. The chance of an object moving from one state to another is known as a *transition probability* (Fig. 8.1), and it is these that we must estimate, since they determine the behaviour of the collection as a whole, in both the short and long term. Further details can be found in the appendix (pp. 210–23). Our estimates must be precise enough to give a clear indication of the trends in conservation status of the collection, e.g. is it deteriorating, or stable, or is the overall condition actually improving? This in turn depends on the sizes of the transition probabilities encountered in a particular collection, and on their variability. Not enough work has yet been done to indicate the sort of values that might be involved.

### Method of measurement

The usual method of measurement is directly on to a 'form' – either a pre-printed proforma or a 'form' that is part of a computer database or spreadsheet (Fig. 8.2). To prevent transcription errors, a data-entry device such as a *Psion* palm-top computer, that can easily be carried round a store, may be very useful. Definitions of the various condition categories should be provided in a way that the surveyor can take with him round the store, to minimise variability both 'between' and 'within' surveyors (p. 194–5).

### The frame

It would be possible to select either a simple random sample or a systematic sample (p. 21) by choosing objects from a catalogue or database, and then looking for those objects in the store, but this is likely to be a very inefficient way of selecting samples. It is better to employ a more structured approach, and to use *multi-stage* (probably two-stage) sampling (p. 33). The first step is to divide the store into *primary units*, which must be easy to define and recognise. How easy it is to do so will depend on the level of organisation of the store (p. 194). These units should normally correspond to store locations (p. 194); they should not be so large that one of them may include zones of different environmental conditions, since the effect of such conditions is something that

---

In the second year,   3.4% (i.e. 34% × 0.10) move from *little* to *low*,
1.7% (i.e. 34% × 0.05) move from *little* to *high*,
5.0% (i.e. 25% × 0.20) move from *low* to *high*,
2.5% (i.e. 25% × 0.10) move from *low* to *urgent*,
5.75% (i.e. 23% × 0.25) move from *little* to *low*,
so that at the end of the year the percentages in the four priorities are 28.9, 20.9, 23.95 and 26.25 respectively (*bottom chart*).

COLLECTION CONDITION SURVEY    Initials: _____    Date: _____    Conservation Section: PAP    Survey code: ___90 P___

Collection: ___PHO___

**The Museum of London**    Store: ___HPH___

Sub-collection: ___Henry Grant___

Priority codes

Damage factors:
MAJor: torn, very badly creased
MINor: slighter form of physical damage
BIOlogical: mould, pests (past or present — priority will reflect activity)
CHEMical: deterioration of support or image
SURface damage: flaking, lifting, crackled, scratched
DISfigured: stained, abraded, faded
OLD: sub-standard repairs
ACCretions: dirt or other

Run/group/loc ___1/4/7___

Storage type: Arch/Gen/Mass

1. URGENT  Actively deteriorating
2. HIGH    Remedial work needed to arrest deterioration
3. LOW     Needs repair/restoration before display
4. LITTLE  Superficial cleaning only, or none

Number per priority:
1 __0__  2 __2__  3 __9__  4 __12__

Work totals:    Treat __6__    Rem __—__    Mount __23__    Clean __1__

Total in location: ___121___
Total surveyed: ___23___

| Image No. | Simple Name | Process | Major | Min | Bio | Chem | Surf | Disf | Old | Accr | Work | Priority | Remarks |
|---|---|---|---|---|---|---|---|---|---|---|---|---|---|
| 1610/19 | Photo | Gest | ✓ | | | ✓ | | | | | MT | 3 | |
| 2050/3 | " | " | | ✓ | | | | | | | M | 4 | |
| 2109/23 | " | " | | | | | ✓ | | | | M | 4 | |
| 1801/44 | " | " | | ✓ | | | | ✓ | | | CM | 3 | |
| 1610/4 | " | " | | ✓ | | | | | | | M | 4 | |
| 2109/15 | " | " | | | | | | | | ✓ | M | 4 | |
| 2886/61 | " | " | | | | | | | | | M | 4 | |
| 1574/10 | " | " | | ✓ | | ✓ | ✓ | | | | TM | 2 | |
| 2508/38 | " | " | | ✓ | | ✓ | | | | | TM | 3 | |
| 2652/8 | " | " | | ✓ | | ✓ | | | | | TM | 3 | |
| 2109/2 | " | " | | | | | | | | | M | 4 | |
| 1610/13 | " | " | | | | | | | | | M | 4 | |

Fig. 8.2 Example of a recording form for a collection condition survey (Museum of London).

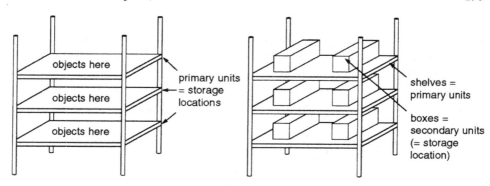

Fig. 8.3 Organisation of a store into primary units (storage location) and objects, or into primary units, secondary units and objects.

we are trying to isolate. In a large and complex store, we may need to define first primary units, and within them *secondary units* (corresponding to store locations as defined above) (Fig. 8.3). Within each unit, objects should be uniquely identified; there may be a problem if several objects (e.g. coins, nails) have been accessioned under one number. If they can be recognised as distinct, they can be given sub-numbers (e.g. n.1, n.2, etc.), but, bearing in mind that they may have to be re-surveyed at a later date, it may be necessary to survey them 'in bulk' and to give an overall assessment of their condition. Otherwise it may not be possible to ascertain which object was the one surveyed previously, and so to assess any change in its condition.

It is important, in setting up the frame, to minimise the possibility of subjective decisions by the surveyor(s) in the choice of objects for the sample. In practice, this means that there should be a set order, or route, through the primary (and secondary) units, and a set procedure for defining an order to the objects within a sampling unit. This is particularly important if, as is often the case, the sample is to be chosen by *systematic sampling* (p. 21). Otherwise, it is surprisingly easy for a surveyor subconsciously to arrange the contents of a location so as to select those in the best condition, or perhaps the worst (or perhaps those whose recording involves the least work).

### Selection of the sample

We must at this stage decide on two *sampling fractions* (p. 22): the proportion of primary units to be selected, and the proportion of objects to be selected in each primary unit (if the frame includes secondary units, then there will be *three* sampling fractions to be decided). Decisions must also be made about whether to employ simple random sampling for both primary units and objects, or whether some other method might be more appropriate, such as *pps* (or *ppes*) sampling for primary units (see p. 34), and *systematic sampling* (p. 21) for objects. As always, there is a balance between efficiency (which does not necessarily mean the smallest sample in terms of numbers of objects, but the one that achieves the required sampling errors (p. 30) for the least effort) and simplicity, both in taking the sample and in analysing the results. It is important that the surveyors understand what they are doing, and why; and over-complex design may only cause confusion, which may lead to errors in its execution.

At one extreme, we might decide to sample *all* primary units, or, at the other, to sample all objects within the chosen primary units (thus creating *cluster samples*, p. 30). Another extreme would be to sample only *one* object from each primary unit, which might be the case if the pilot survey showed the within-unit variation to be very low; it is very unlikely that a design would specify only one primary unit. But most likely, the optimal design will fall somewhere between these extremes. The mathematical details of choosing the two sampling fractions are given in the appendix (pp. 222–3); we note here simply that the more variation there is *within* primary units, the higher the sampling fraction within them will have to be, while the higher the variation *between* units, the more units will have to be chosen. We also note that a realistic design must take into account the cost of various activities, such as the locating of units and objects, as well as of actually surveying the chosen objects.

There may be an argument for selecting the primary units by pps or ppes (p. 34) rather than by simple random sampling, particularly if they vary greatly in size (i.e. in numbers of objects).

Systematic sampling is an attractive option for sampling within units. It is quick and simple to carry out, is easy for the surveyor to understand, and involves little use of random numbers, except perhaps in the choice of starting point. It is unlikely, as may occur in purely spatial sampling (p. 22), that the sampling interval will coincide with some regularity in the objects, thus leading to unreliable results. The main danger, mentioned above (p. 199), is that it may allow the surveyor subconsciously to choose particular objects by defining a particular route through the primary unit. This can easily be dealt with by specifying a route that is to be followed through each primary unit, for example, in lines front-to-back or side-to-side (Fig. 8.4).

The idea of adaptive sampling (p. 34) seems to hold some promise in this field, although it has not yet been used. Although the 'space' of the store has been made one-dimensional by the definition of a route through it (in contrast to the more usual two-dimensional situation, for example of chapters 4 and 5), this does not preclude the use of adaptive sampling. It would be possible, for example, to define a neighbourhood as the objects immediately before and after the chosen object along the route, and the condition as the assignment of the chosen object to the 'worst' condition category. Sampling would then continue until a 'string' (the analogy of a network) of objects in the 'worst' condition had been identified, bounded at each end by an object in less bad

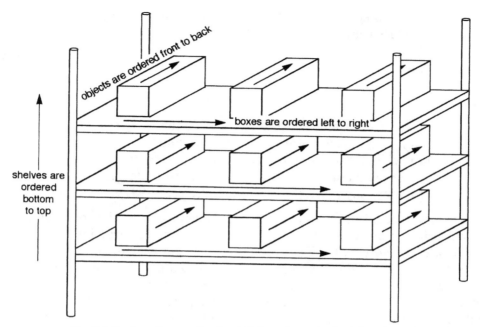

objects are ordered front to back

boxes are ordered left to right

shelves are ordered bottom to top

Fig. 8.4 Systematic sampling by defining a 'route' to be taken through a collection.

condition. This approach would be very suitable if objects in the 'worst' condition did in fact occur in localised clusters, perhaps owing to local storage conditions or to the infective spread of some destructive condition.

For a dynamic survey, we are into the topic of *repeated sampling* (Cochran 1963, 341–52), where we may wish to estimate one or more of three aspects:

1  the change in the numbers of objects in each category, from one survey to the next,
2  the average numbers in each category over a run of surveys,
3  the number in each category at the most recent survey.

We are likely to be interested in 1 (so that we can estimate transition probabilities) and 3 (because the present condition of the collection is always likely to be of interest), but not in 2. Cochran (1963, 342) gives the optimum sampling strategy for each situation:

for 1, it is best to retain the same sample from one survey to the next;
for 3, replacing part of the sample at each survey may give the best results.

If (as here) the interest lies in both 1 and 3, he recommends retaining a large proportion of the sample (e.g. $\frac{2}{3}$, or $\frac{3}{4}$, or $\frac{4}{5}$) from one survey to the next. I favour a high proportion such as $\frac{4}{5}$. Expressing the proportion as a simple fraction in this way makes it easy to integrate the approach with systematic sampling, since the selected objects can be numbered 1, 2, 3, 4, 5, 1, . . . , and after the first survey the '1s' can be replaced by the next object, after the second survey the '2s' can be replaced, and so on (Orton 1996, 152).

### The pre-test

The main issues in selecting the sample will be:

(a)   to achieve an efficient balance between sampling primary units and sampling objects within primary units, and

(b)   to achieve a sample size that can be surveyed in the time available, since the main constraint is often surveyor time, for which special funding may well have to be sought (Keene 1991).

The first is a technical issue related to the balance of variation between and within primary units (pp. 197, 222); some estimates of variability, however rough, are therefore useful. The second is important because a design can be ruined if there is not time to complete the designed programme of work. It is important to have estimates, not only of the time taken to survey and record an actual object (which can be a surprisingly small part of the overall time taken), but of the 'overheads' of locating and identifying both primary units and objects within them.

For both reasons, it is important that a small pilot study should be undertaken. It will also have the beneficial effect of highlighting any errors or omissions in the recording form (p. 197). However hard one tries, it is almost impossible to devise a 'fool-proof' form without actually testing it in a practical situation. The requirements and organisation of a pilot survey are discussed in detail by Keene (1991, Appendix B).

### Organisation of the fieldwork

It should be clear by now that the main ingredients of a successful survey should be in place well before the survey starts. They include: clear aims and objectives (p. 193), an unambiguous sampling frame and sampling procedure (p. 197), clear and workable definitions of the categories of condition and damage (p. 194), some idea of the variability of the collection (p. 195), a documentation system (whether on paper or computer) that ensures that all the necessary information is collected (p. 197), and a procedure for analysis of the results (p. 203). If, as is often the case, the work is to be done by staff brought in on short-term contracts, then attention must be paid to their training and motivation. If possible, it is a good idea for surveyors to work in pairs, one examining objects and the other recording the outcomes, and occasionally exchanging tasks. This can reduce the feelings of loneliness and isolation that may arise, and provide a check against gross errors of recording. In the Museum of London surveys, it was found that this way of working was more than twice as fast as surveyors working by themselves (Keene and Orton 1992, 165).

### Summary and analysis of the data

The procedure for summary and analysis must be settled before a survey starts, and if possible tested on the pilot survey (p. 202). Nothing is more futile and dispiriting than collecting a large body of data and then being unable to analyse it. The main aim is likely to be to produce tables showing the proportions of objects in each category, both for the collection as a whole and probably for sub-collections and/or different materials. These may be linked to estimates of total numbers to show (for example) implications for future conservation needs. Formal statistical tests, such as that of the significance of the difference in the proportion in a certain category between two sub-collections, or two materials, may be required (p. 24). Graphical output can be used to supplement the tables, to make particular points more immediately apparent to the reader, but it should not be seen as a substitute.

Ideally, all these requirements should be met by a single computer package, such as one of the survey analysis packages now available (e.g. Anon. 1989). Alternatively, it is quite straightforward to carry out data entry and initial analysis on a spreadsheet (Microsoft *Works* was used for this stage at the Museum of London), although a more sophisticated package may be needed for advanced analyses (*Systat* was used at the Museum of London, see Keene 1991, 27). Graphical output is part of all modern packages, although care must be exercised over the choice of graphical format – some, such as the unnecessary use of three-dimensional graphics, can obscure rather than clarify (Orton 1999).

### Information gained for future surveys

Unlike in the field situation, surveys should always be undertaken on the assumption that future surveys will be carried out on the same material, either as part of a planned long-term programme, or as another 'one-off' decided on at a later date. It seems very unlikely that a museum, having once surveyed the condition of its collections, would decide never to do so again. The implications are that arrangements must be made for the long-term maintenance of the sampling frame. In particular it should be possible, without enormous effort, to reidentify a specific object that has been sampled in a previous survey, to assess any change in condition (any subsequent survey is likely to include a proportion of objects that were examined in a previous survey, see p. 201). Also, important information may be gained about the relative variation between and within primary units, which will be of help in designing future surveys, as will data on the time taken to accomplish various tasks, such as locating and surveying objects. In a sense, each survey can be seen as a pilot towards the next one, and the keeping of comprehensive and accessible records will make the task much easier in the future.

### A case study

For a case study I have chosen the survey of the Social History/Applied Art Collection at the Museum of London (Keene 1991; Keene and Orton 1992). This was an extremely heterogeneous collection, consisting of an estimated total of about 50,000 objects, of a wide variety of classes, from nearly 3000 locations in eight separate stores. The resources available were two person-months, including time for the pilot survey and writing up. The pilot survey examined all the objects (a total of 684) from 42 locations and took about 30 person-hours. It provided information on the between- and within-location variability in the condition of objects, as well as indirect information on the average time taken to examine an object, and the overhead times per location and per store (p. 223). Some difficulty was encountered in estimating these parameters; the figures finally used to design the main sample were (a) over-head per store – 1 hour, (b) overhead per location – 0.3 hours (i.e. 18 minutes), (c) time per object – 0.013 hours (just under one minute).

Application of Cochran's formula (**8.5**) suggested that the average number of objects to be surveyed per location should be four; in the heat of the moment an arithmetical error led to a figure of two being used. This implied that the sampling fraction for objects at each location should be 1 in 8, and to make the correct total workload, the sampling fraction for locations should be 1 in 4. In actual numbers, these translate to a sample of 1500 objects from 750 locations, which, it was estimated, would have given a standard deviation of 1% on the proportion of objects in the 'urgent' and 'high' categories taken together.

In the event, a rather larger sample of 2449 objects from 991 locations (average 2.5 per location) was taken, probably reflecting an increase in speed as the surveyor became familiar with the procedures. The estimate of the proportion in the two categories of interest was 18.2% (compared to 13.1% in the pilot survey), with a standard deviation of 0.85%. In other words, one could be 95% certain that the proportion in these categories in the collection as a whole lay between 16.5% and 19.9%. It is interesting to note that there is very little difference between the standard deviation based on an average of two objects per location and one based on an average of four objects per location. This is because the standard deviation is fairly insensitive to variation in the ratio of the two sampling fractions, provided that the overall workload is kept the same – a reassuring feature of two-stage sampling, since our estimates of the workload parameters may be rather vague, and (as here) mistakes may be made in the calculation.

Out of interest, we also calculated the standard deviation that would have

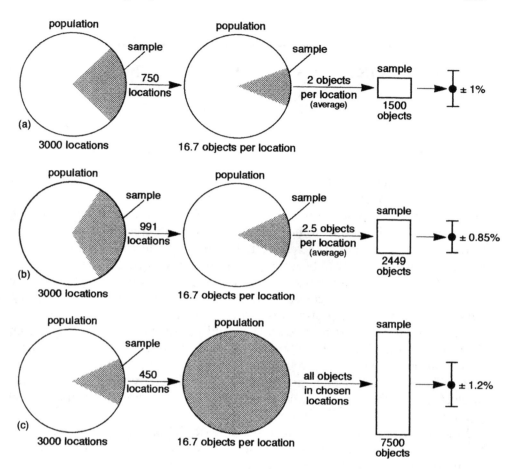

Fig. 8.5 The Museum of London Social History collection survey. Comparison of design and precision for (a) optimum survey, (b) actual survey, (c) scaled-up pilot survey.

been achieved if we had simply scaled up the pilot survey to fit the time available. This would have resulted in a sample of all the objects (a total of about 7500) from 450 locations, and would have had a standard deviation of about 1.2%, which is higher than that of the planned survey of only 1500 objects. The various sample designs and outcomes are compared in Fig. 8.5. This shows that there would be no point in examining more than a few objects from each location, because the variation within the collection was mostly concentrated between locations rather than within them; in other words, objects at the same location tended to be in similar condition.

**9**

---

# BEYOND RANDOM SAMPLING

### Introduction

Well, you have made it. Here we are at the final chapter, ready to review what we have learnt from this survey of the role of sampling in archaeological theory and practice, and to see how it might be applied in the future, both in the discipline as a whole and in individual professional careers. I hope that you have read at least some of the chapters that are outside your own immediate practical concerns, and are beginning to see how a knowledge of work undertaken at other scales can broaden your vision and expand your ideas. At the same time, it should be recognised that the scales defined here are arbitrary, devised for the purposes of structuring this book. In reality, of course, there is a continuum, and work at no one scale should be considered in isolation from the others. In this chapter I shall try to highlight what I consider to be the main opportunities provided for archaeologists both by recent (and some not-so-recent) developments in statistical sampling theory and by rapid developments in electronic technology, as well as some of the problems in archaeological practice that remain to be overcome.

First, though, I must pause to re-emphasise the centrality of sampling to both archaeological theory and practice. We saw in chapter 3 how sampling theory can make a useful contribution to debates about archaeological inference in the face of distorting factors imposed by site formation processes. Its main value is in providing a language and a frame of reference within which such problems can be discussed, rather than in definitive answers. The remaining chapters show that sampling is an essential approach in the struggle to balance the needs of archaeological research with the limitations of archaeological resources, at whatever scale one is primarily working. The point is also made that increased resources (however welcome they may be) are not the whole answer, since data only make sense within a theoretical framework, and in any project a point will come where the accumulation of additional data beyond the needs of the questions being asked cannot be justified. Sampling theory is about assessing the level of resources needed to provide answers to questions, and about the efficient use of such resources.

This should give the lie to anyone who thinks that:

(a) sampling was a product of the New Archaeology, and
(b) its value has faded with the fading of New Archaeological thinking.

206

Certainly, explicit sampling came to prominence in the New Archaeology era of the 1960s and 1970s, but that came from a desire to make explicit, and to formalise, some existing archaeological practices, especially the regional survey. The CRM approach in the USA, and its British counterpart, the PPG 16 regime, provide a forum in which sound sampling practice is still needed on a day-to-day basis. More overtly theoretical projects, not driven by the demands of development, still require a consideration of sampling as part of their research design, whatever their theoretical basis. Sampling *is* still on the agenda, even if it is not discussed as openly or explicitly as it was, say, in the 1970s and 1980s.

## Opportunities

Statistical sampling theory has not stood still since it made its first major impact on the worlds of industry and research in the 1940s and 1950s. First came the idea of *pps sampling* (p. 34), which enabled spatial samplers to break out from the rigid regime of 'geometrically correct' quadrats and transects. It became perfectly possible to incorporate those tiresome natural boundaries, such as coastlines and rivers, into a sample design, and to use topographical or man-made features (provided they had some guarantee of longevity) as a basis for the definition of sampling units. But archaeologists struggled on in a sort of self-imposed straitjacket of very rigid and inflexible sample designs, occasionally ridiculed by other archaeologists (e.g. Hole 1980) but never, it seems, actually doing anything about it. The feeling that archaeologists are in some sense 'missing out' on what are by now quite old advances in theory was one of my motivations for proposing this book (p. 11).

Imagine my surprise and delight, then, in discovering the flexibility and intuitive appeal of adaptive sampling (pp. 34, 213). Here is an approach which allows the design of a sample to modify itself in the light of initial findings, yet remains statistically rigorous – perhaps one can have one's cake and eat it, after all. This is something that field archaeologists in particular must take into their repertoires, and which those working at other scales should certainly seriously consider. The two case studies presented here (pp. 93, 133) are both reworkings of old data; although they have the benefit of allowing comparisons to be made with more conventional approaches to sampling, they still leave a need for a show-case application to a fresh problem. Who will be first? But archaeologists must also learn from history, and not just take on board the '1996' view of adaptive sampling, and ignore any future developments in it. For example, the method developed in chapter 4 (p. 94) to cope with 'large' sites is new in statistical as well as archaeological terms, and other developments in statistical theory may well be needed to accommodate it to archaeological needs. The challenge is there.

Another example of serendipity in the timing of this book is the emergence, at long last, of a practical use of Bayesian statistics (p. 16) in sample survey (p. 119). There has long been a need for a way to formalise our existing knowledge about (for example) a development area, so that when the time comes to investigate it, we can make best use of the resources available. In principle, Bayesian statistics, with its deceptively simple basis of

$$\text{prior belief} + \text{data} = \text{posterior belief},$$

provides a way forward, but practical implementation has been a long time coming. Looking at the underlying mathematics, one can begin to understand why. Nevertheless, it is here now, and offers potential benefits (not least, the tempting offer of 'free' sampling units) to those prepared to master it. Once again, who will take up the challenge?

The last of my opportunities lies not in advances in theory but in new technology. The current development of *personal data assistants* (PDAs) that can locate themselves in the field, record data and transmit it to base could revolutionise the way in which extensive fieldwork is done, within a few years (p. 83). No doubt the technology will be expensive at first, but its widespread adoption in other areas (e.g. agriculture, tourism) is likely to drive costs down to an affordable level quite quickly. Or so I hope.

### Problems

The main outstanding problems seem to concentrate around the nature of much of archaeological sampling as *cluster sampling* (p. 30). This is an inevitable consequence of the fact that, very often, we do not have an explicit population of archaeological objects from which to sample, but must sample more general entities (e.g. territory) and, so to speak, pick up the archaeology on the way. The issue was recognised relatively earlier in the context of regional survey (Mueller 1975a). The fact of cluster sampling in itself does not matter; it has a well-developed theory (see p. 212) which can be, and often is, applied to such problems. It is most often at the smaller scales that it can go unrecognised. The problem then is that inappropriate statistical formulae are used to analyse the resulting data (p. 166). The outcome is likely to be that the variability of the data is under-stated, which can result in different populations being assessed as 'statistically different', when they may in fact be 'statistically the same'. There are practical implications, since there is no way in which margins of error ($\pm$) can be put on (for example) proportions of species in a feature, based on one sample, however large, or on proportions of different types of inclusions in a ceramic vessel, based on one thin-section. Several samples are needed just to assess the level of variability within the feature or vessel; it may well be that each sample can then be quite small, and still give sufficient power to discriminate our feature or vessel from other types of feature or vessel.

Before the field archaeologists get too smug about this, a serious problem at the scale of the site evaluation (p. 115) must be pointed out. It seems to me that most evaluations lack any sort of formal design criteria, i.e. formal and justifiable reasons why a certain design of trenches and/or test-pits is thought to be adequate for a particular site. The effect is that we have no way of telling whether (for example) PPG 16 is succeeding in its aim of minimising the unrecorded destruction of significant archaeological remains (SARS, see p. 119) in Britain. There are two 'loop-holes' which may allow this to happen:

(a)   failure to select for evaluation development sites which contain SARS;

(b)   failure of evaluations to detect SARS on development sites which contain them.

The former is not really a sampling issue, but the second is very much so. The point is impossible to check directly – it would require the total excavation of a sample of evaluated sites to discover what has been 'missed', which is impractical for many reasons. Experiments have only been able to check areas where initial investigations suggested SARS were likely to be found (p. 124). A more realistic, but perhaps archaeologically less satisfying, approach is through the idea of 'quality assurance'. In this approach, the brief would contain a definition of SAR that was appropriate for the particular situation, and a required probability that, should such a SAR exist on the development site, the evaluation would actually detect it. Contractors bidding for the job would have to show that their project design met these criteria. Of course, this idea is at present hopelessly idealistic – most curators or contractors would not be able to tell whether a particular design met such criteria or not. But if the practice is to achieve a level of academic credibility and overcome the doubts that have been expressed about it, it must move in this direction. Chapter 5 has provided suggestions as to how this might be done, including the use of Bayesian statistics to reduce the workload through the incorporation of existing knowledge.

## Farewell

And now it really is time to finish. I hope that you have enjoyed reading this book as much as I have enjoyed writing it, and that you have not been too disappointed by the lack of detailed step-by-step instructions. It has been my intention to liberate, not to replace one straitjacket by another, but also to point out the limits within which that freedom can be exercised. The important thing is to grasp securely the principles involved, and then to ask how they can be applied in one's particular circumstances. There is much to be done before the potential for sampling in archaeology can be fully exploited; I hope that you feel you can take your part in this venture and I wish you every joy and success.

# Appendix

The purpose of this appendix is to bring together the mathematical formulae that would otherwise break up the flow of the main text of the book. They are arranged here according to the chapter from which they are referred.

### From chapter 2

We start with those that are needed in order to calculate estimates and their standard errors, sample sizes and allocations, under a variety of circumstances.

#### Notation

A conventional notation, as employed by Cochran (1963), is used here. It denotes characteristics of the population by upper case letters, and those of the sample by lower case. The size of a population is $N$ units, and that of a sample is $n$ units. The letter $y$ is used to denote a variable, $x$ a second variable, and so on; the subscript $i$ denotes their value on the $i$th member of the population or of the sample, as appropriate. The population total is called $\bar{Y}$ and its mean ; its variance is denoted by $S^2$.

The 'hat' (e.g. $\hat{Y}$) is used to denote an estimate. The sampling fraction is $f = n/N$.

#### Simple random sampling

Estimate: the population mean is estimated by the sample mean, i.e.

$$\hat{\bar{Y}} = \bar{y} = \sum_1^n y_i/n$$

and the population total by

$$\hat{Y} = N\bar{y} \tag{2.1}$$

and the standard errors are estimated by

$$s_{\bar{y}} = (\sqrt{1-f})s/\sqrt{n}$$
$$s_{\hat{Y}} = (N\sqrt{1-f})s/\sqrt{n} \tag{2.2}$$

where $s$ is the sample standard deviation, defined by

$$s^2 = \sum_{i=1}^{n} (y_i - \bar{y})^2/(n-1)$$

If we know the value of the variance $V$ that we require the sample mean to have, we can use equation **2.2** to solve for the required sample size $n$. This is best done in two stages: first on the assumption that the sampling fraction $f$ is so small that it can safely be ignored, leading to

$$n_0 = s^2/V$$

and if $n_0/N$ is not small, we make the correction

$$n = n_0/(1 + (n_0/N)) \tag{2.3}$$

We may also want to estimate the proportion of items that belong to a particular class (e.g. the proportion of sites of a particular period). If the total number of items in a class is $A$, and the number of that class in our sample is $a$, then the estimate of the proportion $P = A/N$ is

$$p = a/n, \tag{2.4}$$

and its variance is

$$v(p) = \frac{(N-n)}{(n-1)N}pq \tag{2.5}$$

where $q$ is defined as $q = 1 - p$.

Note that in this situation, we do not need an explicit sample standard deviation, as it is in effect provided through the values of $p$ and $q$. The number $a$ is said to have a *binomial distribution* (e.g. Cochran 1963, 54).

The formula for the required sample size now becomes

$$n_0 = pq/V$$

with the correction

$$n = n_0/(1 + (n_0/N)) \tag{2.6}$$

if it is not small.

### Stratified sampling

The number of strata is $L$, and they are denoted by the subscript $h$, so that $f_h = n_h/N_h$ for $h = 1, \ldots, L$. The 'weights' of the strata in the population are $W_h = N_h/N$, and in the sample are $w_h = n_h/n$.

The estimate of the population mean is

$$\hat{\bar{Y}} = (\Sigma_1^L N_h \bar{y}_h)/N \tag{2.7}$$

and its variance is estimated by

$$v(\hat{\bar{Y}}) \equiv s_{\hat{\bar{Y}}}^2 = (\Sigma_1^L N_h(N_h - n_h)s_h^2/n_h)/N^2 \tag{2.8}$$

and its standard error is just the square root of this.

There are analogous formulae for estimating proportions from stratified samples (Cochran 1963, 106–7).

Optimum allocation (i.e. the values of $n_h$ which minimise this variance for a given total sample size $n$) is given by

$$n_h = n(N_h S_h)/\Sigma_1^L N_h S_h \tag{2.9}$$

on the assumption that the cost of sampling a unit in each stratum is the same. A more complicated formula for variable costs was given by Cochran (1963, 96).

If the required variance of the sample mean is $V$, then the required sample size is given by (for proportional allocation, i.e. $w_h = W_h$)

$$n_0 = \Sigma W_h s_h^2/V \tag{2.10}$$

with the correction $n = n_0/(1 + (n_0/N))$ if needed.
For optimum allocation $w_h \propto W_h s_h$ and the formula is

$$n = (\Sigma W_h s_h)^2/(V + (\Sigma W_h s_h^2)/N) \tag{2.11}$$

*Cluster sampling*

We need some further notation: we use $M_i$ to denote the number of elements in the $i$th unit, and $M_0$ to denote the total number of elements in the population. The item total for the $i$th unit is

$$y_i = \Sigma_{j=1}^{M_i} y_{ij} = M_i \bar{y}_i$$

Then one estimate of the population mean per element is the sample mean per element, i.e.

$$\hat{\bar{Y}}_R = \Sigma_1^n y_i/\Sigma_1^n M_i \tag{2.12}$$

whose variance is given by

$$v(\hat{\bar{Y}}_R) \approx \left(\frac{N^2(1-f)}{nM_0^2}\right)\frac{\Sigma_1^N M_i^2(\bar{y}_i - \bar{\bar{Y}})^2}{N-1} \tag{2.13}$$

and which is known as the *ratio to size estimate*. It is often superior to the *unbiased estimate*

$$\hat{\bar{Y}} = \hat{Y}/M_0 = \frac{N}{nM_0}\Sigma_{i=1}^n y_i$$

and to the unweighted mean of the unit means

$$\bar{y}' = (\bar{y}_1 + \bar{y}_2 + \ldots + \bar{y}_n)/n$$

The same approach applies to cluster sampling for proportions (Cochran 1963, 64–5 and 247–8).

The estimate

$$\hat{p} = \Sigma_{i=1}^n a_i/\Sigma_{i=1}^n m_i \tag{2.14}$$

is a ratio estimate, whose variance is given by the formula

$$v(\hat{p}) \approx \left(\frac{1-f}{n\bar{M}^2}\right)\left(\frac{\Sigma_{i=1}^N M_i^2(p_i - P)^2}{N-1}\right) \tag{2.15}$$

where $\bar{M} = \Sigma M_i/N$ is the average size of cluster.
This can be estimated by

$$v(\hat{p}) \approx \left(\frac{1-f}{n\bar{m}^2}\right)\left(\frac{\Sigma a_i^2 - 2\hat{p}\Sigma a_i m_i + \hat{p}^2\Sigma m_i^2}{n-1}\right) \tag{2.16}$$

where $\bar{m} = \Sigma m_i/n$ is the average number of objects per cluster in the sample. If the sample is compared with a simple random sample of $n\bar{M}$ objects, then the change in variance is given by

$$\frac{v_{clus}(p)}{v_{ran}(p)} \approx \frac{\Sigma M_i^2(p_i - P)^2}{N\bar{M}PQ} \tag{2.17}$$

### Sampling with probability proportional to size (pps)

There are several possible estimators of the mean per element; one of the best is also one of the simplest – the sample mean $\bar{y}_i$. Unfortunately, the formula for its variance is not so simple

$$v(\bar{y}_i) = \frac{1}{M_0}\left[\Sigma_{i=1}^N(M_i - m_i)\frac{S_{2i}^2}{m_i} + \Sigma_{i=1}^N M_i(\bar{Y}_i - \bar{\bar{Y}})^2\right] \tag{2.18}$$

where $S_{2i}^2 = \frac{1}{M_i - 1}\Sigma_{j=1}^{M_i}(y_{ij} - \bar{Y}_i)^2$

(Cochran 1963, 294–5).

### Adaptive cluster sampling

We need some extra notation, taken from Thompson and Seber (1996, 96): the number of networks in the sample is $\kappa$, the number of units in the $k$th network is $x_k$, and the sum of the $y$-values in the $k$th network is $y_k^*$. The number of units in the initial sample is $n_1$.

Then an unbiased estimate of the average per unit is $\mu$, estimated by

$$\hat{\mu} = \frac{1}{N} \sum_{k=1}^{\kappa} \frac{y_k^*}{\alpha_k}, \tag{2.19}$$

where $\alpha_k = 1 - \left[ \binom{N - x_k}{n_1} \Big/ \binom{N}{n_1} \right]$.

Its precision is given by

$$v(\hat{\mu}) = \frac{1}{N^2} \left[ \sum_{j=1}^{\kappa} \sum_{k=1}^{\kappa} \frac{y_j^* y_k^*}{\alpha_{jk}} \left( \frac{\alpha_{jk}}{\alpha_j \alpha_k} - 1 \right) \right] \tag{2.20}$$

### Ratio estimates

Here we use $x$ to denote the auxiliary variable. If we want to estimate the population mean value of $y_i$, the formula is

$$\hat{\bar{Y}}_R = \frac{y}{x} \bar{X} \tag{2.21}$$

and the variance is estimated by

$$v(\hat{\bar{Y}}_R) \approx \frac{N(N - n)}{n(n - 1)} \sum_{i=1}^{n} (y_i - \hat{R} x_i)^2 \tag{2.22}$$

### Adjusting for imperfect detectability

We use here the notation of Thompson and Seber (1996, 211–33): the number of objects in unit $i$ is $\tau_i$, and the number detected by the observer is $y_i$. We wish to estimate

$$\tau = \sum_{i=1}^{N} \tau_i = N\mu$$

the total number of objects in the study region.

The detection probability is denoted by $g$ where $g < 1$.

The estimator that would be used if $g = 1$ is called $\tau_0$, and its variance is called $v_0$.

Then the new estimator is

$$\hat{\tau} = \frac{\tau_0}{g} \tag{2.23}$$

and its variance is estimated by

$$v(\hat{t}) = \frac{v_0}{g} + \frac{\hat{t}(1-g)}{g} \tag{2.24}$$

## From chapter 3

*The Petersen (or Lincoln) and related indices*

The aim of such indices is to estimate the number of animals in an original population from the numbers of 'left' and 'right' examples of a particular element. The notation is:

> $L$ = total number of left examples of a particular element found
> $R$ = total number of right examples of a particular element found
> $P$ = number of matching pairs present
> $N$ = estimate of number of animals in original population.

Then Krantz's estimate is

$$N_K = (L^2 + R^2)/2P \tag{3.1}$$

while the Petersen Index gives the estimate

$$N_P = LR/P \text{ if } P > 0,$$

$$\text{or} = (L+1)(R+1) \text{ if } P = 0 \tag{3.2}$$

It can be shown that $N_K \geq N_P$, with equality if and only if $L = R$.

Also, if $L = R = P$, then $N_P = \text{MNI}$.

A separate estimate can be made for each element. If they agree with each other (within the limits implied by their confidence intervals), they can be combined to give a more precise estimate, If not, that is in itself interesting information, and the reasons for the differences should be sought.

    The Petersen Index started life as a way of estimating the size of a living population by the method of capture and recapture. A sample of $n_1$ animals is captured, tagged in some way and then released into the wild. At a later date, a second sample of $n_2$ animals is captured and examined. The number of those recaptured (i.e. those with tags) is counted and called $m$. Then the proportion of tagged animals in the population is estimated to be $m/n_2$. But since the number of tagged animals is known to be $n_1$, the estimate of the size of the population is this number divided by the proportion, i.e.

$$n_1 \, n_2/m.$$

    In the archaeological analogy, the place of the first sample is taken by the 'left' elements, and that of the second sample by the 'right' elements (or *vice versa*, since the equation is symmetrical). Matched pairs correspond to animals that were captured for both samples.

*The exponential distribution*

Suppose that a population of objects decays in such a way that the probability of any particular object decaying remains the same over time. In other words, the probability of a particular object decaying within the next unit of time (say, within the next year) is the same however old that object happens to be. If this probability is denoted by the symbol $\lambda$, then the probability that it decays after $x$ years is given by the equation

$$p(x|\lambda) = \lambda e^{-\lambda x} \tag{3.3}$$

This is known as the *exponential distribution* (sometimes, the *negative exponential distribution*) (Patel *et al.* 1976, 87). The mean age at which the objects decay is $1/\lambda$, and the half-life is $0.693/\lambda$.

This is the simplest of many models that are used to represent the process of decay, as it represents the situation in which there is 'no ageing', i.e. the probability of decay neither increases with age ('positive ageing') nor decreases with age ('negative aging'). It is thus often used as a default model in situations where little is known or understood about the processes of aging.

**From chapter 4**

*Optimal layout of test units in a rectangular survey*

Here we follow the notation and argument of Krakker *et al.* (1983), as corrected slightly by Kintigh (1988). The length of the survey area is $L$ and its width $W$; the interval between test units along a row is $i$ and the spacing between rows is $s$. For a square grid and a 'staggered grid' (see Fig. 4.7) $i = s$, while for a hexagonal grid $s = i\sqrt{3/2} \approx 0.866i$. Then the maximum diameter $d$ of a site that does not have to be intersected is:

$$
\begin{array}{lll}
\text{square grid} & d = i\sqrt{2} \approx 1.414i, & = s\sqrt{2} \approx 1.414s \\
\text{staggered grid} & d = 1.25i & = 1.25s \\
\text{hexagonal grid} & d = 2i/\sqrt{3} \approx 1.155i & = 1.33s
\end{array}
\tag{4.1}
$$

**From chapter 5**

*Discovery probabilities*

Suppose that a population consists of $N$ sampling units, of which $M$ contain items of archaeological interest (e.g. sites in a region, features in a site). Suppose we want to be $p\%$ (e.g. 90%) certain of discovering at least one such unit in our sample. How big does the sample $n$ have to be? The formula is

$$n = \log(1 - p)/\log\left(1 - \frac{M}{N}\right) \tag{5.1}$$

(note that this is mathematically the same as the formula given by Read (1986, 484) and Shott (1987, 365), although it appears slightly different from them, as they do from each other).

This formula is the same as the one for the minimum size of 'small' units (mathematical points) needed to intersect, with chosen probability, the proportion $M/N$ of a development area that is occupied by archaeological remains, which formula is given by Orton (forthcoming) as:

$$N = \log(1 - p)/\log(1 - \theta_p) \qquad (5.2)$$

where $\theta$ is the proportion of the development area that is occupied by archaeological remains, and $\theta_p$ is the upper confidence limit for the estimate of $\theta$, given that no archaeological remains are found by the sample.

In the Bayesian situation, the parameter $\theta$ is modeled as a beta distribution (Patel *et al.* 1976, 136) with parameters $a$ and $b$. Nicholson and Barry (1995, 75) showed that if $a$ is set to the value 1, different prior beliefs about $\theta$ are represented by different values of $b$. The value $b = 1$ corresponds to a prior belief that all values of $\theta$ between 0 and 1 are equally likely. As $b$ increases, values $\theta$ of greater than 0.5 become increasingly less likely. For example, 'a prior belief expressed as being 95% sure that $\theta$ is less than 0.1 gives $b = 28.4$'. They also showed that the value of $b$ acts as 'the sample size of a hypothetical survey from which the species was absent' (1995, 76). Thus the prior beliefs can provide 'free' sampling units. The archaeological implications are discussed by Orton (forthcoming).

### Nance's Discovery Model

Nance (1981, 154–5) considered the situation where $K$ out of $N$ potential sampling units contain some item class, and units are randomly selected until $x$ units containing the item class are discovered. He asked the question for the case when $x = 1$, i.e. it is only necessary to discover the class once : 'what is the number, $n$, of units that must be examined to discover the item class?' (his notation has been changed slightly to bring it in line with that of this Appendix). He stated, for a finite population, that this number is given by the negative hypergeometric distribution (Patel *et al.* 1976, 206), whose expected value is

$$E[n] = xN/(k - 1) \qquad (5.3)$$

He gave an example in which $N = 100$, $k = 5$ and $x = 1$. Application of the formula gives the answer to be about 17 units.

He also considered the probability that at least one unit contains the item class of interest for various sample sizes, where the item class occurs in 1, 2, 5, 10 and 20% of the sampling units in the population, for a grid of 625 units. Denoting the proportion of units in the population containing the item class by $p$, and setting $q = 1 - p$, he calculated the probability using the binomial approximation:

$$\text{probability} = 1 - q^n \tag{5.4}$$

*Predicting the probability of failing to detect any features*

This is closely related to (**5.4**). Here $p$ is the proportion of quadrats containing a feature; in this example $p = 55/576 = 0.0955$. So the probability that a selected quadrat does not contain a feature is $q = 1 - p = 1 - .0955 = 0.9045$. This means that the probability that none of an initial selection of 20 quadrats contains a feature is

$$(0.9045)^{20} = 0.134,$$

that the probability that none of an simple random selection of 40 quadrats contains a feature is

$$(0.9045)^{40} = 0.018. \tag{5.5}$$

## From chapter 6

*Watson's formula for the numbers of bone fragments of different lengths*

Watson (1972, 221) denoted length by $L$ and frequency by $F$. The parameter $b$ depends only on sample size, while $a$ is site-specific but, in the sites considered by Watson, always lay between 1.5 and 1.8.

Then $L$ and $F$ are related by $\log_{10}F = (b - L)\log_{10}a$ \hfill (6.1)

For scaling factors, $d$ denotes the number of diagnostic fragments from a species, whose length is greater than a chosen arbitrary value (which must be greater than the critical length), and $D$ denotes the total number of diagnostic fragments of that species. The subscripts $u$ and $s$ denote unsieved and sieved samples respectively.

$$\text{Then } D_u = D_s d_u/d_s \tag{6.2}$$

*Differences between assemblages*

Suppose we measure a variable $Y$ on two samples $A$ and $B$, of sizes $n_A$ and $n_B$, and obtain values $y_{Ai}, i = 1, \ldots, n_A$ and $y_{Bj}, j = 1, \ldots, n_B$.

We are interested in the difference between $\bar{Y}_A$ and $\bar{Y}_B$, but only if it is greater than some critical value $C$.

A pilot samples gives us estimates $s_A^2$ and $s_B^2$ of the variances of the two samples.

The question is 'how big do our samples have to be, so that we can be $x$ certain ($x$ is less than 1, but only by a little, e.g. $x = 0.9$ or 90%) of saying that $\bar{Y}_A$ and $\bar{Y}_B$ are different, if the true difference between them is greater than $C$?'

We assume that the samples are of such size that the distributions of $\bar{y}_A$ and $\bar{y}_B$ are approximately Normal, but that the fpc can be ignored.

We approach this question by considering the null hypothesis $H_0$: $\bar{Y}_A = \bar{Y}_B$ or the simpler but equivalent null hypothesis $Y = 0$, where $Y = \bar{Y}_A - \bar{Y}_B$.

We want the probability of rejecting $H_0$, when $Y < -C$ or $Y > C$, to be more than $x$, and express this as $P(\text{reject } H_0 | |Y| > C) > x$.

We need a further condition, the probability of rejecting $H_0$ when $Y = 0$, which we want to be small, say $\alpha$. Finally, we need a test value of $y$, which we call $k$, such that we reject $H_0$ when $|y| > k$.

This leads to the equations

$$P(|y| > k | Y = 0) = \alpha,$$
$$P(|y| < k | Y = C) = x$$

which in turn lead to the equations

$$2\alpha = 1 - N(k/s) \text{ and}$$
$$x = ((k - C)/s) \text{ where N is the Normal distribution function.}$$

These can be solved to give values for $k$ and $s$ in terms of $C$, $x$ and $a$. To find $n_A$ and $n_B$, we note that

$$s^2 = (s_A^2/n_A) + (s_B^2/n_B)$$

and that the total sample size will be smallest when $n_B = (s_B^2/s_A^2)n_A$ and solve these equations for $n_A$ and $n_B$         **(6.3)**

### Measures of diversity
### Notation

The total number of classes (taxa, etc.) in a population is $T$, and in a sample is $t$. The 'importance value' (Cruz-Uribe 1988, 180) of the $i$th class in the population is $N_i$, and in the sample is $n_i$, and the overall totals are $N$ and $n$ respectively. The importance value is usually a count, but may be some other measure of quantity, such as an MNI (see p. 53).

The proportions are denoted by $P_i = N_i/N$, $p_i = n_i/n$.

### Richness

The richness of a sample $= t$ and the richness index $= t - 1/\log(n)$         **(6.4)**

*Shannon index*

The Shannon index is

$$H = - \sum_{i=1}^{t} (n_i/n) \log(n_i/n) = - \sum_{i=1}^{t} p_i \log(p_i) \tag{6.5}$$

It is sometimes replaced by $H/H_{max}$, where $H_{max}$ is its maximum possible value, $= \log(t)$.
The outcome, $J = H/H_{max}$ is sometimes called the *evenness* (Kintigh 1989, 29).

*Simpson's index*

Simpson's index of concentration is given by Rindos (1989, 17)

$$C = \sum_{i=1}^{t} \{n_i(n_i - 1)\}/\{n(n - 1)\} \tag{6.6}$$

since this is the opposite of diversity, $-\log(C)$ can be used as an index of diversity (Pielou 1975).

*Niche width*

The niche width measure of heterogeneity (Hardesty 1975, 77) is given by

$$\text{niche width} = 1/\sum_{i=1}^{t} p_i^2 \tag{6.7}$$

*Rarefaction analysis*

The distribution of individuals in a set of rarefied samples of fixed size follows the hypergeometric distribution (Patel *et al.* 1976, 205) because the rarefied samples are randomly drawn with replacement from a known finite population.

*Notation*

$E(T_n)$ is the expected number of object types in a sample of $n$ objects selected at random without replacement from a total of $N$ objects containing $T$ types.

$$\text{Then } E(T_n) = \sum_{i=1}^{T} 1 - \left[ \frac{(N - N_i)!(N - n)!}{(N - N_i - n)!N!} \right] \tag{6.8}$$

and

$$\text{var}(T_n) = \left(\frac{N}{n}\right)^{-1}\left[\sum_{i=1}^{T}\binom{N-N_i}{n}\left[1 - \binom{N-N_i}{n}\Big/\binom{N}{n}\right]\right.$$

$$\left. + 2\sum_{i=1}^{T}\sum_{j=i+1}^{T}\left[\binom{N-N_i-N_j}{n} - \frac{\binom{N-N_i}{n}\binom{N-N_j}{n}}{\binom{N}{n}}\right]\right]$$

(6.9)

If $n$ is much less than $N$ (e.g. $n/N < 0.1$), we can use the multinomial distribution (Patel *et al.* 1976, 182) as an approximation to the hypergeometric (i.e. use sampling *with* replacement).

### From chapter 8

*Markov chains and transition probabilities*

The number of objects at the time of a census, held at time 0 is $N(0)$, of which $N_i(0)$ are in the $i$th category ($i = 1, 2, 3, 4$). The number $N_j(t)$ in the $j$th category at time $t$ is given by

$$N_j(t) = \sum_i N_i(t-1)p_{ij}, \ i = 1, \ldots 4, j = 1, \ldots, 4, t = 1, 2, \ldots \quad (8.1)$$

or in matrix notation

$$N'(t) = N'(t-1)P.$$

The transition matrix $P$ is initially given the form

$$P = \begin{matrix} p_{11} & p_{12} & p_{13} & p_{14} \\ 0 & p_{22} & p_{23} & p_{24} \\ 0 & 0 & p_{33} & p_{34} \\ 0 & 0 & 0 & p_{44} \end{matrix}$$

where $\sum_j p_{ij} = 1$ for $i = 1, \ldots, 4$.

The $p_{ij}$ are known as the *transition probabilities* from the state $i$ to the state $j$ in one interval of time, e.g. from $t = 1$ to $t = 2$, or from $t = 2$ to $t = 3$, etc.
For any one stratum, we suppose that the population at the time of the survey is $N$, and that a sample of size $n$ is selected. The number in the $i$th category at the time of the census we call $n_{i.}$, the number in the $j$th category at the survey we call $n_{.j}$, and the number in the $i$th category at the census and in the $j$th at the survey we call $n_{ij}$.

Then we can estimate the transition probabilities $\{p_{ij}\}$ by

$$p_{ij} = n_{ij}/n_i$$

and the numbers $N_j$ in each category by

$$\hat{N}_j = \sum_i N_i \hat{p}_{ij} \tag{8.2}$$

adjusting if necessary to allow for acquisitions and disposals.

This approach to the estimation of the $N_j$ is an example of ratio estimation (p. 38), and gives better estimates than the simpler approach

$$\hat{N}_j = N(n_{.j}/n)$$

at least for the sorts of values of $\{p_{ij}\}$ that are likely to be encountered.

   This theory is appropriate for a census followed by a single survey; for repeated surveys we have to take account of the 'matched' and the 'unmatched' parts of the sample, i.e. the part present in both the present and the previous surveys, and the part present only in the present survey. A method was suggested by Orton (1996, 151); a more advanced method was given by Klotz and Sharples (1994).

This section is adapted from Orton (1996).

### Two-stage sampling

We use the notation that was established for *cluster sampling*, and in particular cluster sampling for proportions (p. 213).

We sample a proportion $f_1$ of the storage locations, and then a proportion $f_2$ of the objects at each location. Since the proportion $f_2$ is the same for all locations, this is a *self-weighting sample*. To estimate the overall proportion $P$ we use the ratio-to-size estimate

$$\hat{P} = \sum_i M_i P_i / \sum_i M_i = p \tag{8.3}$$

(hence the term self-weighting).

A general formula for the variance is given by Cochran (1963, 302). By defining a dummy variable

$$y_{ij} = 1 \text{ if object } j \text{ in location } i \text{ belongs to the chosen category,}$$
$$= 0 \text{ otherwise,}$$

we have

$$p_i = \bar{y}_i$$

and his formula becomes

$$v(\hat{P}) = (1 - f_1)\Sigma\frac{M_i^2(p_i - \hat{p})^2}{n\bar{M}^2(n - 1)} + f_1(1 - f_2)\Sigma\frac{M_i(m_i/(m_i - 1))p_iq_i}{n^2\bar{m}\bar{M}} \quad (8.4)$$

The overall size of the sample depends on the resources available and the time needed to undertake each aspect of the survey. This is best expressed as (a) a fixed overhead $c_0$ per store, (b) an overhead $c_1$ per storage location, and (c) a time per object $c_2$. Cochran (1963, 314) gives the formula for optimum allocation as

$$\bar{m}_{opt} = (s_2/\sqrt{s_b^2 - s_2^2/\bar{M}})\sqrt{c_1/c_2} \quad (8.5)$$

where $\bar{m}$ is the average number of objects sampled per location, $s_2^2$ is the within-location variance and $s_b^2$ is the between-location variance. The overhead $c_0$ does not enter this equation directly, but must be subtracted from the total time available before the size of the sample is calculated. The factors $c_1$ and $c_2$ can be estimated, e.g by using linear regression .

This section is adapted from Keene and Orton 1992.

# BIBLIOGRAPHY

Adams, M. 1991. 'A logic of archaeological inference', *Journal of Theoretical Archaeology* 2: 1–11.

Adams, R. McC. 1981. *Heartland of Cities: Surveys of Ancient Settlement and Land Use on the Central Floodplain of the Euphrates* (Chicago: University of Chicago Press).

Addyman, P. V. and Leigh, D. 1973. 'The Anglo-Saxon village at Chalton, Hampshire: second interim report', *Medieval Archaeology* 17: 1–25.

Addyman, P. V. and Leigh, D. and Hughes, M. F. 1972. 'Anglo-Saxon house at Chalton', *Medieval Archaeology* 16: 1–31.

Aitken, M. J. 1990. *Science-Based Dating in Archaeology* (Harlow: Longman).

Aldenderfer, M. S. 1987. 'On the structure of archeological data', in Aldenderfer, M. S. (ed.) *Quantitative Research in Archaeology* (Newbury Park: Sage Publications), 89–113.

Altman, N., Dwyer, J. P., Beckes, M. R. and Hake, R. D. 1982. 'ASP: a simplified computer sampling package for the field archaeologist', *Journal of Field Archaeology* 9 (1): 137–43.

Ammerman, A. J. 1981. 'Surveys and archaeological research', *Annual Review of Anthropology* 10: 63–88.

1985. 'Plow-zone experiments in Calabria, Italy', *Journal of Field Archaeology* 12 (1): 33–40.

Ammerman, A. J., Gifford, D. P. and Voorrips, A. 1978. 'Towards an evaluation of sampling strategies: simulated excavations of a Kenyan pastoralist site', in Hodder, I. (ed.) *Simulation Studies in Archaeology* (Cambridge: Cambridge University Press), 123–32.

Anon. 1984. 'Library of Congress surveys collections', *The Abbey Newsletter: Bookbinding and Conservation* 8: 5.

1985. 'Archives' plan stresses storage conditions', *The Abbey Newsletter: Bookbinding and Conservation* 9: 2.

1989. *The Rothamsted General Survey Program (RGSP)* (Rothamsted, Herts: Lawes Agricultural Trust).

1991. *The Conservation Assessment: A Tool for Planning, Implementing and Fundraising* (Washington, DC: Getty Conservation Institute and National Institute for Conservation of Cultural Property).

1994. 'The Martian Chronicles I', *Bulletin of the Monuments at Risk Survey*. http://csweb.bournemouth.ac.uk/consci/text_mars/martian1.htm 30.6.97.

1995a. 'The Martian Chronicles II', *Bulletin of the Monuments at Risk Survey*. http://csweb.bournemouth.ac.uk/consci/text_mars/martian2.htm 30.6.97.

1995b. 'The Martian Chronicles III', *Bulletin of the Monuments at Risk Survey*. http://csweb.bournemouth.ac.uk/consci/text_mars/martian3.htm 30.6.97.

Arrhenius, O. 1923. 'Statistical investigation in the constitution of plant associations', *Ecology* 4: 68–73.

Asch, D. L. 1975. 'On sample size problems and the uses of nonprobabilistic sampling', in Mueller, J. W. (ed.) *Sampling in Archaeology* (Tucson: University of Arizona Press), 170–91.

Ascher, R. 1968. 'Time's arrow and the archaeology of a contemporary community', in Chang, K. C. (ed.) *Settlement Archaeology* (Palo Alto: National Press Books), 43–52.

Astill, G. and Davies, W. 1985. 'The East Brittany Survey: Oust–Vilaine Watershed', in Macready, S. and Thompson, F. H. (eds.) *Archaeological Field Survey in Britain and Abroad* (London: Society of Antiquaries of London), 101–9.

Aston, M. A. 1995. 'General introduction', in Aston, M. A. and Gerrard, C. M. (eds.) *The Shapwick Project: The Sixth Report* (Bristol: University of Bristol Department for Continuing Education), 5–6.

Aston, M. A. and Gerrard, C. M. (eds.) 1995. *The Shapwick Project: The Sixth Report* (Bristol: University of Bristol Department for Continuing Education).

Bailey, G. N. 1975. 'The role of molluscs in coastal economies: the results of a midden analysis in Australia', *Journal of Archaeological Science* 2 (1): 45–62.

Bamps, A. 1883. *La Céramique américaine au point de vue des éléments constitutifs de la pâte et de sa fabrication*, Congrès des Américanistes, Cinquième Session.

Barclay, K., Biddle, M. and Orton, C. 1990. 'The chronological and spatial distribution of the objects', in Biddle, M. (ed.) *Object and Economy in Medieval Winchester*. Winchester Studies 7ii (Oxford: Clarendon Press), 42–73.

Barker, G. 1975. 'To sieve or not to sieve', *Antiquity* 49: 61–3.

1991. 'Approaches to area survey', in Barker, G. and Lloyd, J. (eds.) *Roman Landscapes: Archaeological Survey in the Mediterranean Region*. British School at Rome Archaeological Monograph 2 (London: British School at Rome), 1–10.

1995. 'The Biferno Valley Survey: methodologies', in Barker, G. (ed.) *A Mediterranean Valley: Landscape Archaeology and Annales History in the Biferno Valley* (London: Leicester University Press), 40–61.

Barker, G. and Lloyd, J. (eds.) 1991. *Roman Landscapes: Archaeological Survey in the Mediterranean Region*. British School at Rome Archaeological Monographs 2 (London: British School at Rome).

Barker, P. 1975. 'Excavations on the site of the Baths Basilica at Wroxeter 1966–74: an interim report', *Britannia* 6: 106–17.

1977. *Techniques of Archaeological Excavation* (London: Batsford).

Barry, J. and Nicholson, M. 1993. 'Measuring the probability of patch detection for four spatial sampling designs', *Journal of Applied Statistics* 20 (3): 353–62.

Bastelaar, D. A. van 1877. *Les Couverts, lustres, vernis, enduits, engobes, etc., de nature organique employés en céramique chez les Romains* (Anvers).

Baxter, M. J. 1993. 'Comment on D. Tangri and R. V. S. Wright. "Multivariate analysis of compositional data . . .", *Archaeometry* 35 (1): 112–15.

1994. *Exploratory Multivariate Analysis in Archaeology* (Edinburgh: Edinburgh University Press).

Bayes, T. R. 1763. 'An essay towards solving a problem in the doctrine of chances', *Philosophical Transactions of the Royal Society* 53: 370–418.

Bayliss, A. and Orton, C. 1994. 'Strategic considerations in dating, or "How many dates do I need?"', *Bulletin of the Institute of Archaeology* 31: 151–67.

Beardah, C. C. and Baxter, M. J. 1996. 'MATLAB routines for kernel density estimation and the graphical representation of archaeological data', in Kamermans, H. and Fennema, K. (eds.) *Interfacing the Past: Computer Applications and Quantitative Methods in Archaeology CAA 95*, Analecta Praehistorica Leidensia 28, 179–84.

Beck, C. and Jones, G. T. 1989. 'Bias and archaeological classification', *American Antiquity* 54 (2): 244–62.

Bell, M. and King, N. 1996. 'The MARS Project – an interface with England's past', in Kamermans, H. and Fennema, K. (eds.) *Interfacing the Past: Computer Applications and Quantitative Methods in Archaeology CAA 95*, Analecta Praehistorica Leidensia 28, 87–91.

Bellhouse, D. R. 1980. 'Sampling studies in archaeology', *Archaeometry* 22 (2): 123–32.

Bellhouse, D. and Finlayson, W. D. 1979. 'An empirical study of probability sampling designs:

preliminary results from the Draper site', *Canadian Journal of Archaeology* 3: 105–23.

Belli, F. E. 1997. 'GPS and GIS as aids for mapping archaeological sites', *Archaeological Computing Newsletter* 47: 5–10.

Benfer, R. A. 1975. 'Sampling and classification', in Mueller, J. W. (ed.) *Sampling in Archaeology* (Tucson: University of Arizona Press), 227–47.

Benson, D. and Miles, D. 1974. *The Upper Thames Valley* (Oxford: Oxford Archaeological Unit).

Betts, I. M. 1982. 'Roman brick and tile: a study in fabric variability', in Freestone, I., Johns, C. and Potter, T. (eds.) *Current Research in Ceramics: Thin-Section Studies. The British Museum Seminar 1980*. British Museum Occasional Papers 32, 63–71.

Biddle, M. and Hudson, D. M. with Heighway, C. M. 1973. *The Future of London's Past: A Survey of the Archaeological Implications of Planning and Development in The Nation's Capital* (Worcester: Rescue).

Biddle, M. and Kjølbye-Biddle, B. 1969. 'Metres, areas and robbing', *World Archaeology* 1 (2): 208–19.

Binford, L. R. 1964. 'A consideration of archaeological research design', *American Antiquity* 29 (4): 425–41.

Binford, L. R., Binford, S. R., Whallon, R. C. and Hardin, M. A. 1970. *Archaeology at Hatchery West*. Memoirs of the Society for American Archaeology 24.

Bintliff, J. 1985. 'The Boeotia Survey', in Macready, S. and Thompson, F. H. (eds.) *Archaeological Field Survey in Britain and Abroad* (London: Society of Antiquaries of London), 196–216.

1992. 'Appearance and reality: understanding the buried landscape through new techniques in field survey', in Bernardi, M. (ed.) *Archaeologia del Paesaggio* (Florence: Insegna del Giglio), 89–137.

Bintliff, J. and Snodgrass, A. M. 1985. 'The Cambridge/Bradford Boeotian expedition: the first four years', *Journal of Field Archaeology* 12 (2): 123–61.

1988. 'Off-site pottery distributions: a regional and inter-regional perspective', *Current Anthropology*, 29: 506–13.

Birks, H. J. B. and Line, J. M. 1992. 'The use of rarefaction analysis for estimating palynological richness from Quaternary pollen-analytical data', *Holocene* 2 (1): 1–10.

Bjelajac, V., Luby, E. M. and Ray, R. 1996. 'A validation test of a field-based phosphate analysis technique', *Journal of Archaeological Science* 23 (2): 243–8.

Boaz, J. S. and Uleberg, E. 1993. 'Gardermoen Project – use of a GIS system in antiquities registration and research', in Andresen, J., Madsen, T. and Scollar, I. (eds.) *Computing the Past: Computer Applications and Quantitative Methods in Archaeology CAA 92* (Aarhus: Aarhus University Press), 177–82.

Boismier, W. A. 1997. *Modelling the Effects of Tillage Processes on Artefact Distribution in the Ploughzone: A Simulation Study of Tillage-induced Pattern Formation*. British Archaeological Reports British Series 259 (Oxford: Archaeopress).

Boismier, W. A. and Reilly, P. 1988. 'Expanding the role of computer graphics in the analysis of survey data', in Ruggles, C. L. N. and Rahtz, S. P. Q. (eds.) *Computer and Quantitative Methods in Archaeology 1987*. British Archaeological Reports International Series 393 (Oxford: BAR), 221–5.

Bordes, F. and Fitte, P. 1964. 'Microlithes du Magdalénien Supérieur de la Gare de Couze', in Ripoll Perello, E. (ed.) *Miscelanea en homenaje al Abate Henri Brieul* 1 (Barcelona: Instituto de Prehistoria y Arquelogia), 259–367.

Bowley, A. L. 1906. 'Address to the Economic Science and Statistics Section of the British Association for the Advancement of Science', *Journal of the Royal Statistical Society* 69: 548–57.

Bowley, A. L. 1926. 'Measurement of the precision attained in sampling', *Bulletin of the*

*International Statistical Institute* 22, Livre I.

Bradley, R. 1984. 'Sieving for soil marks', *Oxford Journal of Archaeology* 3 (3): 71–6.

Bradley, R., Durden, T. and Spencer, N. 1994. 'The creative use of bias in field survey', *Antiquity* 68 (259): 343–6.

Braidwood, R. J., Wilson, J. and Allen, T. (eds.) 1937. *Mounds of the Plain of Antioch: An Archaeological Survey*. Oriental Institute Publications 28 (Chicago: University of Chicago Press).

Brand, V. 1992. *Buildings at Risk: A Sample Survey* (London: English Heritage).

Brandt, R., Groenewoudt, B. J. and Kvamme, K. 1992. 'An experiment in archaeological site location: modelling in the Netherlands using GIS techniques', *World Archaeology* 24 (2): 268–82.

Briuer, F. L. and Mathers, C. 1996. *Trends and Patterns in Cultural Resource Significance: An Historical Perspective and Annotated Bibliography*. Institute for Water Resources Report 96–EL-1 (Alexandria, Virginia: US Army Corps of Engineers).

Bromund, R. H., Bower, N. W. and Smith, R. H. 1976. 'Inclusions in ancient ceramics: an approach to the problem of sampling for chemical analysis', *Archaeometry* 18 (2): 218–21.

Brongniart, M. A. 1844. *Traité des arts céramiques, ou des poteries, considérées dans leur histoires, leur pratique et leur théorie* (Paris).

Brown, J. A. 1975. 'Deep-site excavation strategy as a sampling problem', in Mueller, J. W. (ed.) *Sampling in Archaeology* (Tucson: University of Arizona Press), 155–69.

Brzezinski, W., Dulinicz, M., Kobylinski, Z., Lichy, B. and Moszczynski, A. 1984. 'Multistage strategy for sampling settlement sites: an example from Poland', *Proceedings of the Prehistoric Society* 50: 377–82.

Buck, C. E., Cavanagh, W. G. and Litton, C. D. 1988. 'The spatial analysis of site phosphate data', in Rahtz, S. P. Q. (ed.) *Computer and Quantitative Methods in Archaeology 1988*. British Archaeological Reports International Series 446 (Oxford: BAR), 151–60.

1996. *Bayesian Approach to Interpreting Archaeological Data* (Chichester: John Wiley & Sons Ltd).

Burton, R. J. 1977. 'ARCHSAMP: a general purpose sampling simulation program', *Newsletter of Computing Archaeology* 13 (2): 1–23.

Carver, M. O. H. 1981. 'Sampling towns: an optimistic strategy', in Clack, P. and Haselgrove, S. (eds.) *Approaches to the Urban Past*. Department of Archaeology Durham University Occasional Papers 2 (Durham: Durham University Press), 65–91.

Carver, S. J., Cornelius, S. C., Heywood, D. I. and Sear, D. A. 1995. 'Using computers and Geographical Information Systems for expedition fieldwork', *Geographical Journal* 161 (2): 167–76.

Casteel, R. W. 1970. 'Core and column sampling', *American Antiquity* 35 (4): 465–7.

1972. 'Some biases in the recovery of archaeological faunal remains', *Proceedings of the Prehistoric Society* 38: 382–8.

1976. 'Comparison of columns and whole unit samples for recovering fish remains', *World Archaeology* 8 (2): 192–6.

1977. 'Characterisation of faunal assemblages and the minimum number of individuals determined from paired elements: continuing problems in archaeology', *Journal of Archaeological Science* 4 (2): 125–34.

Champion, T. 1978. 'Strategies for sampling a Saxon settlement: a retrospective view of Chalton', in Cherry, J. F., Gamble, C. and Shennan, S. (eds.) *Sampling in Contemporary British Archaeology*. British Archaeological Reports British Series 50 (Oxford: BAR), 207–25.

Champion, T., Cuming, P. and Shennan, S. J. 1995. *Planning for the Past 3: Decision-Making and Field Methods in Archaeological Evaluation* (Southampton: English Heritage and University of Southampton).

Chaplin, R. E. 1971. *The Study of Animal Bones from Archaeological Sites* (London: Seminar Press).

Charters, S., Evershed, R. P., Goad, L. J., Leyden, A. and Blinkhorn, P. W. 1993. 'Quantification and distribution of lipid in archaeological ceramics: implications for sampling potsherds for organic residue analyses and the classification of vessel use', *Archaeometry* 35 (2): 211–23.

Chartkoff, J. L. 1978. 'Transect interval sampling in forests', *American Antiquity* 43 (1): 46–53.

Chase, P. G. and Hagaman, R. M. 1987. 'Minimum number of individuals and its alternatives: a probability theory perspective', *Ossa* 13: 75–86.

Chenhall, R. G. 1975. 'A rationale for archaeological sampling', in Mueller, J. W. (ed.) *Sampling in Archaeology* (Tucson: University of Arizona Press), 3–25.

Cherry, J. F. 1975. 'Efficient soil searching: some comments', *Antiquity* 49: 217–19.

  1978. 'Questions of efficiency and integration in assemblage sampling', in Cherry, J. F., Gamble, C. and Shennan, S. (eds.) *Sampling in Contemporary British Archaeology*. British Archaeological Reports British Series 50 (Oxford: BAR), 293–320.

  1982. 'A preliminary definition of site distribution on Melos', in Renfrew, C. and Wagstaff, M. (eds.) *An Island Polity: The Archaeology of Exploitation in Melos* (Cambridge: Cambridge University Press), 10–23.

Cherry, J. F., Gamble, C. and Shennan, S. (eds.) 1978. *Sampling in Contemporary British Archaeology*. British Archaeological Reports British Series 50 (Oxford: BAR).

Cherry, J. F. and Shennan, S. 1978. 'Sampling cultural systems: some perspectives on the application of probabilistic regional survey in Britain', in Cherry, J. F., Gamble, C. and Shennan, S. (eds.) *Sampling in Contemporary British Archaeology*. British Archaeological Reports British Series 50 (Oxford: BAR), 17–48.

Claassen, C. 1991. 'Normative thinking and shell-bearing sites', *Archaeological Method and Theory* 3: 249–98.

Clark, A. J. 1996. *Seeing Beneath the Soil: Prospecting Methods in Archaeology* (revised edn) (London: Batsford).

Clark, I. 1979. *Practical Geostatistics* (London: Applied Science Publishers).

Clarke, D. L. 1973. 'Archaeology: the loss of innocence', *Antiquity* 47: 6–18.

Clason, A. T. and Prummel, W. 1977. 'Collecting, sieving and archaeozoological research', *Journal of Archaeological Science* 4 (2): 171–5.

Cleere, H. 1978. 'A survey of surveys', in Darvill, T. C., Parker Pearson, M., Smith, R. W. and Thomas, R. M. (eds.) *New Approaches to Our Past* (Southampton: University of Southampton Archaeology Society), 89–100.

Cochran, W. G. 1942. 'Sampling theory when the sampling units are of unequal sizes', *Journal of the American Statistical Association* 37: 199–212.

  1963. *Sampling Theory* (2nd edn) (New York: John Wiley).

  1976. 'Discussion', in Smith, T. M. F. 'The foundations of survey sampling: a review', *Journal of the Royal Statistical Society* A, 139: 201.

  1977. *Sampling Theory* (3rd edn) (New York: John Wiley).

Collins, M. B. 1975. 'Sources of bias in processual data: an appraisal', in Mueller, J. W. (ed.) *Sampling in Archaeology* (Tucson: University of Arizona Press), 26–32.

Conkey, M. W. 1980. 'The identification of prehistoric hunter-gatherer aggregation sites: the case of Altamira', *Current Anthropology* 21 (5): 609–30.

Cook, S. F. and Treganza, A. E. 1947. 'The quantitative investigation of aboriginal sites: comparative physical and chemical analysis of two Californian Indian mounds', *American Antiquity* 13 (2): 135–41.

  1950. *The Quantitative Investigation of Indian Mounds*. University of California Publications in American Archaeology and Ethnology 40 (5) (Berkeley: University of California Press), 223–61.

Cornwall, I. W. 1958. *Soils for the Archaeologist* (London: Phoenix House).

Courty, M. A., Goldberg, P. and Macphail, R. 1989. *Soils and Micromorphology in Archaeology* (Cambridge: Cambridge University Press).

Cowgill, G. L. 1964. 'The selection of samples from large sherd collections', *American Antiquity* 29 (4): 467–73.

1970. 'Some sampling and reliability problems in archaeology', in Gardin, J. C. (ed.) *Archéologie et calculateurs* (Paris: CNRS), 161–75.

1975. 'A selection of samplers: comments on archaeo-statistics', in Mueller, J. W. (ed.) *Sampling in Archaeology* (Tucson: University of Arizona Press), 258–74.

1977. 'The trouble with significance tests and what we can do about it', *American Antiquity* 42 (3): 350–68.

1990. 'Towards refining concepts of full-coverage survey', in Fish, S. K. and Kowalewski, S. (eds.) *The Archaeology of Regions: A Case Study for Full-Coverage Survey* (Washington, DC: Smithsonian University Press), 249–59.

1994. 'Unknown sampling bias is not a licence to ignore statistical theory', in Johnson, I. (ed.) *Method in the Mountains: Proceedings of UISPP Commission IV Meeting.* Sydney University Archaeological Methods Series 2 (Sydney), 7–11.

Crowther, D., French, C. and Pryor, F. 1985. 'Approaching the Fens the flexible way', in Haselgrove, C., Millett, M. and Smith, I. (eds.) *Archaeology from the Ploughsoil: Studies in the Collection and Interpretation of Field Survey Data* (Sheffield: J. R. Collis), 59–76.

Craft, M. and Jones, S. 1981. *Written Documentation* (Philadelphia: AIC 9th Annual Meeting).

Cruz-Uribe, K. 1988. 'The use and meaning of species diversity and richness in archaeological faunas', *Journal of Archaeological Science* 15 (2): 179–96.

Daniel, G. 1981. *A Short History of Archaeology* (London: Thames and Hudson).

Daniels, S. G. H. 1966. 'An operational scheme for the analysis of large assemblages of archaeological material', *Archaeometry* 9 (2): 151–4.

1972. 'Research design models', in Clarke, D. L. (ed.) *Models in Archaeology* (London: Methuen), 201–29.

1978. 'Implications of error: research design and the structure of archaeology', *World Archaeology* 10 (1): 29–35.

Darvill, T. C. 1979. 'A petrological study of LHS and TFP stamped tiles from the Cotswold region', in McWhirr, A. (ed.) *Roman Brick and Tile: Studies in Manufacture, Distribution and Use in the Western Empire.* British Archaeological Reports International Series 68 (Oxford: BAR), 309–49.

Darvill, T., Burrow, S. and Wildgust, D.-A. 1995. *Planning for the Past 2: An Assessment of Archaeological Assessment Procedures in England 1982–91.* (London: Bournemouth University and English Heritage).

Darvill, T. and Fulton, A. K. 1998. *The Monuments at Risk Survey of England 1995: Summary Report* (London: Bournemouth University and English Heritage).

Darvill, T., Saunders, A. and Startin, B. 1987. 'A question of national importance: approaches to the evaluation of ancient monuments for the monuments protection programme of England', *Antiquity* 61 (233): 393–408.

Darvill, T. and Timby, J. 1982. 'Textural analysis: a review of potentials and limitations', in Freestone, I., Johns, C. and Potter, T. (eds.) *Current Research in Ceramics: Thin-Section Studies. The British Museum Seminar 1980.* British Museum Occasional Papers 32 (London: British Museum), 73–87.

Darvill, T. and Wainwright, G. 1994. 'The Monuments at Risk Survey: an introduction', *Antiquity* 68 (261): 820–4.

1995. 'The MARS Project: An Introduction', http://csweb.bournemouth.ac.uk/consci/ text _ mars/intro.htm 30.6.97.

Darwin, C. 1904. *The Formation of Vegetable Mould through the Action of Worms with Observations on their Habits* (London: Murray).

David, A. (compiler) 1995. *Geophysical Survey in Archaological Field Evaluation*. English Heritage Research and Professional Services Guideline 1 (London: English Heritage).

Davis, B. F. 1935. 'The Roman road from West Wickham to London', *Surrey Archaeological Collections* 43: 61–83.

DeBoer, W. R. 1974. 'Ceramic longevity and archaeological interpretation: an example from the Upper Ucalayi, Peru', *American Antiquity* 39 (2): 335–43.

Dennell, R. W. 1972. 'The interpretation of plant remains: Bulgaria', in Higgs, E. S. (ed.) *Papers in Economic Prehistory* (Cambridge: Cambridge University Press), 149–59.

Department of the Environment 1990. *Planning Policy Guidance 16: Archaeology and Planning* (London: Department of the Environment).

Diamant, S. 1979. 'A short history of archaeological sieving at Francthi Cave', *Journal of Field Archaeology* 6 (2): 203–17.

Dincauze, D., Wobst, M., Hasenstab, R. and Lacy, D. 1981. *Retrospective Assessment of Archaeological Survey Contracts in Massachusetts 1970–79* (3 vols.) (Boston: Massachusetts Historical Commission).

Dobbs, C. A. 1993. Recreating vanished mound groups in the upper Mississippi river valley (USA): integrating historic documents, CADD, and photogrammetric mapping', in Andresen, J., Madsen, T. and Scollar, I. (eds.) *Computing the Past: Computer Applications and Quantitative Methods in Archaeology CAA 92* (Aarhus: Aarhus University Press), 33–44.

Dobney, K., Hall, A., Kenward, H. and Miles, A. 1992. 'A working classification of sample types for environmental archaeology', *Circaea* 9: 24–6.

Dunnell, R. C. 1984. 'The ethics of archaeological significance decisions', in Green, E. L. (ed.) *Ethics and Values in Archaeology* (New York: The Free Press), 62–74.

   1988. 'Low density archaeological records from plowed surfaces: some preliminary considerations', *American Archaeology* 7: 29–38.

   1989. 'Diversity in archaeology: a group of measures in search of an application?', in Leonard, R. D. and Jones, G. T. (eds.) *Quantifying Diversity in Archaeology* (Cambridge: Cambridge University Press), 142–9.

   1990. 'Artifact size and lateral displacement under tillage: comments on the Odell and Cowan experiment', *American Antiquity* 55 (3): 592–4.

Dunnell, R. C. and Dancey, W. S. 1983. 'The siteless survey: a regional scale data collection strategy', in Schiffer, M. B. (ed.) *Advances in Archaeological Method and Theory* 6 (New York: Academic Press), 267–87.

Dunnell, R. C. and Stein, J. K. 1989. 'Theoretical issues in the interpretation of microartifacts', *Geoarchaeology* 4 (1): 31–41.

Ebert, J. I. 1984. 'Remote sensing applications in archaeology', in Schiffer, M. B. (ed.) *Advances in Archaeological Method and Theory* 7 (New York: Academic Press), 293–362.

Efremov, I. A. 1940. 'Taphonomy: a new branch of paleontology', *Pan-American Geologist* 74: 81–93.

Ehrenberg, A. S. C. 1975. *Data Reduction* (London: Wiley).

English Heritage 1995. *Planning for the Past 1: A Review of Archaeological Assessment Procedures in England 1982–91* (London: English Heritage).

Fasham, P. and Monk, N. 1978. 'Sampling for plant remains from Iron Age pits: some results and implications', in Cherry, J. F., Gamble, C. and Shennan, S. (eds.) *Sampling in Contemporary British Archaeology*. British Archaeological Reports British Series 50 (Oxford: BAR), 363–71.

Fasham, P. J., Schadla-Hall, R. T., Shennan, S. J. and Bates, P. J. 1980. *Fieldwalking for Archaeologists* (Winchester: Hampshire Field Club and Archaeological Society).

Fieller, N. R. J. and Nicholson, P. T. 1991. 'Grain size analysis of archaeological pottery: the use of statistical models', in Middleton, A. and Freestone, I. (eds.) *Recent Developments in Ceramic Petrology.* British Museum Occasional Papers, 81 (London: British Museum), 71–111.

Fieller, N. R. J. and Turner, A. 1982. 'Number estimation in vertebrate samples', *Journal of Archaeological Science* 9 (1): 49–62.

Fish, S. K. and Kowalewski, S. (eds.) 1990. *The archaeology of Regions: A Case Study for Full-Coverage Survey* (Washington, DC: Smithsonian University Press).

Fisher, R. A., Corbet, A. S. and Williams, C. B. 1943. 'The relation between the number of species and the number of individuals in a random sample of an animal population', *Journal of Animal Ecology* 12: 42–58.

Fitte, P. and Sonneville-Bordes, D. de 1962. 'Le Magdalénien VI de la Gare de Couze', *L'Anthropologie* 66: 217–54.

Fitzpatrick, A. 1987. 'The structure of a distribution map: problems of sample bias and quantitative studies', in Tomasevic-Buck, T. and Kellner, H.-J. (eds.) 14th congress of RCRF, London and Oxford. *Rei Cretariae Romanae Fautorum Acta* 25–6: 79–112.

Fladmark, K. R. 1982. 'Microdebitage analysis: initial considerations', *Journal of Archaeological Science* 9 (2): 205–20.

Flannery, K. V. 1976a. 'Excavating deep communities by transect samples', in Flannery, K. V. (ed.) *The Early Mesoamerican Village* (New York: Academic Press), 68–72.

Flannery, K. V. (ed.) 1976b. *The Early Mesoamerican Village* (New York: Academic Press).

Foley, R. 1978. 'Incorporating sampling into initial research design: some aspects of spatial archaeology', in Cherry, J. F., Gamble, C. and Shennan, S. (eds.) *Sampling in Contemporary British Archaeology.* British Archaeological Reports British Series 50 (Oxford: BAR), 49–65.

    1981a. *Off-Site Archaeology and Human Adaptation in Eastern Africa: An Analysis of Regional Artefact Density in the Amboseli, Southern Kenya.* British Archaeological Reports International Series 97 (Oxford: BAR).

    1981b. 'A model of regional archaeological structure', *Proceedings of the Prehistoric Society* 47: 1–17.

Folk, R. L. and Ward, W. C. 1957. 'Brazos river bar: a study in the significance of grain size parameters', *Journal of Sedimentary Petrology* 27 (1): 3–26.

Fowler, E. (ed.) 1972. *Field Survey in British Archaeology* (London: Council for British Archaeology).

Fox, Sir C. 1923. *The Archaeology of the Cambridge Region* (Cambridge: Cambridge University Press.

Fraser, D. 1993. 'The British archaeological database', in Hunter, J. and Ralston, L. (eds.) *Archaeological Resource Management in the UK: An Introduction* (Stroud: Institute of Field Archaeologists), 19–29.

Freeman, P. 1988. 'How to simulate if you must', in Ruggles, C. L. N. and Rahtz, S. P. Q. (eds.) *Computer and Quantitative Methods in Archaeology 1987.* British Archaeological Reports International Series 393 (Oxford: BAR), 139–46.

Frink, D. S. 1984. 'Artifact behavior within the plow zone', *Journal of Field Archaeology* 11 (3): 356–63.

Fritz, J. M. 1972. 'Archaeological systems for indirect observation of the past', in Leone, M. P. (ed.) *Contemporary Archaeology* (Carbondale: Southern Illinois University Press), 135–57.

Fulford, M. G. and Hodder, I. 1974. 'A regression analysis of some later Romano-British pottery: a case study', *Oxoniensia* 39: 26–33.

Gaffney, C., Gaffney, V. and Tingle, M. 1985. 'Settlement, economy or behaviour? Micro-regional land use models and the interpretation of surface artefact patterns', in Haselgrove, C., Millett, M. and Smith, I. (eds.) *Archaeology from the Ploughsoil: Studies in the Collection and Interpretation of Field Survey Data* (Sheffield: J. R. Collis), 95–107.

Gaffney, V. and Gaffney, C. 1986. 'From Boeotia to Berkshire: an integrated approach to geophysics and rural field survey', *Prospezione Archaeologiche* 10: 65–70.

Gaffney, V. Gaffney, C. and Corney, M. 1998. 'Changing the Roman landscape: the role of geophysics and remote sensing', in Bayley, J. (ed.) *Science in Archaeology* (London: English Heritage), 145–56.

Gaffney, V. and Leusen, P. M. van 1996. 'Extending GIS methods for regional archaeology: the Wroxeter Hinterlands Project', in Kamermans, H. and Fennema, K. (eds.) *Interfacing the Past: Computer Applications and Quantitative Methods in Archaeology CAA 95*, Analecta Praehistorica Leidensia 28, 297–305.

Gaffney, V., Ostir, K., Podobnikar, T. and Stancic, Z. 1996. 'Satellite imagery and GIS applications in Mediterranean landscapes', in Kamermans, H. and Fennema, K. (eds.) *Interfacing the Past: Computer Applications and Quantitative Methods in Archaeology CAA 95*, Analecta Praehistorica Leidensia 28, 337–42.

Gaffney, V. and Tingle, M. 1985. 'The Maddle Farm (Berks.) Project and micro-regional analysis', in Macready, S. and Thompson, F. H. (eds.) *Archaeological Field Survey in Britain and Abroad* (London: Society of Antiquaries of London), 67–73.

Gallant, T. W. 1986. '"Background noise" and site definition: a contribution to survey methodology', *Journal of Field Archaeology* 13 (4): 403–18.

Gamble, C. 1978. 'Optimising information from studies of faunal remains', in Cherry, J. F., Gamble, C. and Shennan, S. (eds.) *Sampling in Contemporary British Archaeology*. British Archaeological Reports British Series 50 (Oxford: BAR), 321–53.

Gerrard, C. M. 1990. 'Fieldwalking results, methodological experiments and future strategy', in Aston, M. A. (ed.) *The Shapwick Project: A Topographical and Historical Study – 1989 (2nd) Report* (Bristol: University of Bristol Department for Continuing Education), 21–39.

1995. 'Problems and patterns in Shapwick fieldwalking', in Aston, M. A. and Gerrard, C. M. (eds.) *The Shapwick Project: The Sixth Report* (Bristol: University of Bristol Department for Continuing Education), 9–52.

Gifford, D. P. 1981. 'Taphonomy and palaeoecology: a critical review of archaeology's sister discipines', in Schiffer, M. B. (ed.) *Advances in Archaeological Method and Theory* 4 (New York: Academic Press), 365–438.

Gifford, E. W. 1916. 'Composition of California shellmounds', *Publications in American Archaeology and Ethnology* 12 (1) (University of California), 1–29.

Gilbert, A. S. and Singer, B. H. 1982. 'Reassessing zooarchaeological quantification', *World Archaeology* 14 (1): 21–40.

Gladwin, N. 1937. 'Petrography of Snaketown pottery', in Gladwin, H. S. (ed.) *Excavations at Snaketown*. Medallion Papers (Globe, Arizona: Gila Pueblo), 25.

Gladwin, W. and Gladwin, H. S. 1928. *A Method for the Designation of Ruins in the Southwest*. Medallion Papers 1 (Globe, Arizona: Gila Pueblo).

Goodyear, A. C., Raab, L. M. and Klinger, T. C. 1978. 'The status of archaeological research design in cultural resource management', *American Antiquity* 43 (2): 159–73.

Gordon, E. A. 1993. 'Screen size and differential faunal recovery: a Hawaiian example', *Journal of Field Archaeology* 20 (4): 453–60.

Gould, R. A. 1987. 'Archaeological survey by air: a case from the Australian desert', *Journal of Field Archaeology* 14 (4): 431–43.

Grassle, J. F., Patil, G. P., Smith, W. K. and Taillie, C. (eds.) 1979. *Ecological Diversity in Theory and Practice* (Fairland, MD: International Co-operative Publishing House).

Grayson, D. K. 1979. 'On the quantification of vertebrate archaeo-faunas', in Schiffer, M. B. (ed.) *Advances in Archaeological Method and Theory* 2 (New York: Academic Press), 199–237.

1981. 'The effects of sample size on some derived measures in vertebrate faunal analysis',

*Journal of Archaeological Science* 8 (1): 77–88.

1984. *Quantitative Zooarchaeology* (Orlando, FL: Academic Press).

Greenacre, M. J. 1984. *Theory and Applications of Correspondence Analysis* (London: Academic Press).

1993. *Correspondence Analysis in Practice* (London: Academic Press).

Greenwood, P. 1989. 'Uphall Camp, Ilford, Essex: an Iron Age fortification', *London Archaeologist* 6 (4): 94–101.

Greenwood, R. S. 1961. 'Quantitative analysis of shells from a site in Goleta, California', *American Antiquity* 26 (3): 416–20.

Groube, L. M. and Bowden, M. C. B. 1982. *The Archaeology of Rural Dorset: Past, Present and Future.* Dorset Natural History and Archaeological Society Monograph Series 4 (Dorchester : Dorset Natural History and Archaeological Society).

Grupe, G. 1988. 'Impact of the choice of bone sample on trace element data in excavated human skeletons', *Journal of Archaeology Science* 15 (2): 123–9.

Haigh, J. G. B. 1981. 'A scheme for regional survey and site sampling', *Revue d'Archéometrie* 5: 1–9.

1982. 'Procedures for the surface sampling of archaeological sites', in Graham, I. and Webb, E. (eds.) *Computer Applications in Archaeology 1981* (London: Institute of Archaeology), 61–9.

Hall, D. 1985. 'Survey work in eastern England', in Macready, S. and Thompson, F. H. (eds.) *Archaeological Field Survey in Britain and Abroad* (London: Society of Antiquaries of London), 25–44.

1987. 'The Fenland Project Number 2: Fenland landscapes and settlements between Peterborough and March', *East Anglian Archaeology* 35.

Hally, D. J. 1981. 'Plant preservation and the context of paleobotanical samples: a case study', *American Antiquity* 46 (4): 723–42.

Hamond, F. 1978. 'Regional survey strategies: a simulation approach', in Cherry, J. F., Gamble, C. and Shennan, S. (eds.) *Sampling in Contemporary British Archaeology.* British Archaeological Reports British Series 50 (Oxford: BAR), 67–85.

Hansen, M. H. and Hurwitz, W. N. 1943. 'On the theory of sampling from finite populations', *Annals of Mathematical Statistics* 14: 333–62.

Hardesty, D. 1975. 'The Niche Concept: suggestions for its use in human ecology', *Human Ecology* 3 (2): 71–85.

Hartley, H. O. and Rao, J. N. K. 1962. 'Sampling with unequal probabilities and without replacement', *Annals of Mathematical Statistics* 33: 350–74.

Haselgrove, C. 1978. 'Spatial pattern and settlement archaeology: some reflections on sampling design', in Cherry, J. F., Gamble, C. and Shennan, S. (eds.) *Sampling in Contemporary British Archaeology.* British Archaeological Reports British Series 50 (Oxford: BAR), 159–75.

1985. 'Inference from ploughsoil artefact samples', in Haselgrove, C., Millett, M. and Smith, I. (eds.) *Archaeology from the Ploughsoil: Studies in the Collection and Interpretation of Field Survey Data* (Sheffield: J. R. Collis), 7–29.

1989. 'Fieldwork in the Aisne Valley, 1988', *University of Durham and University of Newcastle Archaeological Reports for 1988* (Durham: The University), 221–8.

Haselgrove, C. C., Lowther, P. C. and Scull, C. J. 1990. 'Fieldwork in the Aisne Valley, 1989', *University of Durham and University of Newcastle Archaeological Reports for 1989* (Durham: The University), 6–15.

Haselgrove, C. C., Lowther, P. C., Scull, C. J. and Howard, P. 1990. 'Fieldwork in the Aisne Valley, 1990', *University of Durham and University of Newcastle Archaeological Reports for 1990* (Durham: The University), 2–10.

Haselgrove, C., Millett, M. and Smith, I. (eds.) 1985. *Archaeology from the Ploughsoil: Studies in the Collection and Interpretation of Field Survey Data* (Sheffield: J. R. Collis).

Hassan, F. A. 1978. 'Sediments in archaeology: methods and applications for palaeoenvironmental and cultural analysis', *Journal of Field Archaeology* 5 (2): 197–213.

Hayfield, C. (ed.) 1980. *Fieldwalking as a Method of Archaeological Research*. Directorate of
Ancient Monuments and Historic Buildings Occasional Papers, 2 (London: Department of
the Environment).

Heer, O. 1865. *Die Pflanzen der Pfahlbauten* [Plants of the Lake Dwellings] (Zurich: Separatab-
druk aus demm Neujahrsblatt der Naturwisch. Gesellschaft auf das Jahr 1866).

    1866. 'Abstract on the "Plants of the Lake Dwellings"', in Keller, F. *The Lake Dwellings of
Switzerland and Other Parts of Europe* (London: Longmans, Green, and Co.), 336–54.

Hinchliffe, J. and Schadla-Hall, R. T. (eds.) 1980. *The Past under the Plough*. Directorate of
Ancient Monuments and Historic Buildings Occasional Papers 3 (London: Department of
the Environment).

Hirth, K. G. 1978. 'Problems in data recovery and measurement in settlement archaeology',
*Journal of Field Archaeology* 5 (2): 125–31.

Hodder, I. 1974. 'The distribution of two types of Romano-British coarse pottery in the West
Sussex region', *Sussex Archaeological Collections* 112: 1–11.

Hodder, I. and Orton, C. 1976. *Spatial Analysis in Archaeology* (Cambridge: Cambridge University Press).

Hodges, H. W. M. 1962. 'Thin sections of prehistoric pottery: an empirical study', *Bulletin of the
Institute of Archaeology University of London* 3: 58–68.

Hoffecker, J. F. 1988. 'Applied geomorphology and archaeological survey strategy for sites of
Pleistocene age: an example from central Alaska', *Journal of Archaeological Science* 15 (6):
683–713.

Hoffman, C. 1993. 'Close-interval core sampling: tests of a method for predicting internal site
structure', *Journal of Field Archaeology* 20 (4): 461–73.

Hole, B. 1980. 'Sampling in archaeology: a critique', *Annual Review of Anthropology* 9: 217–34.

Holmes, W. H. 1919. *Handbook of Aboriginal American Antiquities. Part 1: Introductory: The
Lithic Industries*. Bureau of American Ethnology Bulletin 60. Washington, DC: Government Printing Office.

Horton, D. R. 1984. 'Minimum numbers: a consideration', *Journal of Archaeological Science* 11
(3): 255–71.

Howell, T. V. 1993. 'Evaluating the utility of auger testing as a predictor of subsurface artifact
densities', *Journal of Field Archaeology* 20 (4): 475–84.

Inostrantsev, A. A. 1882. *Doistoricheskii chelovek kamennago veka poberezh'ia Ladozhkogo ozera*
(St Petersburg: Stasiulevich).

Jacobsen, T. W. 1974. 'New radiocarbon dates from Franchthi Cave: a preliminary note
regarding collection of samples by means of flotation', *Journal of Field Archaeology* 1(3):
303–4.

Jarman, H. N., Legge, A. J. and Charles, J. A. 1972. 'Retrieval of plant remains from archaeological sites by froth flotation', in Higgs. E. S. (ed.) *Papers in Economic Prehistory* (Cambridge:
Cambridge University Press), 39–48.

Jelks, E. B. 1975. *The Use and Misuse of Random Sampling in Archaeology* (Normal, IL: Jett
Publishing Company).

Jones, A. K. G. 1983. 'A comparison of two on-site methods of wet sieving large archaeological
soil samples', *Science and Archaeology* 25: 9–12.

Jones, G. T., Grayson, D. K. and Beck, C. 1983. 'Artifact class richness and sample size in
archaeological surface assemblages', in Dunnell, R. C. and Grayson, D. K. (eds.) *Lulu Linear
Punctuated: Essays in Honour of George Irving Quimby*. Museum of Anthropology, University of Michigan, Ann Arbor Anthropological Papers 72: 55–73.

Jones, G. T. and Leonard, R. D. 1989. 'The concept of diversity: an introduction', in Leonard,

R. D. and Jones, G. T. (eds.) *Quantifying Diversity in Archaeology* (Cambridge: Cambridge University Press), 1–3.

Jones, M. 1978. 'Sampling in a rescue context: a case study in Oxfordshire', in Cherry, J. F., Gamble, C. and Shennan, S. (eds.) *Sampling in Contemporary British Archaeology*. British Archaeological Reports British Series 50 (Oxford: BAR), 191–205.

Judge, W. J., Ebert, J. I. and Hitchcock, R. K. 1975. 'Sampling in Regional Archaeological Survey', in Mueller, J. W. (ed.) *Sampling in Archaeology* (Tucson: University of Arizona Press), 82–123.

Juhl, K. and Markestad, P. 1991. 'Lies, damned lies and statistics', *Norwegian Archaeological Review*, 24 (2): 113–22.

Kaier, A. N. 1901. 'Sur les méthodes représentatives ou typologiques', *Bulletin of the International Statistical Institute* 13, Livre I, 66.

Kaufman, D. 1998. 'Measuring archaeological diversity: an application of the jackknife technique', *American Antiquity* 63 (1): 73–85.

Keay, S., Creighton, J. and Jordan, D. 1991. 'Sampling ancient towns', *Oxford Journal of Archaeology* 10 (3): 371–83.

Keeley, H. C. M. 1978. 'The cost-effectiveness of certain methods of recovering macroscopic organic remains from archaeological deposits', *Journal of Archaeological Science* 5 (2): 179–83.

Keene, S. 1990a. *Assessing Collection Condition*. Museum of London Conservation Department Research Report.

1990b. *Condition Surveys of the Collections: Summary of Results*. Museum of London Conservation Department Research Report.

1991. *Collection Condition Surveys*. Museum of London Conservation Department Research Report.

Keene, S. and Orton, C. 1985. 'Stability of treated archaeological iron: an assessment', *Studies in Conservation* 30: 136–42.

1992. 'Measuring the condition of museum collections', in Lock, G. and Moffett, J. (eds.) *Computer Applications and Quantitative Methods in Archaeology 1991*. British Archaeological Reports International Series 577 (Oxford: Tempus Reparatum), 163–6.

Keepax, C. 1977. 'Contamination of archaeological deposits by seeds of modern origin with particular reference to flotation machines', *Journal of Archaeological Science* 4 (3): 221–229.

Keighley, J. 1973. 'Some problems in the quantitative interpretation of ceramic data', in Renfrew, C. (ed.) *The Explanation of Culture Change: Models in Prehistory* (London: Duckworth), 131–6.

Keller, D. R. and Rupp, D. W. (eds.) 1983. *Archaeological Survey in the Mediterranean Area*. British Archaeological Reports International Series 155 (Oxford: BAR).

King, T. F., Hickman, P. P. and Berg, G. 1977. *Anthropology in Historic Preservation: Caring for Culture's Clutter* (New York: Academic Press).

Kintigh, K. W. 1984. 'Measuring archaeological diversity by comparison with simulated assemblages', *American Antiquity* 49 (1): 44–54.

1988. 'The effectiveness of subsurface testing: a simulation approach', *American Antiquity* 53 (4): 686–707.

1989. 'Sample size, significance and measure of diversity', in Leonard, R. D. and Jones, G. T. (eds.) *Quantifying Diversity in Archaeology* (Cambridge: Cambridge University Press), 25–36.

Kish, L. 1957. 'Confidence limits for clustered samples', *American Sociological Review* 22: 154–65.

Klein, R. 1987. 'Faunal analysis', *Quarterly Review of Archaeology* 8 (2): 8–9.

Klotz, J. H. and Sharples, L. D. 1994. 'Estimation for a Markov heart transplant model', *Journal of the Royal Statistical Society D* 43 (3): 431–8.

Koloseike, A. 1970. 'Costs of shell analysis', *American Antiquity* 35 (4): 475–80.

Kowalewski, S. A., Blanton, R. E., Feinman, G. and Finster, L. 1983. 'Boundaries, scale and internal organisation', *Journal of Anthropological Archaeology* 2: 32–56.

Krakker, J. J., Shott, M. J. and Welch, P. D. 1983. 'Design and evaluation of shovel-test sampling in regional archaeological survey', *Journal of Field Archaeology* 10 (4): 469–80

Krantz, G. S. 1968. 'A new method of counting mammal bones', *American Journal of Archaeology* 72: 286–8.

Kroeber, A. L. 1916. 'Zuñi potsherds', *Anthropological Papers of the American Museum of Natural History* 18 (1): 1–37.

Krumbein, W. C. 1965. 'Sampling in paleontology', in Kummel, B. and Raup, D. (eds.) *Handbook of Paleontological Techniques* (San Francisco: W. H. Freeman), 137–50.

Lang, N. A. R. 1992. 'Sites and Monuments Records in Britain', in Larsen, C. U. (ed.) *Sites and Monuments: National Archaeological Records* (Copenhagen: National Museum of Denmark), 171–83.

Lange, A. G. 1990. *Plant Remains from a Native Settlement at the Roman Frontier: De Horden near Wijk bij Duurstede: A Numerical Approach* (Amersfoort : ROB).

Lee, J. E. 1866. 'Methods employed in collecting the lake-dwelling antiquities', in Keller, F. *The Lake Dwellings of Switzerland and Other Parts of Europe* (London: Longmans, Green), 9–10.

Leese, M. N. 1983. 'The statistical treatment of grainsize data from pottery', in Aspinall, A. and Warren, S. E. (eds.) *Proceedings of the 22nd Archaeometry Symposium* (Bradford: Schools of Physics and Archaeological Sciences, University of Bradford), 47–55.

Leese, M. N. and Bradley, S. M. 1995. 'Conservation condition surveys at the British Museum', in Huggett, J. and Ryan, N. (eds.) *Computer Applications and Quantitative Methods in Archaeology 1994*. British Archaeological Reports International Series 600 (Oxford: Tempus Reparatum), 81–6.

Lennstrom, H. A. and Hastorf, C. A. 1992. 'Testing old wives' tales in palaeoethnobotany: a comparison of bulk and scatter sampling from Pancán, Peru', *Journal of Archaeological Science* 19 (2): 205–29.

1995. 'Interpretation in context: sampling and analysis in paleoethnobotany', *American Antiquity* 60 (4): 701–21.

Leonard, R. D. 1997. 'The sample size–richness relation: a comment on Plog and Hegman', *American Antiquity* 62 (4): 713–16.

Leonard, R. D. and Jones, G. T. (eds.) 1989. *Quantifying Diversity in Archaeology* (Cambridge: Cambridge University Press).

Leone, M. P. and Potter, P. B. 1992. 'Legitimation and the classification of archaeological sites', *American Antiquity* 57 (1): 137–45.

Leusen, M. van 1993. 'Cartographic modelling in a cell-based GIS', in Andresen, J., Madsen, T. and Scollar, I. (eds.) *Computing the Past: Computer Applications and Quantitative Methods in Archaeology CAA 92* (Aarhus: Aarhus University Press), 105–23.

Levitan, B. 1982. *Excavations at West Hill Uley 1979: The Sieving and Sampling Programme.* Western Archaeology Trust Occasional Papers 10 (Bristol: Western Archaeology Trust).

1983. 'Reducing the workload: sub-sampling animal bone assemblages', *Circaea* 1 (1): 7–12.

Lewarch, D. E. and O'Brien, M. J. 1981. 'The expanding role of surface assemblages in archaeological research', in Schiffer, M. B. (ed.) *Advances in Archaeological Method and Theory* 4 (New York: Academic Press), 297–342.

Liddell, D. 1932. 'Report on the excavation at Hembury Fort, third season, 1932', *Proceedings of the Devon Archaeological Exploration Society* 1: 162–83.

Lie, R. W. 1980. 'Minimum numbers of individuals from osteological samples', *Norwegian Archaeological Review* 13 (1): 24–30.

Lightfoot, K. G. 1986. 'Regional surveys in the Eastern United States: the strengths and weaknesses of implementing sub-surface testing programs', *American Antiquity* 51 (3): 484–504.

1989. 'A defense of shovel-test sampling: a reply to Shott', *American Antiquity* 54 (2): 413–16.

Limp, W. F. 1974. 'Water separation and flotation processes', *Journal of Field Archaeology* 1 (4): 337–42.

1987. 'The identification of archaeological site patterning through the integration of remote sensing, geographic information systems and exploratory data analysis', *Proceedings of the US Army Corps Engineers 6th Remote Sensing Symposium* (Galveston, TX): 232–62.

Lindley, D. V. 1985. *Making Decisions* (2nd edn) (London: Wiley).

Lipe, W. D. 1974. 'A conservation model for American archaeology', *The Kiva* 39 (3–4): 213–45.

Lloyd, S. 1954. 'Mound surveys', *Antiquity* 28: 214–20.

Lock, G. 1995. 'Sampling the sample', in Cunliffe, B. W. *Danebury: An Iron Age Hillfort in Hampshire 6: A Hillfort Community in Perspective*. CBA Research Reports, 102 (London: Council for British Archaeology), 104–17.

Loving, S. H., Kamermans, H. and Voorips, A. 1991. 'Randomizing our walks: the Agro Pontino survey sample design', in Voorrips, A., Loving, S. H. and Kamermans, H. (eds.) *The Agro Pontino Survey Project: Methods and Preliminary Results*. Studies in Prae- en Protohistorie 6 (Amsterdam: University of Amsterdam), 61–78.

Lovis, W. A. 1976. 'Quarter sections and forest: an example of probability sampling in the Northeastern Woodlands', *American Antiquity* 41 (3): 364–72.

Lyall, J. and Powlesland, D. 1996 'The application of high resolution fluxgate gradiometry as an aid to excavation planning and strategy formulation', *Internet Archaeology* 1.

Lyman, R. L. 1994. *Vertebrate Taphonomy* (Cambridge: Cambridge University Press).

1995. 'Determining when rare (zoo-)archaeological data are truly absent', *Journal of Archaeological Method and Theory* 2 (4): 369–424.

Lynch, B. M. 1980. 'Site artifact density and the effectiveness of shovel probes', *Current Anthropology* 21 (4): 516–17.

1981. 'More on shovel probes', *Current Anthropology* 22 (4): 438.

McCartney, P. H. and Glass, M. F. 1990. 'Simulation models and the interpretation of archaeological diversity', *American Antiquity* 55 (3): 521–36.

McCracken, S. and Phillpotts, C. 1995. *Archaeology and Planning in London* (London: Standing Conference on London Archaeology).

McGimsey, C. R. 1972. *Public Archaeology* (New York: Seminar Press).

McGimsey, C. R. and Davis, H. A. 1977. *The Management of the Archaeological Resource: The Airlie House Report*. Special Publication of the Society for American Archaeology (Washington DC).

McManamon, F. P. 1984. 'Discovering sites unseen', in Schiffer, M. B. (ed.) *Advances in Archaeological Method and Theory* 7 (New York: Academic Press), 223–92.

Macready, S. and Thompson, F. H. (eds.) 1985. *Archaeological Field Survey in Britain and Abroad* (London: Society of Antiquaries of London).

Madow, W. G. and Madow, L. H. 1944. 'On the theory of systematic sampling', *Annals of Matematical Statistics* 15: 1–24.

Mallouf, R. J. 1982. 'An analysis of plow-damaged chert artifacts: the Brookeen Creek Cache (41HI86), Hill County, Texas', *Journal of Field Archaeology* 9 (1): 79–98.

Marquardt, W. H. 1978. 'Advances in archaeological seriation', in Schiffer, M. B. (ed.) *Advances in Archaeological Method and Theory* 1 (New York: Academic Press), 257–314.

Marriott, F. H. C. 1989. *A Dictionary of Statistical Terms* (5th edn) (Harlow: Longman Scientific and Technical for the International Statistical Institute).

Massagrande, F. A. 1995a. 'Using GIS with non-systematic survey data: the Mediterranean evidence' (London: University of London unpublished PhD thesis).

1995b. 'A GIS approach to the study of non-systematically collected data: a case study from the Mediterranean', in Huggett, J. and Ryan, N. (eds.) *Computer Applications and Quantitative Methods in Archaeology* 1994. British Archaeological Reports International Series 600 (Oxford: Tempus Reparatum), 147–56.

Mathew, A. J., Woods, A. J. and Oliver, C. 1991. 'Spots before your eyes: new comparison charts for visual percentage estimation in archaeological material', in Middleton, A. and Freestone, I. (eds.) *Recent Developments in Ceramic Petrology*. British Museum Occasional Papers 81: 211–63.

Meighan, C. W., Pendergast, D. M., Swartz, B. K. and Wissler, M. D. 1958. 'Ecological interpretation in archaeology: part 1', *American Antiquity* 24 (1): 1–23.

Meltzer, D. J., Leonard, R. D. and Stratton, S. K. 1992. 'The relationship between sample size and diversity in archaeological assemblages', *Journal of Archaeological Science* 19 (4): 375–87.

Merkel, J. F. 1997. 'Geochemical and stratigraphic sampling strategies for ancient tin smelting', in Budd, P. and Gale, D. *Prehistoric Extractive Metallurgy in Cornwall* (Truro: Cornwall Archaeological Unit), 41–4.

Middleton, A. P., Freestone, I. C. and Leese, M. N. 1985. 'Textural analysis of ceramic thin sections: evaluation of grain sampling procedures', *Archaeometry* 27 (1): 64–74.

Middleton, R. and Winstanley, D. 1993. 'GIS in a landscape archaeology context', in Andresen, J., Madsen, T. and Scollar, I. (eds.) *Computing the Past: Computer Applications and Quantitative Methods in Archaeology CAA 92* (Aarhus: Aarhus University Press), 151–8.

Miksicek, C. H. 1987. 'Formation processes of the archaeobotanical record', in Schiffer, M. B. (ed.) *Advances in Archaeological Method and Theory* 10 (New York: Academic Press), 211–47.

Millett, M. 1985. 'Field Survey Calibration: a contribution', in Haselgrove, C., Millett, M. and Smith, I. (eds.) *Archaeology from the Ploughsoil: Studies in the Collection and Interpretation of Field Survey Data* (Sheffield: J. R. Collis), 31–7.

Millett, M., and Graham, D. 1986. *Excavations on the Romano-British Small Town at Neatham, Hampshire, 1969–79*. Hampshire Field Club and Archaeological Society Monograph 3 (Winchester: Hampshire Field Club).

Mood, A. M. and Graybill, F. A. 1963. *Introduction to the Theory of Statistics* (2nd edn) (New York: McGraw-Hill).

Moorehead, W. K. 1929. *The Cahokia Mounds* (Urbana: University of Illinois Press).

Moorhouse, S. 1986. 'Non-dating uses of medieval pottery', *Medieval Ceramics* 10: 85–124.

Moreno-García, M., Orton, C. R. and Rackham, J. 1996. 'A new statistical tool for the comparison of animal bone assemblages', *Journal of Archaeological Science* 23: 437–53.

Morgan, R. A. 1975. 'The selection and sampling of timber from archaeological sites for identification and tree-ring analysis', *Journal of Archaeological Science* 2 (3): 221–30.

Morris, C. 1975. 'Sampling in the excavation of urban sites: the case at Huánuco Pampa', in Mueller, J. W. (ed.) *Sampling in Archaeology* (Tucson: University of Arizona Press), 192–208.

Muckelroy, K. 1975. 'A systematic approach to the investigation of scattered wreck sites', *International Journal of Nautical Archaeology and Underwater Exploration* 4: 173–90.

Muckle, R. J. 1994. 'Differential recovery of mollusk shell from archaeological sites', *Journal of Field Archaeology* 21 (1): 129–31.

Mueller, J. W. 1974. *The Use of Sampling in Archaeological Survey*. Society for American Archaeology Memoir 28 (Washington, DC: Society for American Archaeology).

1975a. 'Archaeological research as cluster sampling', in Mueller, J. W. (ed.) *Sampling in Archaeology* (Tucson: University of Arizona Press), 33–41.

Mueller, J. W. (ed.) 1975b. *Sampling in Archaeology* (Tucson: University of Arizona Press).

Murphy, P. L. and Wiltshire, P. E. J. 1994. *A Guide to Sampling Archaeological Deposits for Environmental Analysis*. Privately printed.

Nance, J. D. 1979. 'Regional subsampling and statistical inference in forested habitats', *American Antiquity* 44 (1): 172–6.

1981. 'Statistical fact and archaeological faith: two models in small site sampling', *Journal of Field Archaeology* 8 (2): 151–65.

1983. 'Regional sampling in archaeological survey: the statistical perspective', in Schiffer, M. B. (ed.) *Advances in Archaeological Method and Theory* 6 (New York: Academic Press), 289–356.

1987. 'Reliability, validity and quantitative methods in archaeology', in Aldenderfer, M. S. (ed.) *Quantitative Research in Archaeology* (Newbury Park: Sage Publications), 244–93.

1990. 'Statistical sampling in archaeology', in Voorrips, A. (ed.) *Mathematics and Information Science in Archaeology: A Flexible Framework* (Bonn: Holos), 135–63.

Nance, J. D. and Ball, B. F. 1986. 'No surprises? The reliability and validity of test-pit sampling', *American Antiquity* 51 (3): 457–83.

1989. 'A shot in the dark: Shott's comments on Nance and Ball', *American Antiquity* 54 (2): 405–12.

National Audit Office 1987–8. *Management of the Collections of the English National Museums and Galleries* (London: HMSO).

Newey, H., Bradley, S. M. and Leese, M. N. 1993. 'Assessing the condition of archaeological iron: an intercomparison', in Bridgeland, J. (ed.) *Tenth Triennial Meeting of ICOM Committee for Conservation, Washington, D.C.* (Paris: International Council Museums Committee Conservation) Preprints vol. 2: 786–91.

Neyman, J. 1934. 'On the two different aspects of the representative method: the method of stratified sampling and the method of purposive selection', *Journal of the Royal Statistical Society* 97: 558–625.

Nichol, R. K. and Wild, C. J. 1984. '"Numbers of individuals" in faunal analysis: the decay of fish bones in archaeological sites', *Journal of Archaeological Science* 11 (1): 35–51.

Nicholson, M. and Barry, J. 1995. 'Inferences from spatial surveys about the presence of an unobserved species', *Oikos* 72: 74–8.

Noe-Nygaard, N. 1987. 'Taphonomy in archaeology with special emphasis on man as a biasing factor', *Journal of Danish Archaeology* 6: 7–52.

Oakley, K. P. 1933. 'The pottery from the Roman-British site on Thundersbarrow Hill', *Antiquaries Journal*, 13: 134–41.

Obenauer, K. 1936. 'Petrographische Untersuchung der Keramik', in Buttler, W. and Haberey, W. (eds.) *Die Bandkeramische Ansiedlung bei Köln-Lindenthal* (Berlin: de Gruyter), 123–9.

O'Brien, M. J. and Lewarch, D. E. (eds.) 1981. *Plowzone Archaeology: Contributions to Theory and Technique*. Publications in Archaeology 27 (Nashville, Tennessee: Vanderbilt University).

O'Connor, T. 1989. 'Deciding priorities with urban bones: York as a case study', in Serjeantson, D. and Waldron, T. (eds.) *Diet and Crafts in Towns: The Evidence of Animal Remains from the Roman to the Post-medieval Period*. British Archaeological Reports British Series 199 (Oxford: BAR), 189–200.

Odell, G. H. 1992. 'Bewitched by mechanical site-testing devices', *American Antiquity* 57 (4): 692–703.

Odell, G. H. and Cowan, F. 1987. 'Estimating tillage effects on artefact distributions', *American Antiquity* 52 (3): 456–84.

O'Muircheartaigh, C. A. and Francis, D. P. 1981. *Statistics: A Dictionary of Terms and Ideas* (London: Arrow Books).

O'Neil, D. H. 1993. 'Excavation sample size: a cautionary tale', *American Antiquity* 58 (3): 523–9.

Orton, C. 1975. 'Quantitative pottery studies: some progress, problems and prospects', *Science and Archaeology* 16: 30–5.

    1978. 'Is pottery a sample?', in Cherry, J. F., Gamble, C. and Shennan, S. (eds.) *Sampling in Contemporary British Archaeology.* British Archaeological Reports British Series 50 (Oxford: BAR), 399–402.

    1993. 'How many pots make five? – An historical review of pottery quantification', *Archaeometry* 35 (2): 169–84.

    1996. 'Markov models for museums', in Kamermans, H. and Fennema, K. (eds.) *Interfacing the Past: Computer Applications and Quantitative Methods in Archaeology CAA 95.* Analecta Praehistorica Leidensia 28, 149–53.

    1999.'Plus ça change – perceptions of archaeological statistics', in Dingwall, L., Exon, S., Gaffney, V., Laflin, S. and van Leusen, M. (eds) *Archaeology in the Age of the Internet: Computer Applications and Quantitative Methods in Archaeology CAA 97.* British Archaeology Reports International Series 750 (Oxford: Archaeopress), 25–34.

    forthcoming. 'A bayesian approach to a problem of archaeological site evaluation', in Lockyear, K., Sly, T. J. T. and Mihailescu-Bîrliba, V. (eds.) *Computer Applications and Quantitative Methods in Archaeology CAA 96* (Iasi: Edîtura Demiurg).

Orton, C. R. and Tyers, P. A. 1990. 'Statistical analysis of ceramic assemblages', *Archeologia e Calcolatori* 1: 81–110.

Orton, C. R., Tyers, P. A. and Vince, A. G. 1993. *Pottery in Archaeology* (Cambridge: Cambridge University Press).

Palmer, R. 1978. 'Aerial archaeology and sampling', in Cherry, J. F., Gamble, C. and Shennan, S. (eds.) *Sampling in Contemporary British Archaeology.* British Archaeological Reports British Series 50 (Oxford: BAR), 129–48.

Parsons, D. 1977. 'Brixworth and its monastery church', in Dornier, A. (ed.) *Mercian Studies* (Leicester: Leicester University Press), 173–89.

Pascoe, J., Morse, M. and Ryan, N. 1997. 'Using hand-held technology to support student fieldwork', unpublished report presented to the Conference on Mobile Computing in the Field, University of Kent, Canterbury, 26 September 1997.

Patel, J. K., Kapadia, C. H. and Owen, D. B. 1976. *Handbook of Statistical Distributions* (New York: Marcel Dekker).

Payne, S. 1972a. 'Partial recovery and sample bias: the results of some sieving experiments', in Higgs, E. S. (ed.) *Papers in Economic Prehistory* (Cambridge: Cambridge University Press), 49–64.

    1972b. 'On the interpretation of bone samples from archaeological sites', in Higgs. E.S. (ed.) *Papers in Economic Prehistory* (Cambridge: Cambridge University Press), 65–81.

    1975. 'Partial recovery and sample bias', in Clason, A. T. (ed.) *Archaeozoological Studies* (Amsterdam: North-Holland), 7–17.

    1992. *Some Notes on Sampling and Sieving for Animal Bones.* Ancient Monuments Laboratory Report 55/92.

Peacock, D. P. S. 1967. 'The heavy mineral analysis of pottery: a preliminary report', *Archaeometry* 10: 97–100.

    1971 'Petrography of certain coarse pottery', in Cunliffe, B. W. *Excavations at Fishbourne 1961–69* 2: *The Finds* (London: Society of Antiquaries), 255–9.

Peacock, W. 1978. 'Probabilistic sampling in shell middens: a case study from Oronsay, Inner Hebrides', in Cherry, J. F., Gamble, C. and Shennan, S. (eds.) *Sampling in Contemporary British Archaeology.* British Archaeological Reports British Series 50 (Oxford: BAR), 177–90.

Pendleton, M. V. 1983. 'A comment concerning "testing flotation recovery rates"', *American*

*Antiquity* 48 (3): 615–16.

Perkins, P. 1996. 'An image processing technique for the suppression of traces of modern agricultural activity in aerial photographs', in Kamermans, H. and Fennema, K. (eds.) *Interfacing the Past: Computer Applications and Quantitative Methods in Archaeology CAA95*, Analecta Praehistorica Leidensia 28, 139–45.

Peters, C. R. 1970. *Introductory Topics in Probability Sampling Theory for Archaeology* (Anthropology UCLA 2), 33–50.

Phillpotts, C. 1997. 'London evaluation in the 1990s', *London Archaeologist* 8 (5): 137–9.

Pielou, E. C. 1975. *Ecological Diversity* (New York: John Wiley and Sons).

Plog, S. 1976. 'Relative efficiencies of sampling techniques for archaeological surveys', in Flannery, K. V. (ed.) *The Early Mesoamerican Village* (New York: Academic Press), 136–58.
1978 'Sampling in archaeological surveys: a critique', *American Antiquity* 43 (2), 280–5.

Plog, S. and Hegman, M. 1993. 'The sample size–richness relation: the relevance of research questions, sampling strategies and behavioral variation', *American Antiquity* 58 (3): 489–96.
1997. 'An anthropological perspective on the sample size–richness relation: a response to Leonard', *American Antiquity* 62 (4): 717–18.

Plog, S., Plog, F. and Wait, W. 1978. 'Decision making in modern surveys', in Schiffer, M. B. (ed.) *Advances in Archaeological Method and Theory* 1 (New York: Academic Press), 384–421.

Poplin, F. 1976. 'Rémarques théoriques et practiques sur les unites utilisées dans les études d'ostéologie quantitative, particulièrement en archéologie préhistorique', UISPP 9e Congrès, Thèmes Specialisées B, Problèmes Ethnographiques des Vestiges (Nice: Osseux), 124–41.

Powell, S. and Rice, G. E. 1981. 'The incorporation of small contract projects into a regional sampling design', *American Antiquity* 46 (3): 602–610.

Prior, F. 1991. *English Heritage Book of Flag Fen Prehistoric Fenland Centre* (London: Batsford).

Pumpelly, R. (ed.) 1908. *Explorations in Turkestan: Expedition of 1904: Prehistoric Civilizations of Anau: Origins, Growth, and Influence of Environment* (Washington DC: Carnegie Institution of Washington).

Pye, W. D. 1943. 'Rapid methods of making sedimentational analysis of arenaceous sediments', *Journal of Sedimentary Petrology* 13 (3): 85–104.

Ragir, S. 1967. 'A review of techniques for archaeological sampling', in Heizer, R. F. and Graham, J. A. (eds.) *A Guide to Field Methods in Archaeology* (Palo Alto: National Press), 181–98.
1972. 'A review of techniques for archaeological sampling', in Leone, M. P. (ed.) *Contemporary Archaeology* (Carbondale: Southern Illinois University Press), 178–91.

Ramenofsky, A. F., Standifer, L. C., Whitmer, A. M. and Nelson, D. E. 1986. 'A new technique for separating flotation samples', *American Antiquity* 51 (1): 66–72.

Raup, D. 1975. 'Taxonomic diversity estimation using rarefaction', *Paleobiology* 1: 333–42.

Read, D. W. 1986 'Sampling procedures for regional surveys: a problem of representativeness and effectiveness', *Journal of Field Archaeology* 13 (4): 477–91.

Redman, C. L. 1973 'Multistage fieldwork and analytical techniques', *American Antiquity* 38 (1): 61–79.
1974. *Archaeological Sampling Strategies* (Addison-Wesley Modular Publications in Archaeology 55).
1975. 'Productive sampling strategies for archaeological sites', in Mueller, J. W. (ed.) *Sampling in Archaeology* (Tucson: University of Arizona Press), 147–54.
1987. 'Surface collection, sampling, and research design: a retrospective', *American Antiquity* 52 (2): 249–65.

Redman, C. L., Anzalone, R. D. and Rubatone, P. E. 1979. 'Medieval archaeology at Qsar es-Seghir, Morocco', *Journal of Field Archaeology* 6 (1): 1–16.

Redman, C. L. and Watson, P. J. 1970. 'Systematic, intensive surface collection', *American Antiquity* 35 (3): 279–91.

Reece, R. M. 1995. 'Site-finds in Roman Britain', *Britannia* 26: 179–206.

Reid, J. J., Schiffer, M. B. and Neff, J. M. 1975. 'Archaeological considerations of intrasite sampling', in Mueller, J. W. (ed.) *Sampling in Archaeology* (Tucson: University of Arizona Press), 209–24.

Renfrew, C. and Wagstaff, M. (eds.) 1982. *An Island Polity: The Archaeology of Exploitation in Melos* (Cambridge: Cambridge University Press).

Rhoads, J. W. 1992. 'Significant sites and non-site archaeology: a case-study from south-east Australia', *World Archaeology* 24 (2): 198–217

Rhode, D. 1988. 'Measurement of archaeological diversity and the sample-size effect', *American Antiquity* 53 (4): 708–16.

Rick, J. W. 1976. 'Downslope movement and archaeological intrasite spatial analysis', *American Antiquity* 41 (2): 133–44.

Rindos, D. 1989. 'Diversity, variation and selection', in Leonard, R. D. and Jones, G. T. (eds.) *Quantifying Diversity in Archaeology* (Cambridge: Cambridge University Press), 13–23.

Ringrose, T. J. 1993a. 'Bone counts and statistics: a critique', *Journal of Archaeological Science* 20 (2): 121–57.

  1993b. 'Diversity indices and archaeology', in Andresen, J., Madsen, T. and Scollar, I. (eds.) *Computing the Past CAA 92* (Aarhus: Aarhus University Press), 279–85.

Robertson, J. C. 1989. 'Counting London's horn cores: sampling what?', *Post-medieval Archaeology* 23: 1–10.

Rogers, A. R. 1982. 'Data collection and information loss in the study of spatial pattern', *World Archaeology* 14 (2): 249–58.

Rogge, A. E. and Fuller, S. L. 1977. 'Probabilistic survey sampling: making parameter estimates', in Schiffer, M. B. and Gumerman, G. J. (eds.) *Conservation Archaeology* (New York: Academic Press), 227–38.

Roper, D. 1976. 'Lateral displacement of artifacts due to plowing', *American Antiquity* 41 (3): 372–5.

Rütimeyer, L. 1861. *Die Fauna der Pfahlbauten in der Schweiz* [The Fauna of the Swiss Lake-dwellings] (Basle).

  1866. 'Results of the investigation of animal remains from the lake dwellings', in Keller, F. *The Lake Dwellings of Switzerland and Other Parts of Europe* (London: Longmans, Green), 355–62.

Sanders, W. T., Parsons, J. R. and Santley, R. S. 1979. *The Basin of Mexico: Ecological Processes in the Evolution of a Civilization* (New York: Academic Press).

Sayre, E. V., and Dobson, R. W. 1957. 'Neutron activation study of Mediterranean potsherds', *American Journal of Archaeology* 61: 35–41.

Schadla-Hall, T. and Shennan, S. 1978. 'Some suggestions for a sampling approach to archaeological survey in Wessex', in Cherry, J. F., Gamble, C. and Shennan, S. (eds.) *Sampling in Contemporary British Archaeology.* British Archaeological Reports British Series 50 (Oxford: BAR), 87–104.

Schiffer, M. B. 1976. *Behavioural Archaeology* (New York: Academic Press).

  1987. *Formation Processes of the Archaeological Record* (Albuquerque: University of New Mexico Press).

Schiffer, M. B. and Gumerman, G. J. (eds.) 1977. *Conservation Archaeology: A Guide for Cultural Resource Management Studies* (New York: Academic Press).

Schiffer, M. B. and House, J. H. 1975. *The Cache River Archaeological Project: An Experiment in Contract Archaeology.* Arkansas Archaeology Survey, Research Series 8.

1977. 'Cultural resource management and archaeological research: the Cache Project', *Current Anthropology* 18 (1): 43–68.

Schiffer, M. B., Sullivan, A. P. and Klinger, T. C. 1978. 'The design of archaeological surveys', *World Archaeology* 10 (1): 1–28.

Schofield, A. J. 1987. 'The role of palaeoecology in understanding variation in regional survey data', *Circaea* 5: 33–42.

1989. 'Understanding early medieval pottery distributions: cautionary tales and their implications for further research', *Antiquity* 63: 460–70.

1991a. 'Lithic distribution in the upper Meon valley: behavioural response and human adaptation on the Hampshire chalklands', *Proceedings of the Prehistoric Society* 57 (2): 159–78.

Schofield, A. J. (ed.) 1991b. *Interpreting Artefact Scatters: Contributions to Ploughzone Archaeology* (Oxford: Oxbow Books).

Schuldenrein, J. 1991. 'Coring and the identity of cultural-resource environments: a comment on Stein', *American Antiquity* 56 (1): 131–7

Scollar, I., Tabbagh, A., Hesse, A. and Herzog, A. 1989. *Archaeological Prospecting and Remote Sensing* (Cambridge: Cambridge University Press).

Shaffer, B. S. 1992. 'Quarter-inch screening: understanding biases in recovery of vertebrate faunal remains', *American Antiquity* 57 (1): 129–36.

Shaffer, B. S. and Sanchez, J. L. J. 1994. 'Comparison of 1/8″- and 1/4″-mesh recovery of controlled samples of small-to-medium sized mammals', *American Antiquity* 59 (3): 525–30.

Shennan, S. 1980. 'Meeting the plough damage problem: a sampling approach to area-intensive fieldwork', in Hinchliffe, J. and Schadla-Hall, R. T. (eds.) *The Past under the Plough*. Directorate of Ancient Monuments and Historic Buildings Occasional Paper 3 (London: Department of the Environment), 125–33.

1997. *Quantifying Archaeology* (2nd edn) (Edinburgh: Edinburgh University Press).

Shennan, S. J., with Gardiner, J. and Oake, M. 1985. *Experiments in the Collection and Analysis of Archaeological Survey Data: The East Hampshire Survey* (Sheffield: Department of Archaeology and Prehistory, University of Sheffield).

Shepard, A. O. 1942. *Rio Grande Glaze Paint Ware: A Study Illustrating the Place of Ceramic Technological Analysis in Archaeological Research* (Washington: Carnegie Institute of Washington).

Sherwood, S. C. and Ousley, S. D. 1995. 'Quantifying microartifacts using a personal computer', *Geoarchaeology* 10 (6): 423–8.

Sherwood, S. C., Simek, J. F. and Polhemus, R. R. 1995. 'Artifact size and spatial process: macro- and microartifacts in a Mississippian house', *Geoarchaeology* 10 (6): 429–55.

Shott, M. J. 1985. 'Shovel-test sampling as a site discovery technique: A case study from Michigan', *Journal of Field Archaeology* 12 (4): 457–68.

1987. 'Feature discovery and the sampling requirements of archaeological evaluations', *Journal of Field Archaeology* 14 (3): 359–71.

1989a. 'Shovel-test sampling in archaeological survey: comments on Nance and Ball, and Lightfoot', *American Antiquity* 54 (2): 396–404.

1989b. 'Diversity, organization and behavior in the material record: ethnographic and archaeological examples', *Current Anthropology* 30 (3): 283–315.

Smith, T. M. F. 1976. 'The foundations of survey sampling: a review', *Journal of the Royal Statistical Society A* 139: 183–95.

Solomon, H. and Zacks, S. 1970. 'Optimal design of sampling from finite populations: a critical review and indication of new research areas', *Journal of the American Statistical Association* 65: 653–77.

South, S. 1978. 'Research strategies for archaeological pattern recognition on historic sites',

*World Archaeology* 10 (1): 36–50.

Spier, L. 1917. 'An outline for a chronology of Zuñi ruins', *Anthropological Papers of the American Museum of Natural History* 18 (1): 209–331.

Spigelman, M. S. 1996. 'The archaeologist and ancient bio-molecules: field sampling strategies to enhance recovery', *Papers from the Institute of Archaeology* 7: 69–73.

Stafford, C. R. 1995. 'Geoarchaeological perspectives on palaeolandscapes and regional subsurface archaeology', *Journal of Archaeological Method and Theory* 2 (1): 69–104.

Stallibrass. S. M. 1985. 'Some effects of preservational bias on interpretation of animal bones', in Fieller, N., Gilbertson, D. D. and Ralph, N. G. A. (eds.) *Palaeobiological Investigations: Research Design, Methods and Data Analysis*. British Archaeological Reports International Series 266 (Oxford: BAR), 65–72.

Steenstrup, J. 1857. 'Et bidrag til Gerrfuglens, Alca impennis Lin., naturhistorie, og saerligt til kundskaben om dens tidligere Udbredningskreds'. *Vid. Medd. nat. For. Kjobenhavn 1855* (3–7): 33–116.

Stein, J. K. 1986. 'Coring archaeological sites', *American Antiquity* 51 (3): 505–27.

1991. 'Coring in CRM and archaeology: a reminder', *American Antiquity* 56 (1): 138–42.

Stein, J. K. (ed.) 1992. *Deciphering a Shell Midden* (San Diego, CA: Academic Press).

Stein, J. K. and Teltser, P. A. 1989. 'Size distributions of artifact classes: combining macro- and microfractions', *Geoarchaeology* 4 (1): 1–30.

Steinhorst, R. K. and Samuel, M. D. 1989. 'Sightability adjustment methods for aerial surveys of wildlife populations', *Biometrics* 45: 415–25.

Stoltman, J. B. 1989. 'A quantitative approach to the petrographic analysis of ceramic thin sections', *American Antiquity* 54 (1): 147–60.

Stone, G. D. 1981. 'On artifact density and shovel probes', *Current Anthropology* 22 (2): 182–3.

Streeten, A. D. F. 1982. 'Textural analysis: an approach to the characterization of sand-tempered fabrics', in Freestone, I., Johns, C. and Potter, T. (eds.) *Current Research in Ceramics: Thin-Section Studies. The British Museum Seminar 1980*. British Museum Occasional Papers 32 (London: British Museum), 123–34.

Struever, S. 1968. 'Flotation techniques for the recovery of small-scale archaeological remains', *American Antiquity* 33 (3): 353–62.

Suenson-Taylor, K., Sully, D. and Orton, C. 1999. 'Data in conservation: the missing link in the process', *Studies in Conservation* 44: 184–94.

Sullivan, A. P. 1978. 'Inference and evidence in archaeology: a discussion of the conceptual problems', in Schiffer, M. B. (ed.) *Advances in Archaeological Method and Theory* 1 (New York: Academic Press), 183–222.

Sundstrom, L. 1993. 'A simple mathematical procedure for estimating the adequacy of site survey strategies', *Journal of Field Archaeology* 20 (1): 91–6.

Sylvester, R. J. 1991. 'The Fenland Project Number 4: The Wissey Embayment and the Fen Causeway, Norfolk', *East Anglian Archaeology* 52.

Tainter, J. A. and Lucas, G. J. 1983. 'Epistomology of the significance concept', *American Antiquity* 48 (4): 707–19.

Tangri, D. and Wright, R. V. S. 1993. 'Multivariate analysis of compositional data: applied comparisons favour standard principal components analysis over Aitchison's loglinear contrast method', *Archaeometry* 35 (1): 103–12.

Thomas, D. H. 1969. 'Great Basin hunting patterns: a quantitative method for treating faunal remains', *American Antiquity* 34 (4): 392–401.

1975. 'Nonsite sampling in archaeology: up the creek without a site?', in Mueller, J. W. (ed.) *Sampling in Archaeology* (Tucson: University of Arizona Press), 61–81.

1978. 'The awful truth about statistics in archaeology', *American Antiquity* 43 (2): 231–44.

Thompson, S. K. 1988. 'Adaptive sampling', *Proceedings of the Section on Survey Research*

*Methods of the American Statistical Association*: 784–6.

1990. 'Adaptive cluster sampling', *Journal of the American Statistical Association* 85: 1050–9.

1991a. 'Adaptive cluster sampling: designs with primary and secondary units', *Biometrics* 47: 1103–15.

1991b. 'Stratified adaptive cluster sampling', *Biometrika* 78: 389–97.

1993. 'Multivariate aspects of adaptive cluster sampling', in Patil, G. P. and Rao, C. R. (eds.) *Multivariate Environmental Statistics* (New York: North Holland/Elsevier Science Publishers), 561–72.

Thompson, S. K. and Ramsey, F. L. 1987. 'Detectability functions in observing spatial point processes', *Biometrics* 43: 355–62.

Thompson, S. K. and Seber, G. A. F. 1994. 'Detectability in conventional and adaptive sampling', *Biometrics* 50: 712–24.

1996. *Adaptive Sampling* (New York: John Wiley and Sons).

Thorpe, I. J. N. 1997. 'From settlements to monuments: site succession in Late Neolithic and Early Bronze Age Jutland, East Denmark', in Nash, G. (ed.) *Semiotics of Landscape: Archaeology of Mind*. British Archaeological Reports International Series 661 (Oxford: Archaeopress), 71–9.

Tippett, L. C. 1927. *Random Sampling Numbers*. Tracts for Computers 15 (Cambridge: Cambridge University Press).

Tolstoy, P. and Fish, S. K. 1975. 'Surface and subsurface evidence for community size at Coapexco, Mexico', *Journal of Field Archaeology* 2 (1): 97–104.

Torrence, R. 1978. 'Chipping away at some misconceptions about sampling lithic assemblages', in Cherry, J. F., Gamble, C. and Shennan, S. (eds.) *Sampling in Contemporary British Archaeology*. British Archaeological Reports British Series 50 (Oxford: BAR), 373–98.

Treganza, A. E. and Cook, S. F. 1948. 'The quantitative investigation of aboriginal sites: complete excavation with physical and archaeological analysis of a single mound', *American Antiquity* 13 (4): 287–97.

Turner, A. 1984. 'Subsampling animal bone assemblages: reducing the work-load or reducing the information?', *Circaea* 2 (2): 69–75.

1995. 'Statistical analysis of the Shapwick survey data 1989–94', in Aston, M. A. and Gerrard, C. M. (eds.) *The Shapwick Project: The Sixth Report* (Bristol: University of Bristol Department for Continuing Education), 55–70.

Turner, A. and Fieller, N. R. J. 1985. 'Consideration of minimum numbers: a response to Horton', *Journal of Archaeological Science* 12 (6): 477–83.

Tyers, P. A. 1996. *Roman Pottery in Britain* (London: Batsford).

Van der Velde, P. 1987. 'Post-depositional decay: a simulation', *Analecta Praehistorica Leidensia* 20: 168–75.

Veen, M. van der 1984. 'Sampling for seeds', in Zeist, W. van, and Casparie, W. A. (eds.) *Plants and Ancient Man: Studies in Palaeoethnobotany: Proceedings of the Sixth Symposium of the International Work Group for Palaeoethnobotany, Groningen, 30 May–3 June 1983* (Rotterdam: A. A. Balkema), 193–9.

1985. 'Carbonised seeds, sample size and on-site sampling', in Fieller, N., Gilbertson, D. D. and Ralph, N. G. A. (eds.) *Palaeoenvironmental Investigations: Research Design, Methods and Data Analysis*. British Archaeological Reports International Series 258 (Oxford: BAR), 165–74.

Veen, M. van der, and Fieller, N. 1982. 'Sampling seeds', *Journal of Archaeological Science* 9 (3): 287–98.

Verhoeven, A. A. A. 1991. 'Visibility factors affecting artifact recovery in the Agro Pontino Survey', in Voorrips, A., Loving, S. H. and Kamermans, H. (eds.) *The Agro Pontino Survey Project: Methods and Preliminary Results*. Studies in Prae- en Protohistorie 6 (Amsterdam:

University of Amsterdam), 87–97.

Vescelius, G. S. 1960. 'Archaeological sampling: a problem in statistical inference', in Dole, G. E. and Caneiro, R. L. (eds.) *Essays in the Science of Culture in Honor of Leslie A. White* (New York: Cromwell), 457–70.

Villa, P. and Courtin, J. 1983. 'The interpretation of stratified sites: a view from underground', *Journal of Archaeological Science* 10 (3): 267–81.

Von Hagen, V. W. 1973. *Search for the Maya: The story of Stephenson and Catherwood* (Farnborough: Saxon House).

Voorrips, A., Gifford, D. P. and Ammerman, A. P. 1978. 'Towards an evaluation of sampling strategies: simulated excavations using stratified sampling designs', in Cherry, J. F., Gamble, C. and Shennan, S. (eds.) *Sampling in Contemporary British Archaeology*. British Archaeological Reports British Series 50 (Oxford: BAR), 227–61.

Voorrips, A., Loving, S. H. and Kamermans, H. (eds.) 1991. *The Agro Pontino Survey Project: Methods and Preliminary Results*. Studies in Prae- en Protohistorie 6 (Amsterdam: University of Amsterdam).

Wade, K. R. 1973. 'The Thetford ware tradition with special reference to Norfolk'. Unpublished BA thesis, University of Southampton.

　1978. 'Sampling at Ipswich: the origins and growth of the Anglo-Saxon town', in Cherry, J. F., Gamble, C. and Shennan, S. (eds.) *Sampling in Contemporary British Archaeology*. British Archaeological Reports British Series 50 (Oxford: BAR), 279–84.

Wagner, G. E. 1982. 'Testing flotation recovery rates', *American Antiquity* 47 (1): 127–32.

Wagner, W. 1933–8. 'Die petrographische Baustoffuntersuchung als Hilfsmittel zur Klärung der Geschichte historischer Bauten', *Jahrbuch für Volks- und Heimatsforschung Hessen Nassau*: 202–9.

Walker, K. and Bacon, L. 1987. 'A condition survey of specimens in the Horniman Museum', in Black, J. (compiler) *Recent Advances in the Conservation and Analysis of Artefacts* (London: Summer Schools Press), 337–9.

Wandibba, S. 1982. 'Experiments in textural analysis', *Archaeometry* 24 (1): 71–5.

Wandsnider, L. and Ebert, J. I. (eds.) 1988. 'Issues in archaeological surface survey: meshing methods and theory', *American Archaeology* 7.

Warren, R. E. 1990. 'Predictive modelling of archaeological site location: a primer', in Allen, K. M. S., Green, S. W. and Zubrow, E. B. W. (eds.) *Interpreting Space: GIS and Archaeology* (London: Taylor and Francis), 201–15.

Waselkov, G. A. 1987. 'Shell-fish gathering and shell midden archaeology', in Schiffer, M. (ed.) *Advances in Archaeological Method and Theory* 11 (Orlando: Academic Press), 93–210.

Watson, J. P. N. 1972. 'Fragmentation analysis of animal bone samples from archaeological sites', *Archaeometry* 14 (2): 221–8.

　1979. 'The estimation of the relative frequencies of mammalian species: Khirokitia 1972', *Journal of Archaeology Science* 6 (2): 127–37.

Wauchope, R. 1965. *They Found the Buried Cities: Exploration and Excavation in the American Tropics* (Chicago: University of Chicago Press).

Whalen, M. E. 1990. 'Defining buried features before excavation: a case from the American Southwest', *Journal of Field Archaeology* 17 (3): 323–31.

Wheatley, D. W. 1993. 'Going over old ground: GIS, archaeological theory and the act of perception', in Andresen, J., Madsen, T. and Scollar, I. (eds.) *Computing the Past: Computer Applications and Quantitative Methods in Archaeology CAA 92* (Aarhus: Aarhus University Press), 133–8.

　1996. 'Between the lines: the role of GIS-based predictive modelling in the interpretation of extensive survey data', in Kamermans, H. and Fennema, K. (eds.) *Interfacing the Past: Computer Applications and Quantitative Methods in Archaeology CAA 95*. Analecta

Praehistorica Leidensia 28: 275–92.

White, T. E. 1953. 'A method of calculating the dietary percentages of various food animals utilized by aboriginal peoples', *American Antiquity* 18 (4): 396–8.

Wilkinson, T. J. 1982. 'The definition of ancient manured zones by means of extensive sherd sampling techniques', *Journal of Field Archaeology* 9 (3): 323–33.

Willey, G. R. (ed.) 1953. *Prehistoric Settlement Patterns in the Virú Valley, Peru.* Bureau of American Ethnology Bulletin 155 (Washington DC: Smithsonian Institute).

Willey, G. R. 1961. 'Volume in pottery and the selection of samples', *American Antiquity* 27 (2): 230–1.

Willey, G. R. and Phillips, P. 1958. *Method and Theory in American Archaeology* (Chicago: University of Chicago Press).

Williams, D. F. 1977. 'The Romano-British black-burnished industry: an essay on characterization by heavy mineral analysis', in Peacock, D. P. S. (ed.) *Pottery and Early Commerce* (London: Academic Press), 163–240.

Wilson, R. 1978. 'Sampling bone densities at Mingies Ditch, Oxfordshire', in Cherry, J. F., Gamble, C. and Shennan, S. (eds.) *Sampling in Contemporary British Archaeology.* British Archaeological Reports British Series 50 (Oxford: BAR), 355–61.

Winter, M. C. 1976. 'Excavating a shallow community by random sampling quadrats', in Flannery, K. V. (ed.) *The Early Mesoamerican Village* (New York: Academic Press), 62–7.

Wobst, H. M. 1983. 'We can't see the forest for the trees: sampling and the shapes of archaeological distributions', in Moore, J. and Keene, A. (eds.) *Archaeological Hammers and Theories* (New York: Academic Press), 37–85.

Woodman, P. C. 1981–2. 'Sampling strategies and problems of archaeological visibility', *Ulster Journal of Archaeology* 44–5: 179–84.

Yanin, V. L. 1992. 'An introduction to Novgorod archaeology', in Brisbane, M. A. (ed.) *The Archaology of Novgorod, Russia.* Society for Medieval Archaeology Monograph Series 13 (Lincoln: Society for Medieval Archaeology), 1–5.

Yarnell, R. A. 1969. 'Palaeo-ethnobotany in America', in Brothwell, D. and Higgs, E. *Science in Archaeology* (2nd edn) (London: Thames and Hudson), 215–28.

Zubrow, E. and Harbaugh, J. W. 1978. 'Archaeological prospecting: kriging and simulation', in Hodder, I. (ed.) *Simulation Studies in Archaeology* (Cambridge: Cambridge University Press), 109–22.

# INDEX

Abinger Roman villa (Surrey), 116
abundance, 75
accelerated ageing, *see* ageing, accelerated
accessibility, 75, 80
Acconia (Italy), 61
accuracy, 26, 70
Adams, M., 40
Adams, R. McC., 72
adaptive sampling, *see* sampling, adaptive
Addyman, P., 136
aerial photography, *see* photography, aerial
ageing
    accelerated, 62
    negative, 216
    no, 216
    positive, 216
Agro Pontino Survey (Italy), 61, 67, 78–9, 85
air-blowing, 154
Aitken, M. J., 7, 177
Aldenderfer, M. S., 171
allocation
    adaptive, 16
    optimum, 15, 30, 93, 212, 223
    proportional, 30, 93, 212
Altman, N., 113
Alton effect, 70
Ammerman, A. J., 60, 61, 70, 75, 114, 128, 138
analysis
    change-point, 127
    chemical, 177, 183–4
    correspondence, 46, 169, 184
    data, 68, 76, 203, 204
    elemental, 9
    heavy mineral, 177, 184–5
    nearest-neighbour, 99
    neutron activation, 178
    physical, 177
    principal components, 184
    rarefaction, 176, 220
    statistical, 10, 29, 103, 121–2, 168–9, 183–4, 203
    textural, 177, 178–9, 184–90
Anau (Turkmenistan), 149
ancillary data, *see* data, ancillary
animals, 53
    bone, *see* bone, animal
anthropology, 172
antiquarian records, 68, 76, 116
appraisal (of site), 115
archaeology
    assessment, *see* assessment, archaeological

conservation, 69
contract, 6, 69
deposit, *see* deposit, archaeological
field unit, 4, 11
    marine, 113
    'new', 43, 68–9, 206–7
    public, 69
    record, damage to, 83
    significance, *see* significance, archaeological
    urban, 116, 141, 143
archive, project, 100
area, of site, 129
area-counting, *see* counting, area-
area-walking, *see* fieldwalking, by areas
Army Corps of Engineers (USA), 77
Arrhenius, O., 171
artefact, *see* finds; individual categories;
    micro-artefacts
Asch, D. L., 113
Ascher, R., 43
aspect (topographic), 77
assemblage
    composition of, 44–57, 58, 63, 157, 165, 169, 177
    death, 47, 53, 56
    deposited, 53, 56, 58
    excavated, 43
    faunal, 53–6, 128, 138, 159
    fossil, 53, 56
    life, living, 43, 47, 53
    sample, 53
    seed, 157
    surface, 60
assessment, archaeological, 115, 116
    desk-based, 115
assimilation of existing knowledge, 28, 76, 116–17,
    127, 141
assurance, quality, 209
Astill, G., 74
Aston, M. A., 67, 103
attenuation, 58
augering, 61, 71, 131, 139–40
    bucket soil, 139–40
autocorrelation, spatial, 86

Bacon, L., 191
Bailey, G. N., 114
Ball, B. F., 71
Bamps, A., 178
Barclay, K., 44, 50
Barker, G., 67, 74, 79, 83, 85, 152, 160

248

CPSIA information can be obtained
at www.ICGtesting.com
Printed in the USA
LVHW031443020423
743257LV00006B/507